STAR AWARD

This book was presented to

Sherri Bricker

in recognition of her

15 years of dedicated

library service.

May 2012

**Washington-Centerville
Public Library**

HUNT, GATHER, COOK

HUNT, GATHER, COOK

Finding the Forgotten Feast

HANK SHAW

RODALE.

Rodale books may be purchased for
business or promotional use or for special sales.
For information, please write to:
Special Markets Department, Rodale Inc., 733 Third Avenue, New York, NY 10017

Printed in the United States of America
Rodale Inc. makes every effort to use acid-free ∞, recycled paper ♻.

Photographs by Hank Shaw on pages 26, 32, 39, 54, 55, 94, 103, 133, 149, 162, 192, 209, and 264
and all other photographs by Holly A. Heyser
Book design by Christopher Rhoads

Library of Congress Cataloging-in-Publication Data

Shaw, Hank
 Hunt, gather, cook : finding the forgotten feast / Hank Shaw.
    p.   cm.
 Includes index.
 ISBN 978-1-60529-320-2 hardcover
 1. Cooking (Wild foods)   2. Cookbooks.   I. Title.
 TX751.S465   2011
 641.6'91—dc22   2011006485

Distributed to the trade by Macmillan
2   4   6   8   10   9   7   5   3   1   hardcover

We inspire and enable people to improve their lives and the world around them.

www.rodalebooks.com

To Mom and Dad,
who showed me the way and taught me
that all things are possible.

CONTENTS

PART III:
HUNTING FOR FOOD AND FULFILLMENT

INTRODUCTION

We live in an edible world. It's all around us, if you look closely. You can see it in lawns and at the beach. It thrives along every river, on hillsides, and deep in swamps. You can even steal glimpses of it growing between the cracks of abandoned parking lots and on untended mounds of earth forgotten long ago by construction crews. Nature's garden grows, yes, but it also flies through the air, runs through the brush, and swims through the water.

Most have forgotten the feast that lives all around us. Many stalk the supermarket aisles searching, not for real, honest food, but for the latest flavor of frozen dinner or convenience food. Our hunting and gathering is now largely restricted to picking through the produce aisle for the best ear of corn or keeping an eagle's eye out for so-called bargains. But our instincts are strong. We've been hunters and gatherers eons longer than we've been farmers. Esau is far older than Jacob. Who among even the most urban of us has not eyed a ripe blackberry with interest, even lust, while walking along a path on a hot summer's day? I live in a county of nearly two million people, many of whom run, walk, or ride our local bike trail every day. On that trail, I can be assured that much of what I forage for during the year will remain untouched and unnoticed by these masses. But not the blackberry. As soon as they ripen in July, they are gorged upon by passersby. It is the gatherer in us trying to escape.

What stops the blackberry pickers from enjoying the miner's lettuce, mushrooms, or acorns that surround the bramble? Innocent ignorance and a healthy fear of the unknown. But recognizing wild plants, fish, and animals is no different than recognizing the difference between a head of lettuce and a head of cabbage, or the difference between a deer and a horse. If you can pick a blackberry, you can pick other berries. Or dandelions. Digging clams is not such a stretch, nor is fishing. And for many, with fishing comes hunting—the quest for the original free-range, organic meat does not stop at the water's edge.

I am not content to merely be a spectator in nature. I feel compelled to play the part humans were born to play. Gathering acorns. Picking berries. Digging clams. Hunting birds. These are active pursuits that bring me closer to nature and make me deeply aware that we are all part of the natural world. We cannot live outside nature, as estranged as we may feel sometimes, living in cities or subdivisions. The natural world is not a museum, filled with exhibits to be looked at but never touched. It is our home.

I've felt this need to be outside ever since I was a toddler. I am blessed with a father who gave me an overabundance of curiosity, a mother who gave me a love of the outdoors, and sisters who encouraged this from an early age. My mother taught me to fish, and some of my family's finest hours have been digging clams, fishing for stripers, and feasting at the table afterward.

As I grew older, I realized that most people weren't like us. Most people couldn't name any of the plants or animals they saw around them. My father can name every bird within a hundred miles of his house, and my mother made sure there were encyclopedias of natural history on our bookshelves, set low enough so a grade-school kid could reach them. This sort of knowledge is real power. When I walk anywhere, even in cities, my eyes automatically catalog the plants and animals around me: That's a walnut tree. Those are dandelions. Ooh, mourning doves! Wonder if there are crayfish in that stream? Look at that—a giant prickly pear that no one's tending. Someone once said that you have to really want to starve to death in the wilderness, because food is all around you. Knowing your plants and animals can mean life or death.

I want you to have that knowledge. This is why I wrote the book you are holding now. Knowing your plants and animals, learning to forage and fish and hunt, and then understanding what to do with what you have found is, for many, a deeply spiritual experience. It is for me, and for every hunter, angler, and forager I know. Once you acquire this knowledge, you may feel the same way.

What is it you will see, out there in the wild world? You'll witness things while hunting or fishing or foraging you will never experience any other way. A forager must walk off the beaten path. An angler never knows what she'll reel in. A hunter must become invisible and silent. This is why we all have so many stories. The world is endlessly fascinating—it's better than the best nature show you've ever seen. You can smell it, taste it, feel it on your skin and in your hands. As your skills strengthen, you also will begin to notice something in yourself you only dimly knew existed: You will start feeling more like a complete human, capable of foraging for supper, fishing for breakfast, and hunting for the long winter ahead. You will know how to cure meats, make foods from scratch you thought only came in boxes, and make your own wine to wash it all down with. That feeling is you emerging from your secondhand existence, like a fawn taking its first steps.

I am not asking you to forgo the supermarket. I go there every week, largely for flour, sugar, dairy products, and beer. No, I don't make my own beer. Yet. While this book focuses on fishing, foraging, and hunting skills, it also will help you learn how to make more of your meals from basic ingredients, not prepackaged foods. Honest food need not be wild, but it must be made by hand and with love.

I want to help you become a more active participant in the food you eat, the food you feed your family and friends. For the most part, that food does not come "ready to eat." It doesn't have a shiny label and wasn't raised on a factory farm or subjected to genetic modification. It is, as author Michael Pollan puts it, food your grandmother, or really your great-grandmother, would recognize. Our grandparents and great-grandparents knew many of the skills in this book. It's time we relearned them. The basic act of knowing how to find your own food, to feed yourself with a meal you didn't buy, is a small act of freedom in an increasingly regimented and mechanical world.

What, you may ask, is the big deal with wild food? For starters, wild food lived by its own devices. It was not fed a strict diet of anything. It was not fed. It fed itself. It is free from our dubious husbandry and, in most cases, is the better for it. Wild plants such as lamb's-quarters or amaranth are so full of vitamins they make spinach look like a Twinkie. Wild fish are universally recognized by eaters and experts alike as tastier than those reared by aquaculture. Why is it that wild salmon, rather than their pale farmed cousins, are so sought after? Taste. Wild game is not legal to sell in the United States, but those privileged enough to eat it know that, when properly prepared, it is infinitely more savory than its domestic counterparts. Anyone who has eaten both domestic duck and a fat mallard from the marshes knows this as a matter of faith. It is also my firm belief that the more diverse our diets are, the healthier we will be. Introducing wild food to your diet goes a long way toward achieving this goal.

Hunting occupies a full third of this book, and it is for good reason. Hunting is a pursuit utterly opaque to those not raised around it, and many of us who did grow up around hunters often remember those who set a bad example rather than a good one. This is a pity, because *these* are the "good ol' days" of hunting for much of the game that lives in North America, especially whitetail deer. The populations of game in this country are, for the most part, higher than at any time in more than a century. Thankfully, more people interested in local, fresh, and sustainable food are taking up hunting, if for no other reason than that it is more humane. Consider this: Before it was shot, a wild animal led exactly the life nature intended it to live. And a well-placed shot, which kills in seconds, is a far better fate than most deaths in the wild. But if you've never held a gun before, how do you even begin to take that first step into the field? This book provides a primer.

I also spend considerable time on fishing, mostly for the lesser-known species. You won't see tuna, salmon, or codfish in this book. In fact, the only fashionable fish included is the Pacific rock cod, which is still widely available largely because there is only a limited commercial fishery for them. I have been a fisherman all my life, and I have seen firsthand the decline of all but a handful of our fisheries. One reason for this decline is the distressing issue of bycatch, where fishermen catch species they did not intend to, and those fish are just tossed back into the sea, often to die. This happens with recreational anglers, too. I hate waste, so I learned early on that most anything you catch can be delicious, if you know how to cook it. I've always preferred odd fish, and while not all of the species I write about are truly unusual, all can be caught by hook and line, without fear of damaging the resource.

This is, at its core, a book about food. Hunting food, gathering food, and most of all, preparing food. My hope is that this book will be as useful to you in the kitchen as it is in the field. It includes recipes and techniques that will form the foundation of your wild food repertoire. Some are easy, most are more involved. A few are downright fancy. Every recipe will have domestic substitutions, such as chicken for pheasant or beef for venison, but I urge you to try to gather at least some of your own wild ingredients.

Maybe you don't want to hunt. But you can add foraged greens to a meal made with domestic meats. Maybe you forage but don't know how to fish. Now you can add a fresh-caught bass or herring or porgy to your meal. Adding wild food to your meals enlivens the dishes themselves as well as those who eat them. As the great forager Euell Gibbons once said, how can the talk at the table be dull when everything on the plate is a conversation piece? You and your family can't help but be more interested in your food when every meal comes with its own adventure story.

Eating wild foods is not only a rejection of industrial agriculture and the food manu-facturing establishment, it is also a celebration of something truly magical: a meal you cannot buy in a store at any price. And what's more: *You* brought it home, all by yourself.

PART I

FORAGING

FROM

COAST TO COAST

1

WILD GREENS ARE EVERYWHERE

The wonderful thing about wild greens is that they're all around us. Everywhere. Look out the window. I bet you're looking at some now. Even in a big city or a desert. And even in winter. That's why your first forays into foraging ought to begin at home, with something like dandelions or other wild greens. No treks through the uncharted wilderness, no danger. Not yet.

When I say "wild greens," I mean the leaves or stalk of a plant that is best eaten cooked. This separates it in my mental calculus from salad greens both wild and domestic. Some plants, such as dandelions, fit into both camps, depending on the time of year.

Why bother gathering greens when you can just buy them? First off, it's fun. There's a certain "wow" factor when you serve guests an elegant dish of, say, nettle pasta, or empanadas filled with cheese and lamb's-quarters, or dolmades made with mallow leaves instead of grape leaves. Wild greens taste better, too. They tend to be more substantial, stronger in flavor, and more vibrant.

The reason, I think, is nutrition. If Popeye had eaten amaranth or lamb's-quarters instead of spinach, he'd have been even tougher. Spinach is reasonably high in iron, vitamin A, and several other nutrients. But amaranth and lamb's-quarters blow it out of the water, and the vitamin content of nettles is legendary. Many of these greens have traditionally been eaten as a "tonic" in early spring, before new crops are ready and after the winter's storage food has become wan and sad.

You'd be amazed at how many edible plants are out there. Many hundreds, just in North America alone. Edible, yes, but worth gathering? Worth getting into your car, driving somewhere, and searching for them? That's a tall order for a plate of greens. But you rarely need to leave your yard when you want wild greens, and when you do gather greens when you're out and about, it can come as a bonus to go with whatever else you are hunting, fishing, or foraging.

Case in point: Not long ago, my girlfriend, Holly, and I were wandering along the California coast looking for good places to dig clams and catch Dungeness crabs and maybe a few fish. We were having a rough day, walking a lot and finding little, when a lurid green bushy thing caught the corner of my eye. It was a rambling, succulent plant, about 2 feet tall, draping itself over an ice plant.

"I *know* this plant!" I told Holly. I thought I'd seen it in my guidebooks, and it just *looked* edible. Once you learn what larger plant families look like—everything in the mint family has a square stem, for example—you can get a ballpark idea about whether a plant is edible. This plant looked to be in the spinach family. It had large, roughly triangular leaves that were a little fleshy and brittle. I did a test bite: salty (we were in the dunes) but otherwise good. It tasted like spinach.

I did not eat any more of it until I got home and went to my books. This is just common sense. Although there are not too many lethal plants around, it is better to be safe than dashing to the emergency room to get your stomach pumped. When I found the mystery plant in my guidebooks, sure enough, it was New Zealand spinach. (I write more about this particular green in Chapter 4.) That find helped make a tough day worthwhile.

Even if your main interest is looking for meat or fish or fruit, I highly recommend learning your area's wild greens, if only so you can salvage a potentially bad day of foraging with a plate of tasty lamb's-quarters or dandelions or orache.

What follows are some of my favorite wild greens. All are more than edible. They are delicious, pretty, and highly nutritious, and, in some cases, can cost more than $10 a pound in fancy markets. In most places, I will use the Latin names for the plants I describe, because many have all sorts of local or colloquial names; amaranth and lamb's-quarters are both called pigweed by some. Latin makes sure we're all talking about the same plant.

LAMB'S-QUARTERS, AMARANTH, AND ORACHE

Think of these three as wild spinach, which, in the case of lamb's-quarters, is biologically accurate. Their leaves are smaller than domestic spinach, usually no longer than the palm of your hand. All three are annuals, and all put out lots of little seeds, which some Native Americans ground into flour. You might know one domestic species: It's called quinoa. The leaves of each plant are good simply sautéed with olive oil, salt, and maybe some white wine and grated cheese.

If you are in North America, one of these species grows nearby. I guarantee it. All appear in late spring and last through autumn. You should be able to find these plants with little trouble between May and September.

All three plants start as compact seedlings with soft leaves that can be eaten raw, then grow into rather large sprawly bushes, with tougher leaves that bear a passing resemblance to spinach. If you are looking them up in a field guide, lamb's-quarters are in the *Chenopodium* genus, amaranth are *Amaranthus*, and orache is *Atriplex patula*.

Lamb's-quarters, amaranth, and orache all love to grow in disturbed places like roadsides. However, I don't recommend that you forage for them there, unless it is a quiet, largely untraveled road. Plants near highways and heavily trafficked areas can pick up heavy metals, and as a forager you run the risk of gathering a plant some road crew sprayed with pesticides yesterday. That could be deadly.

But fear not, this trio loves your garden, too. I get volunteer amaranth plants in my garden all the time, and I know a swath of lamb's-quarters that grows on the grounds of a nearby park. It's in an out-of-the-way spot, so I know it does not get sprayed. The edges of farm fields are an ideal spot to search for them.

Here are some tips on identifying them:

ORACHE. Orache is the easiest to recognize. It tends to like seaside areas or alkaline soil and has leaves about 3 inches long that are dramatically triangular—they look like a medieval weapon called a halberd or one of those wedge-shaped cheese knives. In some places, it's called mountain spinach; in others, saltbush. Its leaves often taste salty, which is pretty cool when you consider how bland most greens taste. It grows to about 3½ feet tall and becomes a slightly woody shrub. Its seed stalks are weedy and sparse, not dense like those of amaranth. Incidentally, you can grow domestic oraches in your garden. I grow a red variety that is striking in a mixed greens sauté.

AMARANTH. Amaranth is easily identified by a red tinge in the stalk and in the veins of the leaves. Be careful: Don't mistake it for pokeweed in the East, as eating the older leaves of pokeweed will send you to the hospital (although pokeweed's young shoots are delicious). You can identify pokeweed stems by their rich, dark purple; it's the color of blueberries. Amaranth (or pigweed) stems are a more strawberry red, like rhubarb.

Amaranth leaves are less triangular than either lamb's-quarters or orache. They are a gentle spear shape, with prominent alternate veins at regular intervals. It is most people's mental image of what a generic leaf looks like. The plant will grow to 5 feet, and once it sets seeds you can't miss it. The reddish brown seed clusters are dense and long, and often weigh so much they bend the whole plant over. They look a little like sumac. Amaranth seeds are best in mid-autumn, when the plant is dying and the seedpods are dry.

LAMB'S-QUARTERS. Lamb's-quarters share the same general look as amaranth and orache: tall, weedy, with clusters of little seeds and triangular leaves. But there is a telltale way to spot the plant. Look at the underside of the leaves: They should be silvery and ever-so-slightly fuzzy. Another tip? Water beads on their surface. If you drip water on the underside, it looks like a drop of mercury.

In all cases, pick the leaves and young shoots of the plants. I've cut a lamb's-quarters plant down by half, and it seemed unharmed; within a few weeks, it was growing new sprouts everywhere.

The simplest, best way to eat any wild greens is to wash them well, get a few table-spoons of olive oil hot in a large sauté pan, then sauté the greens in a covered pan while they

are still wet. The resulting steam helps the greens wilt quickly. Add salt as soon as they wilt, maybe some minced garlic, maybe some chile pepper, definitely black pepper, and a squeeze of lemon or lime right when you serve it. It is simplicity itself. It takes less than 5 minutes and keeps most of the nutrients in the greens.

WILD SALAD GREENS: DANDELIONS, WILD CHICORIES, AND LETTUCES

Dandelions and their cousins the chicories and wild lettuces are the "gateway drug" to serious foraging. They probably grow in your lawn, you probably know what they look like,

SOME TIPS ON USING GREENS

Variety is the spice of life. I rarely make a dish of sautéed greens from just one type of plant. Instead, I approach a hot sauté the same way I would a mixed green salad: You want something zingy, like mustard or chicory; something substantial, like lamb's-quarters, nettles, or amaranth; and you can spice things up by adding herbs like mint, oregano, basil, parsley, pea or bean shoots, chard, spinach, kale, green onions—you get the point.

Experiment, and find your own favorite combinations. Wild mustard too spicy for you? Look for mallows or dandelions or amaranth instead. Maybe you have lots of chard in your garden, but want something to jazz it up. Add mustard or chicory leaves. Mixing and matching makes for a better sauté.

Blanch your greens before sautéing to set the bright color, although this is not strictly necessary. Blanching is, however, a vital step if you plan to freeze your greens. I blanch lamb's-quarters, amaranth, mallow, and orache for 1 to 2 minutes. Most nettles get 3 to 4 minutes (although smaller, more tender varieties need only 1 to 2 minutes), and mustard, dandelions, wild lettuces, and chicories need 2 to 3 minutes. Curly dock needs a full 5 minutes. Once your greens are blanched, you're ready to use them in other recipes.

and you're aware they can be eaten. Picked young, dandelion greens are great in salads, and by mid-spring become a stewing green par excellence. When I see dandelion greens for $1.49 a bunch at the produce section of the supermarket, I smile. How about free, suckers? You will likely have several dozen dandelions growing in your yard at any given time— more than enough for a few meals.

Dandelions, wild lettuces, and chicories are to winter and early spring what lamb's-quarters, orache, and amaranth are to summer and early fall. In many places, you can get a second crop of dandelions and wild lettuces in late autumn. Look for them just before the snows fly or, in the West, right around Christmas. Nights should still be cool and days not above 70°F. The ideal time to collect yard greens is after a series of cool rains followed by some sunshine. The roots and flowers of both dandelions and chicories are edible, but I will deal with them in another chapter.

One of the best parts about picking these plants is that dandelion greens can often be found growing side by side with young chicory or wild lettuces. A general rule when identifying wild salad greens is that if it looks more or less like a dandelion or escarole leaf, and it is growing in a rosette in your yard, it's probably edible. Pick a leaf and take a bite. It should be a little bitter but not overpoweringly so. Pull the whole plant, if you can—that way, you get your weeding done at the same time you are preserving the leaves. Chicories and dandelions have a thick taproot, while lettuces have root webs much like grass.

Eat young dandelions, chicories, and wild lettuces as a salad, or sauté them briefly the way you would lamb's-quarters, amaranth, or orache.

Fun fact: Most typical yard weeds are European migrants that arrived with settlers and are still eaten back in the Old Country.

NETTLES

One of the hallmarks of nettles is that they are among the first of the fresh green things to sprout each spring. In warm climates, nettles can emerge in winter. The first time I ever ate them was in mid-January, when the nettles near my home in Northern California are about 8 inches high—prime time for picking. Nettles don't emerge until March in most of the country.

Nettles are easy to spot. They grow straight up in large patches, with thin, 4-inch leaves that look a little like lemon balm or mint, only covered with fine stinging hairs. Nettles like wet places and dappled shade. They can emerge as early as late December in Northern California and as late as April in the far north. There are several varieties, some taller, some shorter, some with nastier stings than others. But they are all nettles. And they are all good.

Never grab nettles with your bare hands, or you will be stung. Wear a glove, or use a thick bag as a shield. If the nettles are longer than about 10 inches, use only the top 6 to 8 inches.

To eat nettles, you must first defeat those stinging silica hairs, which will inject you with formic acid—the same acid employed by fire ants. Blanching them will do this and also set and brighten the nettles' striking blue-green color. To blanch nettles, fill your biggest stockpot with water and bring it to a boil, then get the water good and salty. How salty? It should taste like the sea. Grab a bunch of nettles with tongs and dunk them in the boiling water. Let them cook for 1 to 4 minutes, depending on the species of nettle. Regular nettles (*Urtica dioica*) are more substantial than their daintier cousins, the dwarf nettle (*Urtica urens*), and will need longer cooking. Once cooked, transfer the nettles to a bowl of ice water, cool, then drain. Bye-bye, formic acid; hello, delicious wild green.

Like most greenery, nettles shrink massively in the blanching process. Press the cooled, drained nettles to release more water (you can now safely drink the liquid as nettle tea because the formic acid will have dissipated). Dry the nettles on a kitchen towel. Roll the greens in the towel like a salt water taffy wrapper: One end twists one way, the other end twists the opposite way. Squeeeeze! More liquid will run out. Now you have prepped stinging nettles, ready to be frozen in a vacuum-seal bag or resealable plastic bag, or cooked in any number of ways. I do freeze some, as I like to have nettles around all year.

Sound like a lot of work? It's worth it. There is no shortage of information about the benefits of the common stinging nettle. Nettles are especially beloved by my ancestors the Scots, as well as the Italians. But really, most cultures that have nettles prize them. They are unusually high in protein for a green plant, and score well for vitamins C and A, iron, fiber, and a bunch of other goodies. This is why they've often been called a superfood.

So what do you do with these nutritional wonders? You have an array of options. Nettles, simply sautéed and served with olive oil, are pretty but bland. You could, of course, make a nettle soup or nettle tea, but these bore me. Greek cooks, however, add nettles to wild greens pies like spanakopita. Italians make nettles into pesto, use them to enrich a variety of pastas, or add them to a ravioli filling. That's more my style.

THE BRASSICA FAMILY: WILD MUSTARDS AND RADISHES

Brassicas include some of our most important vegetables: cabbage, turnips, broccoli, cauliflower, radishes, and mustard. They all bear four-petaled flowers, usually a canary yellow but also white and lavender. It's this flower, which some have likened to the holy cross, that gives these plants their other common name: cruciferous vegetables. As domestic as our brassicas have become, they have wild cousins that grow all over North America.

If you lived in Northern California, you would not be crazy to think that with just a little neglect, come April the entire region could be blanketed in the yellow, lavender, and white flowers of wild mustards, lettuces, and radishes. One of the prettiest sights I've ever seen was a whole vineyard blanketed in yellow mustard flowers in early spring; it looked like a dream. I've seen similar swaths of wild mustards in Minnesota, New Jersey, Virginia, and Canada. It's a beautiful sight.

From a culinary perspective, there is little difference between a canary-flowered wild mustard and a wild radish (lavender flowers) and a wild lettuce (white flowers). All have a zing to them, though the wild lettuces are a little milder, and all are vital ingredients in a spring greens sauté.

Wild brassicas are, however, an ephemeral pleasure. Eat these mustardy greens in warm weather at your peril, as the heat will make them pungent as hell and bitter. I like hot, and I like bitter, but by late May (or June in northern states), they're too much even for me.

Wild mustard greens are not terribly different from the domestic mustard greens you buy in the supermarket; they're just smaller and spicier. Mustard likes any spot where its pretty little brown seeds can germinate. I have seen wild mustards and radishes on arid hillsides and almost underwater in swamps.

North America's most common wild mustard is black mustard (*Brassica nigra*). If you had the patience to gather the seeds and grind them, they would make the fiercest mustard you've ever tasted. It's what I use to make my own mustard. Brown mustard seeds are a little milder, and most prepared mustard is made from yellow mustard seeds, which are milder still. Gather the seeds in late summer or early autumn, when the pods are dry.

If you have missed prime time for gathering mustard greens, you can watch for the first flush of flowers (say that fast 10 times!), then go and gather "wild broccoli," the tight clusters of unopened flower buds. We've bred broccoli to have that big flower head, but wild mustard does something similar on its own—only the clusters are more like broccoli raab or rapini, with smaller, looser heads and a definite mustard bite. They are delicious blanched for 1 to 2 minutes in salty water, then sautéed in olive oil with lots of garlic. Pick wild broccoli before the weather gets too hot; otherwise, the flower buds will be impossibly bitter.

MISCELLANEOUS GREENS

The plants I mentioned previously are the most common, easiest to identify, and, in most cases, best tasting. But there are literally hundreds of other wild green plants that have a place in the kitchen. Here are a few others worth your time.

VETCH. Vetches are a kind of wild bean that grows all over the country wherever there are nitrogen-poor soils. The little beans they produce are slightly toxic, so it's best to avoid them, but the tips of the growing plants are delicious. Simply snip the last 4 to 6 inches from the end of the plant and add it to a sauté of mixed greens or the stew pot. Vetch leaves are reminiscent of green beans in flavor and are dense and substantial, despite their lithe appearance. Collect them in spring.

CURLY DOCK LEAVES. Curly dock is a root vegetable related to burdock, which the Japanese call *gobo* and eat with great gusto. But the long, slender leaves of the dock, the edges of which resemble the frilly edge of a woman's skirt, are perfectly good wild greens. They will need 5 to 10 minutes of blanching, however, as the leaves are fairly thick, like collards. Dock is in the *Rumex* family, along with sorrel and rhubarb, so it contains a small amount of sour-tasting oxalic acid. I kinda like that; if you don't, move on to another plant. Collect curly dock leaves in spring, or in winter in warm climates like California's.

MALLOWS. Mallow grows alongside other weeds, and its leaves look like those of a geranium, vaguely maple leaf shaped but rounder. Some *Malva* species can grow to 6 feet or taller, sporting giant leaves larger than your hand. These make excellent springtime substitutes for grape leaves when making dolmades. Smaller leaves and the leaves of less gaudy mallows can be picked, chopped, and added to the stew pot. They are slightly fuzzy when raw, which I find off-putting, but the fuzz goes away after blanching. Mallow's flavor is mellow and mild and ever-so-slightly "thick." It's hard to explain, but eating a plate of cooked mallow greens will seem more substantial than eating the same-size plate of dandelion or mustard greens. This could be because mallow is slightly mucilaginous and will thicken a stew the way okra will.

RECIPES

NETTLE OR WILD GREENS RISOTTO

I created this dish for nettles, but it works well with any wild green. Blanched, nettles and most other wild greens will retain their emerald loveliness even after a good 15 minutes of cooking, which makes this dish visually stunning.

The basic structure of this risotto is pretty simple: risotto rice, cooked greens, butter, shallot, garlic, beef stock, and a little pecorino or Parmigiano-Reggiano cheese. You can use an onion instead of a shallot. You can even use vegetable or chicken stock if you want, although the flavor will be less robust.

Serves 2 as a main course, or 4 as an appetizer

- 1 cup nettles or other wild greens
- 3 tablespoons unsalted butter
- 1 large shallot, finely chopped
- 3 cloves garlic, minced
- 1 cup risotto rice (Carnaroli, Arborio, or Vialone Nano)
- 1 teaspoon salt
- 4 cups homemade beef or vegetable stock (if you use store-bought stock, only use 2 cups; otherwise, your risotto will be too salty)
- ¼ cup grated pecorino cheese

Depending on what variety of greens you use, you will need four or five big handfuls to get the 1 cup of cooked greens. Bring a large pot of water to a boil and add a handful of salt. Fill a large bowl with ice water.

Grab the nettles with tongs and add them to the boiling water. Stir around to submerge. Boil for 1 to 2 minutes for dwarf nettles, or 2 to 4 minutes for regular nettles. Amaranth, orache, lamb's-quarters, dandelion, or chicory greens need 3 to 4 minutes.

Fish the greens out with a skimmer or the tongs and immediately dump them into the bowl of ice water. Once they are cool, drain in a colander, and then roll the greens in a clean tea towel. Twist one end of the towel one way and the other end, the other way (like a candy wrapper), squeezing out as much moisture as you can.

Finely chop the greens. Don't use a food processor, or you will get mush. The finer you chop, the smoother your risotto will be. Pick out any stray stems, which will show themselves after you chop the greens.

TO MAKE THE RISOTTO: Heat 2 tablespoons of the butter in a large heavy pot set over medium-high heat. When the butter stops frothing, add the shallot. Cook for 2 to 3 minutes, stirring often, then add the garlic and rice, and stir to combine. Cook, stirring constantly, for 1 minute, or until the rice is well coated.

Stir the salt and 1 cup of the stock into the rice and turn the heat to high. When it starts boiling, turn the heat down to medium and cook, stirring at least every minute or so, until the rice absorbs the stock. Repeat with a second cup of stock.

When the second cup has been absorbed, add the greens and a third cup of stock. If you are using store-bought broth, switch to water so the risotto doesn't become too salty. Stir well to combine. From this point on, you should be stirring constantly to develop the creaminess in the risotto and to distribute the nettles evenly.

When the third addition of liquid has been absorbed, taste the risotto. The rice should be al dente—soft enough so you want to eat it, but still a little firm. Add up to 1 more cup of stock or water, as you want the risotto to have a loose consistency. Add the cheese and the remaining 1 tablespoon butter. Stir everything well and let the butter and cheese melt in the risotto for 2 or 3 minutes, stirring often. Add salt to taste and serve at once.

If you have leftovers, you can stir a beaten egg into the risotto, form into patties or balls, roll in bread crumbs, and fry in olive oil for a traditional Italian treat called *arancini*.

WILD GREENS RAVIOLI

This is a traditional ravioli recipe from the Alto Adige and Trentino regions in the far north of Italy. Because it is so cold there, some farms cultivate rye, which handles the alpine climate better than wheat. That rye finds its way into the pasta for these ravioli, which are made in early spring when stinging nettles are still tender. You can substitute other greens, such as lamb's-quarters, dandelions, or spinach.

The mascarpone is important to this dish. If you absolutely cannot find it, you can substitute ricotta, but it will not be the same.

Serve these ravioli sautéed briefly in simple, high-quality butter and sprinkled with freshly ground black pepper and some grated dry cheese. A white wine from Friuli or some other big white wine would be an ideal accompaniment.

Makes 35–40 ravioli

FILLING

   2 Yukon gold or other waxy potatoes

   4 ounces mascarpone

   A little less than 1 cup finely chopped, blanched stinging nettles or other greens

   Salt and freshly ground black pepper

DOUGH

   5 ounces all-purpose flour (1 heaping cup)

   5 ounces rye flour (1 heaping cup)

   Pinch of salt

   ⅔ cup water

   1 egg

   Olive oil

TO MAKE THE FILLING: Peel and boil the potatoes until they are tender, then set aside to cool.

In a bowl, mash the cooked potatoes, mascarpone, and nettles into a cohesive paste. Do this by hand, not with a food processor, as it is important for the texture. Add salt and pepper to taste.

TO MAKE THE DOUGH: Whisk or sift the flours and salt in a large bowl to combine. Make a well in the center and add the water and egg. Use a fork to stir the egg and water together, then gradually incorporate the flour until you get a shaggy mass.

With your hands, fold the dough over itself until it comes together, then knead for 5 to 8 minutes. Add a little flour if the dough gets sticky.

Coat the dough with a thin film of olive oil and wrap in plastic. Set aside for 1 hour at room temperature, or up to overnight in the fridge. Cut off about one-quarter of the dough and roll it out in a pasta machine. How thick? Your choice. I normally like thin pasta sheets for ravioli, but with this pasta, the green in the filling shows through clearly, so I go only to number 6 on my Atlas pasta maker, three clicks from the thinnest setting.

Cut the pasta sheet in half lengthwise and set aside. Lay one-half of the sheet on your work surface and put a teaspoon of filling every 2 inches or so along the length of the sheet. Get yourself a little bowl of water, and dip your finger in and moisten the pasta all around your filling. Just use a little water, not too much.

Lay the second piece of pasta over the first and press to seal the ravioli, starting from the edges nearest the filling. Try to push out as much air as possible. With a knife, pizza cutter, or circle cutter, cut the sheet into the individual ravioli. Repeat with the rest of the dough and filling. Each raviolo will be roughly a 2-inch circle or square.

You can freeze the ravioli at this point by arranging them in a single layer on a baking sheet and placing it in the freezer until they are solid. Then transfer to a plastic bag, or, better yet, vacuum-seal them. Vacuum-sealed, they will last up to 4 months; in the plastic bag, the ravioli will begin to deteriorate in 2 months.

To cook, boil the ravioli in lots of salty water until they float, and then let them cook on the surface for another 1 or 2 minutes. You can then sauce them any way you want, or serve the ravioli simply, sautéed in a little butter and topped with grated pecorino or Parmigiano-Reggiano cheese and freshly ground black pepper.

2

FRUITS AND BERRIES OF THE WILD

One day, not too long ago, while I was hunting deer at a friend's place, I came across a huge patch of *Opuntia*, the prickly pear cactus. I knew the Sicilians ate them, as did the Spanish and Mexicans, but that was about all I knew about this odd plant. As it happened, the deer were nowhere to be found that day, so I asked my friend if I could collect some of the prickly pears' magenta fruits, which covered the cacti like a Christmas display—one bristling with vicious thorns.

She said yes, and, armed with heavy gardening gloves, I plucked five dozen of the little nasties from the cactus and dropped them into a paper bag. I smashed one on the ground to see what the inside looked like. It was a lurid, doesn't-occur-in-nature magenta. Only it does. Trippy.

I had no idea what to do with these fruits, but I soon learned they make a great base for syrup. That syrup can be used to make drinks, ice cream, sorbet, and even a glaze for a roast pheasant.

Prickly pear is one of the few wild fruits that are identical to the store-bought variety—if you can find them in a store. Most varieties of fruit you can buy in a supermarket have a wild cousin that is smaller and more concentrated in flavor; this is the virtue that makes up for the wild fruit's generally smaller size. Ever eat a tiny woodland strawberry? If you have, you can summon the taste instantly, because there may be no better fruit on earth—or one harder to collect in quantity.

Like greens, berries are an excellent way to begin foraging. I started picking berries as a toddler and have never stopped. For the most part, berries are easy to identify, sweet, and need no cooking or processing to eat. If you've eaten a domestic blackberry, raspberry, strawberry, or blueberry, you can easily identify their wild cousins in the field.

Finding a patch with good berries is special, and divulging the locations of such patches is not something to be taken lightly. If you have foraged for berries or any other fruit, you know that one bush or tree may produce wonderful fruit, while the next may be bland. I once found an unusually sweet patch of gooseberries in Minnesota; I'd stumbled upon it while looking (unsuccessfully) for morel mushrooms. I can still find that patch today, and I've never told another soul where it is.

Never eaten a gooseberry? How about another Minnesota specialty, the highbush cranberry? Or manzanita berries? Or pawpaws, which, while not actually a berry, are still something of a secret fruit along eastern rivers?

North America is home to so many native fruits that all but the most obsessive of foragers will never taste them all. There is the hackberry, the barberry, the mulberry, the mayapple, and so many varieties of gooseberries and currants that even taxonomists have trouble keeping track of them all. There are, of course, wild strawberries, raspberries, blueberries, and blackberries; these you know already. But they have friends, like the huckleberry, cloudberry, dewberry, and thimbleberry. Crab apples are native, as are Juneberries and hawthorn. There is wild plum, goose plum, beach plum, and Canada plum. There is a sweet cherry, sandcherry, chokecherry, and chokeberry. We have wild grapes galore, none more magical than the muscadine of the Deep South. Oregon has a grape that is not a grape. Forest foragers can find the little partridgeberry, while swamp dwellers know well the cranberry. *Diospyros virginiana*, the native persimmon, was a delight of Colonial Americans, and the California Native Americans loved manzanita berries so much that they held festivals in their honor.

Setting aside some of the more obvious wild fruits and berries, here is a selection of unusual fruits that are worth your efforts to find.

WILD GRAPES

You probably have access to wild grapes and don't even know it. Varieties of wild grapes live in nearly every state, although most of the land that makes up the Great Basin is not generally a grapey spot. Southerners are blessed with muscadines, which have a distinct aroma and flavor that is as southern as tupelo honey and grits. All wild grapes are stronger in aroma than domestic grapes, and this comes through powerfully in jellies and syrups.

You can eat them right off the vine, too, though wild grapes tend to have tough skins and lots of seeds.

Don't be tempted to make wild grape wine, however, unless you can will yourself to not compare it to a wine made from *Vitis vinifera*, the variety most commercial wineries use. The aroma of wild grape wine is very different, almost musky, and the sugar levels in wild grapes are unlikely to be as high as in a wine grape. Trust me, you'll be disappointed.

Start searching for grapes in early summer around the edges of meadows or creek bottoms, where vines often drape over trees. You should be able to see nascent grape clusters at that stage. Some vines will be loaded, others nearly bare. Remember those vines and return to them in late summer or early autumn.

I've picked fox grapes (*Vitis labrusca*) on Block Island, Rhode Island, in September, and this is a pretty universal month for harvesting both wild and domestic grapes. The wild grapes near my home in Northern California are edible by August, but most wild grapes won't ripen until late September. Taste grapes from several different clusters, as not all clusters ripen at the same time, and grapes will not ripen further after you pick them.

Gather them in late morning, if possible, and do your best to keep them intact. Busted grapes are sticky and can spontaneously ferment in a few hours. I use a short-bladed, sharp pocketknife or shears to cut the grape clusters, which I then layer gently in a satchel or 5-gallon bucket.

PRICKLY PEARS

Prickly pears live all over the country, not just in deserts. You can find them even in cold climates such as Montana. And they are easy to spot: If the cactus grows in paddles like a beaver's tail, it's an *Opuntia*, and its fruit is edible.

Since my first experiments with those prickly pears I'd gathered after my unsuccessful deer hunt, I learned a lot about the fruit of the *Opuntia* cactus. The first thing I learned is that it stores really well in the fridge. I'd left some in the refrigerator for nearly a month, and it was fine. In the wild, the fruit will stay on the cactus for months, if the birds don't get it. Color is one indication of ripeness: The fruit will turn from green to magenta, red, orange, or yellow. Cut a fruit open to see if it is ripe inside, too: The color will be deep all the way to the center.

The tricky part about prickly pears is learning how to get these little flavor grenades out of their spiky skins. It's not the big, seemingly vicious spines you need to worry about: It's the hairlike glochids covering the fruit that will get you. Imagine a zillion invisible splinters all over your hands. Hateful, evil glochids. Even the name sounds like some monster in a horror film. At first, I sliced off the skins and dropped the magenta centers into a bowl. A better method is to torch the fruits briefly on a grill or burner to burn off the glochids. You can then use a knife to slice off the skins. If you do get the glochids all over you, fellow forager Connie Green offers a great solution in her book *The Wild Table*: Dip the glochid-infested area in melted wax. The glochids will adhere to the wax!

Once the fruits are skinned, you need to separate the seeds from the pulp. Technically, the seeds are edible, but those who say so must have far stronger teeth than I do. It's like eating wood chips. Pulse the skinned fruits in a blender, then push the pulp through a food mill with the coarse plate—the holes in the plate should be just large enough to block the seeds, which the blender will have broken into large pieces. You could stop here, but I am something of a fanatic when it comes to clarity (I developed this particular neurosis from making wine). So I pass the pulpy juice through a fine-mesh sieve, then through cheesecloth into a measuring cup.

After that, I combine the juice with an equal volume of sugar in a saucepan and bring it to a simmer to reduce a little. Prickly pears are loaded with vitamin C, and this is a vitamin that's destroyed by extended heating, so I limit the heat as much as possible. Once the sugar is dissolved, I turn off the heat and add some citric acid.

Why add acid? Third lesson learned: Prickly pears taste like a combination of bubble gum, watermelon, and strawberries, but they totally lack tartness. Without acid, they are not very tasty. Citric acid tastes neutral, while lemon juice, another easy source of acidity, brings other flavors to the party. Either way, the result is pure magenta power.

A natural way to use this syrup is to mix it with tequila in a cocktail—it's cactus and cactus! You can also drizzle some on a plate with a *torchon* of foie gras, make prickly pear sorbet, or use the syrup as a glaze for a game bird.

GOOSEBERRIES AND CURRANTS

An English favorite, currants—and their cousins the gooseberries—grow in cooler regions all over the northern tier of the United States, as well as in mountainous regions. They are not generally known as heat-loving berries. More than 150 species grow around the Northern Hemisphere, and all are edible to some degree. My advice is to forage widely and remember the location of plants with good-tasting fruit.

Currants and gooseberries grow on spiky bushes, and gooseberry bushes are spikier than currant bushes. Both have distinctive leaves that look a little like a crinkly maple leaf with rounded edges. Once you can recognize the leaves, you're in business. Currants set fruit in clusters, while gooseberries tend to set fruit singly. Gooseberries have a little tuft on the bottom, like a billy goat's beard, and are striped like a hot-air balloon. Unripe, gooseberries are smartly tart and pale green, and this is how they are most often marketed. In this condition, they're perfect for jams or jellies. Ripe gooseberries tend to be purplish and are far sweeter. Birds adore them, which might be another reason you rarely see them sold ripe.

Currants, on the other hand, are always sold ripe, and that's how you should pick them. They are generally one of two main colors, black and red, much like Johnnie Walker Scotch. In general, currants are better as a raw berry than are gooseberries.

One gooseberry that grows near my part of Northern California, *Ribes californicum*, does bear delicious fruit, but the fruit itself is protected by alarmingly sharp spikes. Wear gloves when picking them, and then you'll need to cook the berries, which softens the spines. This is a good berry for syrup or jelly, as is its currant cousin, the Sierra currant, which often lives in sight of the California gooseberry. This currant, *Ribes nevadense*, has blue-black fruit (like a purple grape with a bloom on it) that is covered in funny little hairs that look like the stubble on my chin after a day without shaving.

If you expect to escape weirdly prickly gooseberries in the Midwest, you'll be disappointed. While there are some prickle-free varieties, all the gooseberries I found in the woods of Minnesota and Wisconsin were the eastern prickly gooseberry, *Ribes cynosbati*. Though they are perfectly tasty, the prickles keep most people from eating them raw.

Unlike most berries, gooseberries and currants are high in pectin. That means you can use them in jelly or jam with no need to add pectin or a pectin-rich fruit like apples.

MULBERRIES

Until recently, a mere mention of mulberries would get me going. I hate mulberry trees. Mulberries can send out suckers in all directions, sprouting new trees even if you chop down the main trunk. They can conquer your yard and are nearly impossible to kill. What's worse, the fruit is boring, with no acid. Not worth eating.

Such was my belief for years. I was wrong.

One day, while walking around my neighborhood, I found a fruiting mulberry tree in a little park near my house. I picked a few for a trail snack and stopped midstride. I was shocked: These mulberries weren't at all insipid! They were tart and sweet and irresistible.

Ever get one of those "I've been here before" moments? That's what happened to me as I was eating those mulberries. When I was a boy, I used to play in the woods behind my elementary school in New Jersey, and at the edge of those woods stood a mulberry tree. Put me there right now, and I can walk you straight to it. Looking back, I am sure lots of people knew this mulberry, but my friends and I thought of it as our own secret larder. In between "playing army" or whatever, we would gorge ourselves on mulberries, which came into season right as school was ending in late June.

The day after my discovery in the park, I returned with a plastic container and picked 3 cups of mulberries in about 10 minutes. I saw that there would be more ripe berries in a few days. Mulberries don't all ripen at once, and they turn from a light crimson to a deep purple with reddish undertones.

Mulberry trees are easy to recognize: When the berries are ripe, they are the only thing in North America that looks like a blackberry "tree." The trees have a light-colored bark and lightly serrated leaves with prominent, light green veins.

There are several varieties of mulberries in the United States, including a native American mulberry. Colonists brought over the Chinese white mulberry centuries ago in an attempt to raise silkworms, which eat the leaves of these mulberries. Sadly, the worms all died. The trees did not, also sadly. By all accounts, the fruit of the white mulberry lacks any acid at all. So if you stumble upon a white mulberry tree, I recommend that you keep on walking.

Mulberries are super high in vitamin C; reasonably good for iron, potassium, and vitamin K; and they'll give you a little fiber. Mulberries are also high in resveratrol, the substance present in red wine that experts say helps fight cancer. Plus, they taste good.

Once you have a mess of mulberries, you can do all kinds of things with them. Mulberry ice cream is excellent, as is mulberry sauce for venison or hare. You should, however, eat some simply: in a bowl, with cream. Berries and cream is my favorite breakfast in the world. Another excellent idea is to make a mulberry sorbet spiked with homemade elderberry liqueur. It's definitely worth the effort.

Mulberries have a flavor all their own. Though they most resemble blackberries, they are denser, a little chewier, and not as tart. Mulberries possess a kind of high sweetness, an alto to blackberry's baritone. Blackberries are a Cabernet Sauvignon; mulberries are a Pinot Noir.

MANZANITA BERRIES

Manzanita, known to botanists as the *Arctostaphylos* clan, means "little apple" in Spanish. Indeed, the Franciscan friars, who were the first European settlers of California, made a sort of cider from the berries of the manzanita bush. You'll find these bushes growing in great profusion in the Sierra Nevada of California, but other species will grow as far north as British Columbia and as far east as Texas. They are, for the most part, lovers of arid places.

It doesn't matter which species you come across—all manzanita berries are edible. A few species of manzanita are endangered, so pick from large masses of the plants, not isolated individual bushes.

Manzanita is easy to recognize. Depending on species, it can be anything from a ground

cover to a small tree, but it's usually a shrub. The bark and leaves are distinctive: The bark is deep red and flakes off like the aftermath of a bad sunburn, and the evergreen leaves are thick, almost round, and seem to glow under the moonlight. If you touch the trunk, it will often feel cool. The berries look like teeny Granny Smith apples, even developing a pretty blush of red-brown on the sunny side. Manzanita is one of North America's most beautiful bushes.

Most people, even most foragers, don't know that manzanita is edible. Eaten raw, the berries are pretty sawdusty. Manzanita berries are loaded with tannin, too, which will fill your mouth with a dry, felty feeling, especially if you are fool enough to pop a bunch of berries into your mouth raw.

When cooked and strained, however, manzanita makes something that tastes very much like a dry, hard apple cider, only without the alcohol. You can make syrup out of this cider and from there make ice cream or sorbet, or use it as a concentrate for a cooling drink or a manzanita martini.

Here's what you need to know to make manzanita cider.

🌿 Pick berries anywhere from late June in the lowlands to October in high elevations. You want them green with a bit of blush where the berries have been exposed to the sun. Berries in full shade won't get the blush, but you can still pick them.

🌿 Wash the berries, which will be dusty and might have debris on them.

🌿 Crush the berries with a potato masher or in a mortar and pestle. Don't wail on them, just bruise and lightly break the berries. Put the crushed berries in a large pot, cover with boiling water, and let them steep at room temperature overnight.

 The next day, pour the cider through a fine sieve into a bowl. Now do it again, this time through cheesecloth into a Mason jar. Put the lid on the jar and let this sit in the fridge overnight. More sediment will fall to the bottom. Carefully decant the good cider from the jar, leaving as much of the fine sediment in the original jar as possible. The sediment is loaded with tannins, which you want out of your cider.

 Enjoy your cider! Sweeten to taste for a cooling drink. I add 2 tablespoons of sugar for every pint of cider. Or, to make manzanita syrup, heat it and add an equal volume of sugar to the cider.

HIGHBUSH CRANBERRIES

Not actually a member of the cranberry family, the highbush cranberry is a species of *Viburnum*, which is used extensively in landscape plantings. Highbush cranberry bushes live in the understory of older forests and can reach a dozen feet high or more. It is a plant of the far north, although you can sometimes find it in mountainous areas as far south as Virginia. It is most common in upper New England and in the northern parts of Michigan, Wisconsin, and Minnesota.

Minnesota is where I first picked highbush cranberries. I was grouse hunting and came across a leafless bush with grayish bark laden with scarlet berries so bright they seemed unnatural. My friend Chris said they were highbush cranberries. I ate one, and zing! Holy tartness, Batman! It was definitely cranberry-like, with a hint of sweet and something else, something just a little funky.

A highbush cranberry has a single large seed shaped like a lens—far flatter than a typical pit. So if you are wandering around the north woods from September to November and see a bush festooned with brilliant red berries, smash one and look for that telltale pit. Then you'll know you have a highbush cranberry.

In springtime you can identify the bush by its flower clusters, which, if you look closely, form an odd pattern: It'll have a number of five-petaled larger flowers surrounding a tighter cluster of much smaller flowers. The big ones are sterile, and scientists believe they are used to draw pollinators toward the less showy fertile flowers in the center. This is another giveaway that you have a highbush cranberry in front of you.

You can pick the berries as soon as they turn red, but they will be megatart until the plant gets hit by frost a few times. Even then, don't expect them to taste like a strawberry. Highbush cranberries need sugar the same way regular cranberries do. I made syrup out of the berries I picked. To make it, you run the ripe berries through a food mill to separate the seeds from the pulp. For every cup of berry pulp, you add a cup of water and a cup of sugar. Bring to a boil, then simmer for 5 minutes. Turn off the heat, and let this steep until it cools to room temperature. Strain it through cheesecloth set over a bowl to clarify, then pour it in a jar and refrigerate. One of my favorite uses for the syrup is as a glaze for ruffed grouse or other game birds. Roast grouse tastes like the forest, and it was a rare treat to add the sweet-tart funkiness of the highbush cranberries.

The syrup can also become the base of a jelly. An even easier use for highbush cranberries would be to submerge the washed whole berries in vodka to make a compelling liqueur.

ELDERBERRIES

Several varieties of elderberries grow in North America, but the thing to remember is go for the deep blue-black berries, not the red ones. The red elderberry is technically edible, but

every forager I've read who's tried them says they are horrible. It is also important to know that the only edible parts of the blue elderberry are the flowers and the ripe berries. The stems, leaves, and unripe berries are slightly toxic; eating significant amounts can make you nauseous. So get as many of the teeny stems off the berry or flower cluster as you can before you eat them. A few won't matter, but the more thorough you are, the better.

You'll learn more about the most famous use for elderberries—elderberry wine—in Chapter 6. But the deep blue berries have plenty of other uses, such as jams or sauces or as a wonderful ingredient for a sweet after-dinner liqueur. You can eat elderberries fresh, but be warned: Some people get an upset stomach from eating them.

Look for elderberries near wet places—not in a river or a swamp, but next to one. I've found bushes along rivers, on high ground near marshes, along mountain streams, and ringing remote lakes. The shape of the plant can change, but it is generally a tall, sprawly bush, often 10 to 15 feet high. Occasionally, it will become a small tree. Elderberries set fruit on a wide, flat cluster that looks a little like Queen Anne's lace when it is in flower.

The berries do not all ripen at once. In California, you can find green berries on some bushes in May, and late June is the earliest you can expect ripe berries. In most places, they don't ripen until September. But beware, slackers! Deer love elderberries. I've seen a lot of nibbled-off spots on the bushes we pick from. By late September, the only remaining elderberries will be too high for the deer to get, and then you need to worry about birds. So scout your area early and keep watch over it.

The best berries are on stalks that have begun to turn a bit reddish; there will be a few elderberry raisins on them. These will be riper and come off the stems easier. But the larger black berries on stalks with light green stems are also okay.

It is a chore to destem elderberries. It took me more than 3 hours to destem 12 pounds of berries last season. You need to be patient and have a light hand, as the berries are fragile. Work with small portions of each cluster at a time, and gently rake your half-open hand through the berries, letting them fall into a bowl set beneath you. Again, let me stress the word *gently*. Unripe berries hold on to the stem, while ripe ones fall off easily. And you don't want to eat green berries.

What to do with all these berries? Admire them, to start. Poured into a large, flat container, they look like $10,000 worth of caviar: shiny, tiny black orbs. So pretty! Dip your face close, and you will get a strong aroma of wine grapes.

After you have suitably admired your hard-won berries, you can move on to make elderberry wine or elderberry liqueur; a recipe for the latter follows. Elderberry jelly and elderberry syrup are both wonderful, and a shot of elderberry syrup is especially good in a pan sauce for wild duck or venison.

RECIPES

Below are some recipes for syrups, liqueurs, jellies, and sorbets that, while written for specific wild fruits, will also work with many other kinds of fruit. Experiment and use these recipes as guidelines.

PRICKLY PEAR SYRUP

Commercial versions of this syrup are used for fancy margaritas or poured over pancakes, two excellent ideas. I strongly advise you to buy citric acid for this recipe, to keep the flavors pure. You can often find it in the canning aisle of the supermarket under names like Fruit Fresh. You can also buy it at home-brew supply stores.

This recipe is a guide. Prickly pears—indeed all fruits—come in all sizes and sweetness levels, so use your tastebuds and common sense to adjust the ratio as needed. Remember, the basic ratio for a syrup is an equal volume of liquid (fruit pulp and water) to sugar.

When working with prickly pears, wash your counters, any plastic containers, and cutting board frequently because the juice stains like crazy.

Makes 1 quart

25–30 small prickly pears, or 10–15 medium to large ones

3 cups granulated sugar

1 tablespoon citric acid, or the juice of 2 lemons

Peel the prickly pears and puree the pulp in a food processor. This should take about 30 seconds. There will be lots of seeds in there rattling around that you'll need to filter out. Do this by running the contents of the blender through a colander, food mill, or coarse sieve into a large bowl.

For a clear syrup, push the contents of the bowl through a fine-mesh sieve, and for a really clear syrup, strain that through cheesecloth.

You should have about 3 cups of juice. Pour the juice in a heavy pot and add the sugar. For a syrup that will be shelf stable, add an equal amount of granulated sugar to your prickly pear juice. If you like things less sweet, you can add less, but the resulting syrup will not last as long and will need to be refrigerated.

Slowly bring the sugar and juice to a simmer over medium heat. Stir the mixture until the sugar dissolves, and then simmer for 5 minutes. Turn off the heat and let it cool for 20 minutes, or until it is warm enough to taste without burning your tongue. Add citric acid a little at a time and taste as you go. When it is tart enough for you, stop.

While still warm, pour into clean Mason jars and seal with a clean unused lid. This should keep for months in the fridge, or you could process it in a boiling water bath for 10 minutes if you want to keep it in the pantry. To do this, fill a pot large enough to hold the jar of syrup with water. Set something in the pot to keep the jar from touching the bottom; I use a vegetable steamer. Bring the water to a boil, submerge the jar of syrup in it, and boil for 10 minutes. Remove the jar and set on a cutting board. Your lid should pop at some point to indicate you've properly sealed the jar. When the syrup has completely cooled, check the seal by unscrewing the rim, leaving just the lid. Carefully pick up the jar by the lid only. It should stick. If it doesn't, try again with a new lid or store in the fridge.

MULBERRY OR BLACKBERRY SORBET

This recipe works with any soft berry, such as blueberries, blackberries, raspberries, strawberries, or gooseberries. If you are using a hard fruit, such as manzanita, make syrup first by using the Prickly Pear Syrup recipe as a guide. Then start your sorbet with the syrup.

Mulberry sorbet is smooth and deep purple, sexed up a bit by adding a little liqueur. I make this sorbet with wild mulberries from a tree near my house. As for the liqueur, try to find cassis, which is made from blackberries. Many liquor stores carry it.

If you use a lighter-colored fruit for this recipe, such as strawberries, thimbleberries, or gooseberries, use a lighter liquor. Grappa is always a good choice.

Makes 2 pints

1 cup sugar

1 cup water

5 cups mulberries or blackberries, stems removed

¼ cup cassis, elderberry, or blackberry liqueur, or port

Bring the sugar and water to a boil over medium heat. Stir to dissolve the sugar, and let it simmer gently for 3 to 4 minutes. Turn off the heat and let the syrup cool a bit.

Meanwhile, put the berries in a blender. Pour the syrup over them while it is warm but not hot. Blend into a puree. Use a rubber spatula or wooden spoon to push the mixture through a fine-mesh sieve set over a bowl. This removes a lot of the seeds and any remaining stems.

Add the liquor to the bowl and chill the mixture in the fridge for 1 hour or so.

Pour into your ice cream maker and follow its directions. If you don't have an ice cream maker, pour the mixture into a small casserole dish and set in the freezer. When it is frozen—the alcohol will keep the mixture from freezing rock hard—serve by using a fork to scrape it into shaved ice. Technically, this shaving method makes granita, not sorbet, but it's just as good.

ELDERBERRY LIQUEUR

This recipe produces a warm, rich liqueur reminiscent of a tawny port wine, only stronger. Elderberries resemble little grapes, with a similar aroma, bloom on the skin, and color. I always use fresh elderberries for this recipe, although dried or frozen ones work, too. Remember to destem all the berries—the stems are slightly toxic.

Use 100-proof vodka instead of the more traditional 80 proof to get better extraction of flavor from the berries. Everclear and other super-high alcohol spirits work great, too, but are so strong they will knock you on your ass with just a shot. If you can find it, use grappa, which is made from grapes and is a superior base for a fruit liqueur.

Any sweet fruit will work with this recipe. If you use an acidic one like blackberries, omit the lemon rind.

Makes 1 quart

  1 pint elderberries, stems removed

  1 quart 100-proof vodka

  2–3 pieces (1 inch) lemon peel, white pith removed

  Sugar

Put the elderberries in a 1-quart Mason jar and pour in the vodka. Add the lemon peel and seal. Put the jar in a dark cupboard for at least 1 month, or up to 6 months. The alcohol will extract flavor from the elderberries over time, so the longer you let it sit, the inkier it will get.

Check periodically, and when it is the color you want—anything from a Pinot Noir color to downright black—pour the vodka through a strainer lined with cheesecloth into another quart jar. Add at least ¼ cup of sugar. If you want a sweeter liqueur, you can add up to ½ cup. Seal the jar, shake to combine, and put the jar back in the cupboard.

Every day, check the liqueur and shake it to help the sugar dissolve. After a few days, it will have completely dissolved. Your elderberry liqueur is now ready to drink. It keeps for years, but you will drink it up long before then.

3

ACORNS: LOVING THE UNLOVED

I ask you to reconsider the humble acorn. This nut from the oak tree falls to the ground by the thousands, in nearly every state in the nation and in scores of shapes and sizes. You probably walked past several today. Acorns are all around us, yet rare are the people who can say they've ever eaten them. Eating acorns is uncommon even among dedicated foragers.

Oh, I know what you're thinking: They're poisonous. Intolerably bitter. Flavorless. Too much work to shell. Too much work to process. Not worth the effort. Mealy.

None of this is true. Making acorns good to eat is far easier than many other cooking tasks we do cheerfully on a weekend and can take far less time than you might think.

I first learned that acorns could be eaten as a high school student, when my class went on a field trip to see a 300-year-old white oak tree, planted when the town was newly founded. It was the biggest tree I had ever seen, and I was astounded at the sea of fallen acorns around it. I pointed at them and asked the teacher, "Can you eat those?"

"Some people do," she said. Who? "Indians, I think."

This was New Jersey in the 1980s. I'd never even met an Indian, let alone met one who ate acorns, and I soon lost interest in eating acorns. Some years later, while reading Euell Gibbons, I learned again that yes, acorns can be eaten. But even the great Euell largely wrote off acorns as too much work. Still, every so often I'd eye a giant oak standing amid a swath of acorns and wonder.

Finally, a few years ago, Holly and I sat down at Incanto, a fancy restaurant in San Francisco. Looking over the menu, I stopped short: "Acorn Soup." I asked the waitress if this was acorn squash soup. "No, it is made with acorns. The chef made it himself." I ordered the soup, and it was good—pureed, thick, like a woodland version of potato-leek soup. Monochromatic, yes, but tasty. I asked the chef, Chris Cosentino, how he did it. Cosentino said it took several days of leaching to remove the bitterness from the acorns.

Several days?! I went back to Gibbons's book and reread the chapter on acorns. According to Gibbons, it took hours, not days. He just boiled the acorns in several changes of water. I became determined to repeat Cosentino's soup, using Gibbons's method.

A year went by. I was busily collecting green olives with my friend Elise when I stumbled on a huge fall of California valley oak acorns. Within minutes, we'd gathered about 10 pounds. Game on! A few weeks later, I processed the acorns one morning while watching college football. Without missing a play, I had them ready to eat by the end of the game. Anyone who has ever made his own stock or homemade pasta, filleted a fish, braised beef short ribs, baked and decorated a layer cake, or planted a garden can process acorns.

Turns out we can learn something about processing acorns by watching squirrels, who love them very much. Squirrels don't bury every acorn they find. Scientists observing squirrel behavior in the East noticed something unusual. The fuzzy varmints would seek out white oak acorns and gorge themselves—then dash off to find and bury the acorns of other oaks, mainly the red oak. Why? Turns out white oak acorns are low in the bitter tannins that give all acorns such a bad name. Red oak acorns tend to be high in tannins. But tannins are water soluble. So by burying the red oak acorns, the squirrel hid them from the stealing blue jays (and rival squirrels) and plunked them into water-rich soil. After rain and snow and freezing and thawing, the tannins leach into the soil and leave the red oak acorn sweet enough to eat.

This brilliant feat performed by what is essentially a bushy-tailed rat is the best way of showing you that there are acorns and then there are acorns. Some really are so bitter or small that they're not worth eating. But others, like the eastern white oak, the bellota oaks of Europe, and the Emory oak of the Southwest, are sweet enough to need minimal or, in rare cases, no processing.

Unlocking the secret of acorns goes a long way toward solving what I call the Forager's Dilemma. If you are a skilled hunter-gatherer, finding meat and fish is not terribly difficult. And wild greens, berries, and other yummy plants are pretty easy to find, too. Where things get tricky is that third leg of the nutritional stool: starch. For the most part, finding a sufficient supply of this staff of life is no easy task in the wild. Unless you are near a swamp—where there are several wild sources of carbohydrates, such as the cattail and the arrowhead plant—there is no easier way to collect sufficient starch for a whole year than to collect and process acorns. This is what many Native American groups did, especially in California. Keep in mind that I am not suggesting you give up wheat or potatoes or rice for a diet of acorns. But as a piece of a diverse diet, acorns deserve a place in serious modern cooking.

Chestnuts and acorns share enough culinary traits that any chestnut recipe can become an acorn recipe. In fact, acorns have been used interchangeably with chestnuts in Europe and North Africa for millennia. They are still eaten with some frequency in Korea. While not easy to find, you can suss out a few acorn recipes from the Berbers, Spanish, Italians, and French. Farther north, the Germans drink an acorn coffee.

With few exceptions, however, acorns have been stigmatized as famine food nearly everywhere in the world. North African Berbers still use acorns, however. I corresponded with Paula Wolfert, who wrote the great *Couscous and Other Good Food from Morocco*—the sine qua non of Moroccan cookbooks—and she said that Berbers will sometimes make couscous from acorn flour. Linda Berzok, who wrote *American Indian Food*, says that the Native Americans around Tucson, Arizona, sell roasted acorns from the Emory oak, which they say are so sweet they don't need leaching. An expert on Mexican food told me that in Chihuahua they do the same thing; the Emory oak lives there, too.

My first experiment with acorns was as a coffee substitute. I collected the acorns, then shelled, leached, dried, and ground them into flour. Then I put 2 tablespoons in a press pot and poured boiling water over it. I let the mixture steep for a few minutes and poured it into a coffee cup. It was not black, like the chicory coffee I often make. In fact, it looked like it already had a little cream in it. I put some sugar in the cup and tasted it . . . and I'll be damned if it didn't taste uncannily like tea with cream in it. But that's just one of many ways to make acorns shine in the kitchen.

COLLECTING AND PROCESSING ACORNS

Using acorns as food pretty much falls into three categories: eating acorns as nuts (they are a lot like chestnuts), making acorn flour, and cooking in acorn oil.

First, you need to get yourself a supply of acorns. Go find some oak trees—they're the ones with all the acorns that have fallen down around them. But what kind of oak is it? Oaks come in so many varieties you should check the leaves against a guidebook. A general rule is that the leaves of white oaks, the acorns of which tend to be less bitter, have soft edges, while the leaves of the red oaks, the acorns of which tend to be more bitter, have spiny or pointy edges. Western oaks also fall into these categories: For example, valley oaks are in the white oak family, while live oaks belong to the red oak tribe. Tan oaks are their own thing, but their acorns generally taste more like red oaks'.

When can you gather acorns? Start as early as Labor Day, while many are still green but fully formed; then again in fall when they, well, fall; in winter, when there is no snow to cover them; and even in spring, when they are beginning to sprout. Suellen Ocean, who wrote a very useful book called *Acorns and Eat 'Em*, says she likes to collect tan oak acorns in February and March, after many have begun sprouting. She says acorns with sprouts between 1 and 2 inches long are still good to eat, but discard any acorn meats that have turned green. This is sound advice. Spring gathering has an added bonus: Recently sprouted acorns have begun to turn their starch into sugar and are foolproof. "If it is sprouted, it's a good acorn and I haven't wasted time gathering wormy ones," she says.

A word on worms. When I gathered all those valley oak acorns in October, little did I know that I had gathered scores already infected with the larva of the oak weevil. They're nasty little maggoty things, and you can tell they are inside your acorn if there is a little hole in the shell. Discard any acorns with holes, and move on. Also toss any fallen acorns that still have their "hats" on. The oak may have jettisoned this acorn because it was infected or otherwise defective. Note that a split shell is not necessarily an indicator of a rotten acorn.

You need to know what kind of oak you are dealing with. Different oaks bear acorns with different shapes, so that can help you determine which sort of oak it is as well as the leaves can. Not all oaks will set acorns every year, so you won't find acorns from every species every year.

Acorns are a wild food, and as such you must contend with their tremendous variability, both in species and even among individuals of the same species. Some oaks bear acorns so low in bitter tannins that they can be eaten with only one or two changes of water. Legend says that California's Native Americans fought over these trees. One mature valley oak can drop 2,000 pounds of acorns in a really good year. A ton of sweet acorns may well be worth fighting over.

University of California, Riverside professor David Bainbridge wrote in a 1986 academic paper that, depending on the species, acorns can range in fat content from 1.1 to 31.3 percent, protein from 2.3 percent to 8.6 percent, and carbohydrates from 32.7 to 89.7 percent. That is a wide disparity, which means that in the kitchen, you treat acorns from different species very,

very differently. A fatty acorn will make a meal, like ground almonds. A carb-rich acorn—like valley oak acorns—makes a drier flour, more like chestnut or chickpea flour.

CHARACTERISTICS OF VARIOUS OAKS

For the most part, all acorns can be used interchangeably. The fattier ones taste better when used as something other than flour, and the sweetest ones need the least processing. Here's a general breakdown.

"SWEETEST" ACORNS (MEANING LOWEST IN TANNIN): East Coast white oak, the Emory oak of the Southwest, the pin oak of the South, the valley and blue oaks of California, the burr oak of the Midwest, and the cork oak and the bellota oak of Europe. California readers should keep their eyes peeled for the many cork oaks and burr oaks planted in towns and cities there.

LARGEST ACORNS: Valley oaks and their acorns are huge, as are white oaks. Burr oak acorns are large, too, as are those of the California black oak.

FATTIEST ACORNS: There is not a lot of detailed data on the eastern species, although I have read that the Algonquin Indians used red oak acorns for oil. In the West, the fattiest acorns are from the live oaks, both the coastal and the interior live oak, as well as the California black oak, *Quercus kelloggii*. Be certain to refrigerate anything made from these acorns, as the rich oil turns rancid fast.

SHELLING ACORNS

Shelling acorns is the most onerous part of dealing with them. They have an elastic shell that resists normal nutcrackers. Unless you buy a fancy nutcracker, which you should do if you plan to process large amounts of acorns, whacking them with a hammer is the best way to open up the nuts. Some people use a knife, but that seems dangerous given how slick the surface of an acorn can be.

TANNINS

With a few exceptions, all acorns must be leached with water multiple times to remove bitter tannins. Those tannins not only will make your mouth feel and taste like felt, but also can make you a bit nauseous and possibly constipate you for days.

Getting the tannins out is the big barrier to cooking with acorns. The fastest method is hot-water leaching. After shelling, drop the acorn meats directly into a stockpot two-thirds full of water. Fill the pot about one-third of the way with shelled acorns and boil the water, which will turn dark. As soon as the water boils, pour it into the sink, leaving the acorns in the pot. It's okay if you still have a little water left over in the pot. Repeat the process. It requires about five changes of water to get valley oak acorns to taste like chestnuts. Don't even begin to taste test your acorns until four changes of water, and some, such as live oaks, need as many as a dozen; I avoid these acorns for this reason. Choose the "sweetest" acorns from the list on page 37 for the least amount of work and the fewest changes of water.

Are there other methods of leaching? You bet, including outlandish ones like grinding the raw acorns into flour and hanging them in a sack set in the flush tank of your toilet—whenever you flush, it leaches more tannin out. Ingenious, but I'll pass. Apparently Cosentino, the chef who introduced me to acorn soup, leached his in a kettle set under a gently running faucet for several days, but that seems like a waste of water to me.

One other method I like is to grind the raw acorns into flour by mixing them with some water in a blender. Blitz this until it looks like a coffee milkshake. Pour the mixture into a tall container, such as a 1-quart Mason jar or, preferably, something larger, filling it halfway. Fill the rest of the container to the brim with cool water. Seal and shake vigorously to mix. Put the container in the fridge and let it settle. Every day for a week, carefully pour off the water, leaving the flour at the bottom of the container. Add more water, seal, shake, and set in the fridge. This method takes longer, but it preserves some heat-soluble flavors and starches in the acorns. Cold-leached flour sticks to itself better than hot-leached flour, so it is preferable for baked goods. Check your flour after a week. It should taste bland, but without any bitterness or felty tannins drying your mouth. If there are any, keep changing the water until all the bitterness is gone.

DRYING

Once your acorns are free of tannins, you need to dry them or they will rot. Big pieces can be patted dry on a tea towel. If it is hot out, lay the acorn pieces out on baking sheets and dry in the sun. You could also put them in an oven set on Warm for several hours.

I often roast pieces of acorn that I do not intend to make into flour. Roasting brings out the sugars in acorns and protects them from deteriorating. Roast acorns at 300°F for about an hour. Watch your acorns after about 30 minutes, however, as some species will roast faster than others, and you do not want to burn them.

You dry cold-water leached acorn flour by filling the jar with water, shaking, and then pouring everything into a colander that has cheesecloth set inside it. Let the water drain for a few minutes, then gather the edges of the cheesecloth into a ball. Squeeze it tight to get more water out, then spread the flour onto a baking sheet. Set the sheet in the hot sun, or in an oven set on Warm for 3 to 4 hours. Stir from time to time and break up clumps.

FLOUR OR PIECES

Once dry, pieces of acorn need only be put in a sealed container in the fridge, or vacuum-sealed and frozen. The dried flour will need further grinding.

Pieces can be used in a wild game soup. Ruffed grouse and acorns go well together.

They are also good as nut substitutes, chopped into meatballs and as part of a turkey stuffing, or pureed in a smooth acorn soup. You might use chopped acorn pieces with venison meatballs. Deer eat acorns, and it's a general rule in cooking that whatever a critter had been eating will go well with its meat, like pigeons and barley, duck and wild rice, and striped bass and crab, to name a few.

But as good as acorn pieces are, I prefer the flour. I normally use my strongest coffee grinder to pulverize the roasted acorn pieces. It takes about 90 seconds to turn pieces into usable flour. The rough meal you make when using the cold-water leaching method requires only about 30 seconds in the coffee grinder to turn into usable flour. You will want to sift the ground acorns through your finest-mesh sieve to remove larger pieces. Keep doing this until you have no more chunks. Beware, all you owners of grain mills: Roasted acorns could break your mill, as a roasted acorn is far harder than the hull of normal grain. And grinding unroasted acorns that have a high fat content will gunk up the mill.

Store the flour in jars in the fridge. The fat in acorns will go rancid fast if you leave the flour at room temperature.

There are many uses for acorn flour. I make an acorn flour flatbread modeled after an Italian *piadina*, essentially an Italian flour tortilla. Acorn flour pasta has a nutty, dark, unrefined taste best suited for rustic shapes such as orecchiette or cavatelli. Acorn pasta spaghetti served in a rich venison broth is another wonderful use for the flour. It looks like a Japanese beef soup with soba noodles.

RECIPES

ACORN FLATBREADS

This recipe is based on a specialty of Romagna, a flatbread called a *piadina*. Acorn flour makes the breads dark and nutty. Note that acorn flour has no gluten and the flatbreads will simply disintegrate if you try to make an acorn-only *piadina*.

Makes 6–8

  2¼ cups unbleached all-purpose or bread flour

  ¾ cup acorn or chestnut flour

  1½ teaspoons salt

  3 tablespoons olive oil

  1 cup water

Sift the flours and salt together in a large bowl and make a well in the center. Add the oil and water in the center of the well and combine with a fork. When the dough becomes a shaggy mass, bring it together with your hands, then knead in the bowl until the dough picks up most of the flour stuck to the sides of the bowl. Transfer the dough to a floured surface and knead for another 3 to 5 minutes. Use a bit more flour if it is too sticky. You want a smooth, elastic dough that resembles a soft pasta dough.

Lightly coat the dough with more olive oil, wrap in plastic, and set aside at room temperature for at least 1 hour. (The dough can be refrigerated for up to 2 days.)

Cut the dough into 6 to 8 equal parts. Roll them out one at a time with a rolling pin and then your hands. You want them about ⅛-inch thick, but they need not be perfect, as this is a rustic bread.

Lightly oil a griddle or cast-iron pan set over medium heat. Cook the *piadine* one or two at a time for 2 to 3 minutes, or until the underside begins to get nice and brown. Flip and cook for another 1 to 2 minutes.

Keep the piadine wrapped in towels so they stay warm while you make the rest. Serve with some cheese, fresh herbs, scallions, and some high-quality olive oil.

ACORN OR CHESTNUT FLOUR PASTA

In Puglia, Italy, this pasta was made when times were hard. It is a rough, rustic pasta that cries out to be served with mushrooms or game, or both. Ideally, you would choose wild boar, venison, wood duck, or mallard—something that actually eats acorns. In terms of pasta shape, all sorts of variations work, from hand-formed orecchiette to a thick spaghetti. This recipe is for a simple tagliatelle or pappardelle. If you want a similar effect with store-bought flour, use chestnut flour, which you can buy at good Italian grocery stores or online.

Serves 4

> 1½ cups all-purpose flour
>
> ½ cup acorn or chestnut flour
>
> Pinch of salt
>
> 1½ cups cool water
>
> Olive oil

Mix the flours and salt in a large bowl and make a well in the center.

Pour the water into the well and combine with the flours with a fork. When the dough becomes a shaggy mass, bring it together with your hands, then knead in the bowl until the dough picks up most of the flour stuck to the sides of the bowl. Transfer the dough to a floured surface and knead for another 3 to 5 minutes, or until the dough is no longer sticky and forms a smooth, elastic mass.

Lightly coat the dough in olive oil and cover with plastic wrap. Let it sit at room temperature for at least 1 hour and preferably 2 hours. Acorn flour needs a little longer to hydrate because it is coarser. This dough will also keep in the fridge for a day.

Cut off about one-quarter of the dough ball and run it through your pasta maker. Rub a little all-purpose flour on the pasta sheets if they get a little sticky. For tagliatelle or pappardelle, roll the pasta sheet through the next-to-thinnest setting on your pasta maker. Move the sheet to a floured surface and make sure it will not stick to itself, using a little more flour if needed. Cut the edges of the sheet square and roll it loosely, the way you would roll a carpet. Using a sharp chef's knife, cut your noodles. Tagliatelle is about ¼-inch wide, and pappardelle is about ½-inch wide.

Fluff out the freshly cut pasta to separate. Dust with a little more flour. Gently pick up the pasta and twirl into a loose pile. Set aside while you roll out and cut the remaining dough.

To cook, bring a large pot of water to a boil. Add enough salt to make the water taste like the sea. Add about half the pasta to the boiling water, and use tongs to keep it from sticking to itself. When the pasta floats, let it cook for 1 minute, then serve immediately with your favorite sauce.

Eat any unused pasta soon. This pasta does not freeze well, but it will hold, gently placed in a plastic bag, in the fridge for a few days. The longer this pasta dries, the more brittle it becomes.

ACORN SOUP WITH PORCINI AND BRANDY

Acorn soup is the first way I ever ate acorns. It was at a fancy restaurant in San Francisco called Incanto, and while I never did get the chef's recipe, I like this one even better. It is a smooth soup, deeply earthy and nutty from the combination of acorn "grits"—chopped-up pieces that have had the bitter tannins removed—and porcini mushrooms. A dollop of crème fraîche, sour cream, or even regular cream rounds everything out. Chestnuts are a good substitute if you don't have your own stash of acorns.

Serves 6–8

> 1 ounce dried porcini mushrooms, soaked in 1 cup hot water
>
> 4 tablespoons unsalted butter
>
> 1 large carrot, peeled and chopped
>
> 2 celery stalks, chopped
>
> 1 medium onion, chopped
>
> Salt
>
> 3 cups acorn bits
>
> ¼ cup pear or apple brandy
>
> 2 bay leaves
>
> 1 quart chicken, beef, mushroom, or vegetable stock
>
> ½ teaspoon ground red pepper
>
> ½ cup crème fraîche or sour cream
>
> A few dill fronds

Soak the porcini in the hot water for 1 hour before starting. When soft, remove the mushrooms and squeeze out excess water into the soaking bowl. Strain the soaking water through a paper towel into a clean bowl and reserve.

Heat the butter in a soup pot over medium-high heat. Add the carrot, celery, and onion, and cook, stirring frequently, for 3 to 4 minutes. Sprinkle salt over the vegetables as they cook. Add the mushrooms and acorn bits and stir to combine. Cook, stirring, for 2 minutes longer.

Add the brandy and boil it hard until it is almost gone. Then add the bay leaves, stock, ground red pepper, and the reserved mushroom soaking water. Simmer gently, uncovered, for 1 hour.

Puree the soup in a blender (or use an immersion blender). If you want to get fancy, pass it through a fine-mesh sieve. Put the soup back in the pot. If the soup is too thin, simmer it until you get a soup the consistency of melted ice cream. If it is too thick, add some water and heat through.

To finish, turn off the heat and mix in the crème fraîche or sour cream. You can add regular cream if you'd like, but I like the acidic twang of the sour cream. Add more salt if needed and garnish with the dill.

4

BEACH PEAS, SEA ROCKETS, AND MEMORIES

My early memories of foraging are like glimpses of clear sky through a swiftly shifting fog. I remember eating wild food for the first time as a little boy—a strangely disembodied image of myself munching beach peas on a breezy summer's day, shortly after walking off the ferry from New London, Connecticut, to Block Island, Rhode Island. I was 5.

It is as hazy as all 5-year-olds' memories are, but I see myself lagging behind my sisters on a sun-drenched road, looking all around me. I can still smell the salt air. Towering over me is a giant nest of shoots and vines, decorated with the most beautiful magenta flowers I'd yet seen in my short life. Then I see the plump little peas dangling from the bush, and I knew I liked sweet peas (mashed peas was apparently one of my favorite baby foods). Crunch, crunch, crunch. I began gorging myself on the peas, pods and all. I remember them being sweet and juicy, a wonderful break from what seemed like a long journey.

I've since made that journey scores of times. The little road from Block Island's New Harbor dock to the main road that belts the island is maybe a quarter mile. But all these years later, that beach pea bush is still there, or rather some descendant of it. And every time I walk past it in June, I stop to honor that memory with a handful of juicy little beach peas.

Block Island, a little island near Nantucket that's the shape of a pork chop with a bite taken out of it, is an earthly paradise for foraging, especially for seaside plants. I've walked almost every square foot of the island, and it's impossible to go more than a few yards without coming across something edible. I learned my seaside foraging there, and have taken the lessons I learned on The Block up and down the Atlantic coast. I've only recently begun to explore the California coast, where I live now, but I am happy to say that my friend the beach pea, *Lathyrus maritimus*, lives there, too.

What follows in this chapter are my idiosyncratic experiences with delicious things that grow where the soil is sandy and the air is salty. These are the plants I long for when I am inland, the plants I wish I had in my yard; some will even grow there. But a beach pea in a garden would seem sad to me, a wild thing chained to an orderly row and a regular watering schedule.

BEACH PEAS

My first love. These are exactly what they sound like: peas that live near the ocean on sandy soil, often pure sand. The literature has them variously as *Lathyrus maritimus* or *littoralis* or even *japonicus*. They live along the Pacific from Canada to Southern California, and on the Atlantic coast from Labrador down to New Jersey.

They are easy to spot, as they look and taste exactly like regular garden peas, only smaller. In some places, there is a beach-dwelling vetch that looks similar, but it will have even smaller "peas" and be bitter. You can eat the young growing tops of vetch, but its little peas are slightly toxic.

A few sources say that beach peas themselves are slightly toxic, but my family and I

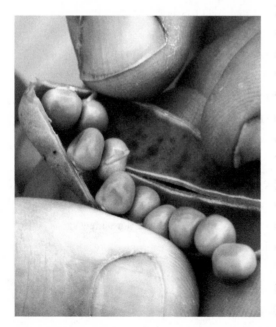

have gorged ourselves on them repeatedly since I was a toddler and we've suffered no ill effects. How best to eat them? Raw, of course. If you catch them young enough, even the pods are sweet, although you will want to strip the string off the side like you would with any pea. You can also cook these briefly like snow peas. The most grandiose recipe I've ever done with young beach peas is a simple stir-fry with freshly shucked clams, an onion, butter, and salt.

There is a very short window when beach peas are both sweet and plentiful. English peas are like this, too, but they've been bred to stay ripe longer. A perfect beach pea looks fat and glossy. When the shell yellows, they are still edible but will taste more starchy than sweet.

Keep in mind, beach peas are small—even smaller than the *petit pois* you see in some markets. If you want a big dish of beach peas, you will need to gather a lot, and you will need to shanghai everyone you know into shelling them. After that, don't mess with them too much. Maybe a splash of white wine and butter and salt, but nothing more.

Beach peas don't all ripen at once, so if you keep your eye on several bushes, you will be able to pick peas from late June through August, depending on where you are.

BAYBERRY BUSH
AND CALIFORNIA BAY

Though these are most definitely not the same plant, they serve the same purpose in the kitchen. Bayberry and California bay are used as substitutes for the European bay laurel, but the flavor and aroma of all three plants are distinctly different. I consider bayberry to be the finest of them all. European bay is excellent, too, but not as sweet-smelling as bayberry. California bay has a bit of a eucalyptus air about it, a camphorous, medicinal aroma that can ruin a dish if overused.

Bayberry and California bay are medium-to-large bushes that have a scraggly air about them. California bay can grow into a small tree, while bayberry tends to be stubbier, rarely taller than 4 feet. Bayberry can grow in vast swaths in the dunes and just behind them. The leaves of all kinds of bay look and feel similar, so use the bay leaves in your cupboard as a guide. All are simple leaves the shape of a spear point and are thick, almost leathery. All will smell strongly.

Bayberry and California bay grow abundantly along the coasts, bayberry along the Atlantic and California bay in, of course, California. California bay can grow several miles inland, too, so don't be surprised to see it at the edge of a coastal woodland.

Pick bay leaves in the morning on days that are about to be warm and dry. This is the best time to catch the leaves when they are at their most aromatic. Dry them in the shade until they are brittle, and use them where you would bay leaves. California bay and bayberry will keep for a year or more in a tightly covered jar.

Bayberry possesses an astoundingly wonderful scent. One of my most memorable meals was a simple dish of clams that Holly and I had collected that day, steamed in white wine and flavored with butter and a handful of bayberry leaves, plucked right from a nearby bush.

You can pulverize bay leaves and add them to sausage. I once made a dry-cured salami from a wild boar I'd shot in Monterey County, seasoned with native white sage that grew not a hundred yards from where the hog fell, as well as with California bay from a bush that grew just a few miles away. It remains my finest salami ever.

RUGOSA ROSE

Beach roses are unmistakable: huge, disheveled bushes dotted with plain-Jane white, pink, or magenta roses. These are not the fancy roses you buy in a store, and to an untrained eye, rugosa's simple flowers don't really look like roses.

Rugosas are Asian immigrants brought to the Atlantic by New England ship captains in the 18th century, and they have naturalized themselves on our dunes ever since. I have seen them occasionally on the Pacific coast, and you can buy rugosa roses from catalogs and grow them inland. In New England, they grow in masses, covering the dunes with a fragrant-but-impassable hedge of forest green leaves and pretty pink blossoms.

You can treat these blossoms the way you would any rose petals. I like filling a Mason jar with them and covering them with 100-proof vodka or even pure grain alcohol. Be sure to snip off the white part at the base of each petal—it is bitter and will foul your liqueur. Steep the mixture for 2 weeks in a dark place and strain it through cheesecloth. Then add sugar to taste and store it for another month before drinking; sugar dissolves slowly in alcohol. The aroma from this heady liqueur is a lovely end to a delicate meal and definitely makes a romantic impression for a date.

The best part of the rose comes in late summer when the flowers give way to the hips, the fruit of the rose. All roses make hips, but rugosa roses are special: They make enormous scarlet hips with a thick, juicy outer flesh that surrounds the astringent seeds. The seeds, incidentally, were once used to make itching powder. Rugosa rose hips are delicious eaten right off the bush. You nibble the outer flesh and leave the seeds for the birds.

The flesh of rugosa rose hips is easily stripped off the central seed cluster, which looks a lot like the seed cluster of a bell pepper. I use rose hips to make syrups, sauces, or jams. They are loaded with vitamin C, but extended cooking kills off most of this, so treat your rose hips gently.

To make a batch of rose hip syrup, strip the flesh off rugosa rose hips until you have a quart. Puree the rose hip flesh in a food processor. Pour 1 quart of water and an equal volume of sugar into a pot, stir it well, and bring it to a boil. Turn off the heat once the sugar has dissolved and stir in the rose hip puree. Cover and let the syrup steep until it cools to room temperature. Pour the mass into a jelly bag or very fine-mesh sieve set over a bowl, and let it drip overnight in the fridge. Taste it, and if the syrup isn't tart enough for you, add some lemon juice or citric acid (available in beer-brewing shops) a little at a time, tasting until you get the acidity you want. Seal and store in the fridge. It'll keep for a year.

KELP

Kelp is the kind of seaweed you find dried in large sheets in Asian markets, where it is called kombu. It is fairly thick, ranging from rich brown to dark olive in color, and very salty. The Japanese eat kombu in salads and pickles, but I am not a fan of the texture, which can be a little rubbery.

Where kelp shines in my estimation is in its ability to bring the sea home with you. One of the secrets to my seafood cooking is that, whenever possible, I cook with seawater, which I have boiled and strained first to kill any wee beasties. Seawater imparts flavor to pasta, risotto, or soup that tap water with added salt simply lacks. Trace minerals and microscopic plants and animals are the source of seawater's power.

Adding dried kelp to your broths can give you a similar strength. Classic Japanese dashi broth requires a piece of dried kombu kelp, and this is a wise practice. Kelp is loaded with nutrients, notably glutamates and potassium, and kelp will add both a briny flavor and a certain umami—that fifth taste of savoriness—to whatever you are cooking.

Note that there are several varieties of kelp, from the giant *Macrocystis pyrifera* that grows in the great forests off the California coast to the smaller *Laminaria digitata* that grows along the Atlantic coast. Look for wide, flat seaweed. I find bull kelp, *Nereocystis luetkeana*, to be the best tasting. The parts you want to collect are the thick, wavy fronds that are attached to a single, thick stem, which attaches to the sea bottom. Bull kelp is typically olive brown. No seaweed is poisonous, so errors in identification are not harmful. The only seaweed you want to avoid is the *Desmarestia* clan, which look frondy like dill or fennel. They are pretty bitter and sour-tasting.

Gather kelp off the sand at low tide, or cut some fronds off the rocks, leaving the rest of the plant alone. Don't denude an area. Follow the forager's code of picking a little here and there, leaving more than you take. A good alternative to picking live kelp is to comb the beach after the strong full-moon tides and pick pieces that have drifted ashore. Once you've collected kelp, while it's still wet use scissors or a knife to cut it into 3- to 6-inch rectangles or squares. Keep them moist in seawater (I fill a 1-quart Mason jar with seawater and put the kelp in that), or wrap in a damp cloth until you get home.

Once home, lay them out in the hot sun or on a baking sheet in an oven set at Warm, until they are fully dry and will snap in half when bent. Store in a cool, dry cupboard in a sealed bag or jar.

Use pieces of dried kelp like seafood bouillon cubes. When making a seafood risotto, get the water or broth hot, drop a piece of kelp in, and bring it to a bare simmer for a few minutes. Do not let it boil or its flavor will become too strong and ruin your broth. Taste the broth every few minutes, and remove the kelp when you're pleased with the flavor. You can reuse the piece of kelp several times. Just lay it flat on a paper towel to dry again.

Another use I learned from my sister is to add a piece of kelp to a crab or lobster boil, which adds a lot to the flavor. It works just as well when steaming open shellfish such as mussels or clams. This time, you leave the kelp in, even at a full boil.

Dried kelp will last more than a year properly stored.

SEA ROCKETS

A lot of wild mustards and radishes grow along both seacoasts, among them the sea rocket, a cousin of the common arugula. Sadly, I rarely seem to get to sea rockets in winter and the earliest weeks of spring, when the leaves are tasty. If you are around the beach then, check the dunes for a scraggly plant with leaves that look a little like a wild lettuce: The thick, fleshy leaves have an elongated palm shape with ragged edges. If you are on the Pacific coast, look for leaves that are like succulent versions of wild arugula, a long central leaf core with many opposite branching leaflets. Take a small bite of the leaves. If they're zippy and mustardy like arugula, you have your greens for dinner.

If, however, you don't make it to the beach until the weather warms, have no fear. Though the leaves are likely to be impossibly mustardy and bitter by then, the plant will most likely be sporting a mass of purplish white flowers. The flowers make the plant easier to identify. Like all brassicas (cabbage, broccoli, and mustard), they have four petals in a cross shape. You can eat the flowers, and they make a nice garnish on a salad, but what you really want are the young seedpods.

The pods look a little like a tiny okra pod. They will be at the bottom of a flower stalk and are often ready to eat when the top of the stalk is still flowering. Try one. It'll be crunchy, mustardy, and a little garlicky. Gather all the ones that are just about fully formed. Check by squishing some large pods at the bottom of stalks. If you find hard seeds, those are too old. Skip the freshly formed pods, too, as they need to grow a bit to develop their full flavor. I tend to pick from the middle of the stalk. If you collect enough, you can pickle them. A recipe for pickles follows at the end of the chapter.

You can also sauté sea rocket pods briefly in olive oil, then add lemon juice, salt, and freshly ground black pepper right at the end. It's a lovely little side dish.

NEW ZEALAND SPINACH

Legend has it that this odd transplant from the South Sea Islands of the Pacific was brought to the California coast by Captain Cook's expedition. In reality, the plant probably floated its way to the West Coast on the ocean currents. The good captain did indeed bring *Tetragonia tetragonioides* to Europe, however, which is why you've been able to see it occasionally in gardens for nearly 200 years. Several seed companies I know of sell seeds for it, but New Zealand spinach seeds are tricky to germinate—they can literally float for thousands of miles before sprouting in the wild.

At first glance, it doesn't look edible. New Zealand spinach is a lurid spring green, brittle,

and a little succulent, meaning the leaves are thick and a bit fleshy. But at second glance, you will notice that the leaves are dead ringers for domestic spinach. Take a bite and you'll get a massive hit of salt, a little crunch, and something bitter.

But when you cook this seaside potherb, it is the hit of the party. New Zealand spinach is stouter than domestic spinach, and when boiled briefly and then sautéed, it loses any bitterness and becomes toothsome and flavorful, like spinach on steroids.

Gather New Zealand spinach anytime

you see it, but it's best from March to September. It grows all year long on the West Coast.

After they're picked, keep the base of the stalks wrapped in a damp paper towel and the leaves will stay fresh and crunchy for several days in the fridge. You can freeze it after blanching in boiling water, too. If you are on the Atlantic coast, use orache instead (see Chapter 1), as it is as common there as New Zealand spinach is in the West.

SALTWORT, GLASSWORT, SEA BEANS, OR CHICKEN FEET

Saltwort—also known as glasswort, samphire, chicken feet, or sea bean—is one of my all-time favorite vegetables. It doesn't look like it ought to be eaten. The plant looks (and is) prehistoric: no leaves, just a sprawling, succulent series of many-jointed fingers reaching for sunlight while their feet are bathed in sand and saltwater.

Look for saltwort on either the Atlantic or Pacific coasts between March and September, and pick only the top few inches of the little plant, which can get bushy over time. Try to avoid the reddish stalks, as they are often tough.

Saltwort lives in protected places like back bays where it can be washed by high tides. On especially high tides, I've found patches almost completely underwater. There are several species of the plant, and the one I find most in California is *Salicornia subterminalis*. It also has an East Coast cousin called sea blite, *Suaeda linearis*, which is more delicate but tastes very similar. All grow relatively low to the ground, no higher than a foot or so, but they tend to sprawl in vast patches. I know a patch in Northern California that's twice the size of a football field.

Once you collect your saltwort, put them in a plastic bag in the fridge with a damp paper towel around them. They will last more than a week that way. Good thing, too, as this is a seriously tasty veggie. Raw saltwort is crunchy and very salty, as its name suggests. It can be tough to properly clean the little stalks, so before eating you'll want to blanch the plant in boiling water for 30 seconds to 1 minute, then shock it in a bowl of ice water. Cooked this way, the plant looks and tastes a lot like perfectly al dente, salty green beans. Crunchy, briny, with something else . . . soda ash, as it turns out.

A moment for a bit of trivia: Saltwort earned its name *glasswort* because it has a lot of alkaline soda in it, which glassmakers need for their art. The plant was once burned and its ashes used as a source of soda. I'm relating this because saltwort also grows in the alkali flats of the Great Basin between Colorado and the Sierra Nevada. An edible species of glasswort that looks similar to its seaside cousin grows in the white, alkali wetlands there. I've even found saltwort growing in an alkaline marsh in Manitoba, Canada.

Anyway, once you have your blanched saltwort, all you really need to do is dress it with your best olive oil and add a little lemon juice, balsamic vinegar, or other acidic component, plus a few grinds of black pepper. No extra salt needed.

Saltwort is not so good cooked for much longer. It gets flabby, so leave this vegetable for flash cooking. What you can do is pickle the little stalks to preserve your harvest. This is common in Ireland and Scotland, and you could use any of your favorite pickling recipes for cucumbers. My recipe is below.

RECIPES

PICKLED SEA BEANS OR SEA ROCKET PODS

This is a pretty standard pickle, good for both sea rocket pods and saltwort. If you are inland, you can also use it for purslane, another succulent plant. Keep the proportions of salt, vinegar, and water and you can then vary the flavors to your liking. This recipe can be halved.

Makes 6 pints

About 3 pounds saltwort stalks or sea rocket pods

3½ cups water

3½ cups distilled or white wine vinegar

6 cloves

6 large cloves garlic, smashed

3 tablespoons roughly cracked black peppercorns

6 large strips lemon or orange peel, about the length of the fruit

2 tablespoons kosher salt (omit for saltwort)

Fill a large stockpot with water, add a handful of salt, and bring to a boil. Prepare
a large bowl with ice water. Blanch the saltwort or sea rocket pods in the water for
30 seconds, then dump them into the ice water.

Bring to a boil the 3½ cups water and the vinegar. Add the cloves, garlic, peppercorns,
and lemon peel. Add the salt if you
are pickling sea rocket pods. Let this
boil for 5 minutes.

Turn off the heat. Using tongs, fish
out a clove, a piece of lemon zest, and
a smashed garlic clove for each jar.
Pack the veggies into the jars, leaving
about a ½-inch space at the top of the
jars. Pour in the hot vinegar solution.
The saltwort or sea rockets should be
completely submerged.

Seal the jars and process them in a
boiling-water bath for 10 minutes.
Store for at least 3 weeks before
eating, to allow the flavors to meld.
Unopened, the pickles should last a
year. Store in the fridge after
opening. Once opened, the pickles
should last several months in
the fridge.

ROSE PETAL ICE CREAM

If there was an award for most romantic ice cream, this rose petal ice cream would win hands down. Delicate, strongly aromatic—dainty, really—it is ideal for a romantic meal, Valentine's Day, or even a wedding reception.

Any rose petals work here, but I prefer to make this with either wild rugosa rose petals or wild rambling rose petals. If you use rugosa rose petals, try to get the magenta ones. The color will seep into the cream to give your ice cream just a touch of pink.

You must trim the white end off each rose petal where it attaches to the central flower. This is bitter and will ruin your ice cream.

You will need an ice cream maker for this recipe.

Makes about 1 quart

    2 cups cream

    2 cups milk

    ⅔ cup sugar

    1 cup trimmed rose petals, loosely packed

    1 piece (1-inch) vanilla bean, scraped

    4–5 egg yolks

    1 teaspoon rose flower water

Heat the cream, milk, and sugar in a heavy-bottomed pot to 170°F, or to the point at which it steams but does not simmer. Turn off the heat, add the rose petals, the vanilla bean, and the scraped insides of the bean. Stir well, cover, and let cool for 1 hour.

Move the mixture to a container and refrigerate for at least 4 hours, or up to overnight.

Strain the mixture to remove the vanilla bean and the rose petals. Heat the mixture to 160°F. As it is heating, beat the egg yolks in a medium bowl to combine. When the cream has hit its temperature, you will need to temper the eggs so they don't scramble when added to the pot. Hold a ladle in one hand and a whisk in the other. Ladle a little hot cream into the bowl while whisking the eggs vigorously. Whisk in 2 full ladles, then pour the egg-cream mixture into the pot and stir well. Cook gently, stirring often, for 5 minutes. Do not let it simmer.

Remove from the heat and allow to cool. Add the rose flower water. Strain the mixture one more time before putting it into an ice cream maker. Churn it until it has the consistency of soft-serve ice cream, then remove to a large bowl. Freeze and eat!

5

MISCELLANEOUS WILD PLANTS

Sometimes good food doesn't fit into easy categories or, as in the case of the black walnut, is the only member of a larger category (nuts, in this case) that I regularly use. Here is a collection of my favorite oddities you won't want to miss.

MADRONE BARK

Ever eat a tree? Not much about cooking excites me more than experimenting with a new ingredient, especially when that ingredient is not only new to me, but new to the rest of the culinary world as well. It's a rush, that feeling—real or imagined—that I am adding something new to our collective knowledge of food, rather than rehashing the genius of those who came before me. Madrone bark has been one of the most exciting of these experiences.

Arbutus menziesii is a tree native to California, Oregon, and Washington. It is a long-lived evergreen cousin of manzanita, and every summer as the tree grows, its bark bursts off the trunk into curls that look like a paper-thin cinnamon stick. The Native Americans who first lived here gathered madrone bark to make a tea they used topically to treat sores and internally to cure a sore throat.

Madrone trees live only on the West Coast and even there only in sporadic locations on the slopes of the Coastal Range, the west side of the Cascades and the Sierra Nevada. Madrone's orange-red bark is the first thing you notice when you've found the tree. Even long after the bark has burst, stray curls will stick to the trunk, making the tree look like it has a skin disease. Madrone leaves are thick and leathery, and bear a superficial resemblance to the bay leaves in your spice rack. In late winter, the trees come alive with sprays of pretty little white bell-shaped flowers, very similar to manzanita or blueberry flowers. The flowers are edible, if a little tannic and bland.

But it's the bark you want. Gather it in high summer, as it peels off the trunk. It will already be dry, so you need only keep it in a dry container. I store mine in a plastic bag in the house. Madrone bark will keep its flavor for a year or more.

I know of only a few other cooks working with madrone, notably Ron Zimmerman of The Herbfarm restaurant outside Seattle. Zimmerman uses madrone bark tea to flavor risotto and as an ingredient in ice cream. When working with this bark, the trick is to highlight its subtle flavor without knocking your guests over with woody tannins.

The primary way to use madrone bark is in a tea, which can then be used as a base for other dishes, such as ice cream, syrup, a brine, etc. Its taste is like a combination of cinnamon, mushrooms, wood, tannin, and something else I find hard to pinpoint; a zephyr of fruitiness.

Madrone bark tea gets dark in a hurry. My normal ratio is about 20 bark curls simmered in 2 quarts of water. At that concentration, the tea rapidly turns a rich red mahogany, a little like South African red tea. When I first saw it, I immediately thought about making a Chinese tea egg with this tea. A tea egg is a cool Chinese snack. You boil eggs, then lightly crack the shells all over and simmer the eggs for several hours in a combination of tea, soy sauce, star anise, and lemon peel. My Western interpretation uses madrone bark tea, bay leaves, a star anise, lemon peel, juniper berries, and salt.

You can also use madrone bark tea to brine a wild duck or other game. Madrone brings out woodsy, earthy flavors in grains, notably farro, a primitive wheat related to spelt you can cook like a risotto. Simply substitute the madrone tea for half the broth or water you would normally use.

Other possibilities abound. Grind the bark to a powder and use it as a flavoring in sausage or salami, or grind it with coarse salt to make a finishing salt for venison or beef. And don't be afraid to experiment with madrone in sweet dishes, like Zimmerman's ice cream. Madrone sugar, anyone?

DAYLILIES

I had no idea daylilies tasted so good until, on a trip to see my family in New England, I finally ate some. After a thorough sampling of the flowers, flower buds, young stalks, and root tubers, I can honestly say that the common daylily is every bit as useful as a food crop as it is pretty in the yard.

The common daylily, *Hemerocallis fulva*, as well as its various *Hemerocallis* friends and relatives, originally came from Asia, probably China. Daylilies appear frequently in Chinese cooking, even starring in such famous dishes as moo shu pork and hot and sour soup. Do not confuse daylilies with the bona fide lilies of the *Lilium* tribe, like the Easter lily. If you are unfortunate enough to eat a true lily, you had better hope that the Resurrection is real—many are so toxic they're fatal.

The best way to identify a daylily is to look for its bright orange, tubular flower in weedy, neglected places or along country roads, or in your neighbor's yard. The plants will be 2 to 3 feet tall and, because the flowers only bloom for a single day, there will be withered flowers, fresh flowers, and unopened buds all on the same flower stalk. A smaller species of daylily with yellow flowers is often used as a landscaping plant where I live in California. Daylilies have naturalized in every state east of the Rockies, so you can find them wild there. Remember, in the wild, daylilies will always be orange, never blue or purple. Those are irises, which are toxic.

That trip east was in part a foraging expedition, although I didn't have to go far to find daylilies. All of Cape Ann is coated in them. No high foraging adventure here; we just picked from my sister Lizz's yard. The drama with daylilies is all in the eating.

When you gather a crop of daylilies, first separate the plants into flowers, buds, and tubers. Unlike true lilies, daylilies don't have bulbs, they have normal roots with tubers attached that look like miniature fingerling potatoes. Strip the outer leaves from those plants that have not yet flowered, until you get to the white part.

Most sources say to sauté the unopened flower buds with a little butter or oil and call it a day, and I agree, especially since you should really taste the plant, not any supplemental seasonings. Heat some butter in a sauté pan over medium-high heat, add the lily buds, cook for 3 to 4 minutes, stirring often, sprinkle a little salt over them, and eat. Briefly cooked, the buds have a bit of *knacken*, a German expression meaning a "pop." Yet the insides reminded me of squash blossoms. The taste? Green, with a whiff of radish and a dash of green bean. Honestly, I'd eat this as a side dish any day, any place. It needs nothing else.

The stalks are not as good. They have a texture like lemongrass, only without the wonderful lemon aroma. More like a bland, tough scallion. Certainly edible, and not terrible, but nothing like the buds.

The flowers are more for color than flavor, although they are said to thicken soups the way okra and filé powder do. Some of the little tubers will be the color of fingerling potatoes; others will be pure white, like the inside of a turnip. The white ones taste *exactly* like jicama, or like a sweet, raw potato. The yellow ones will be starchier.

You can cook the tubers the same way as the flower buds: butter, sauté, salt. But add some black pepper the way you would on potatoes—it brings out the flavor dramatically. These are quite possibly the best tubers I've ever eaten, and I am including potatoes. Think really young fingerling potatoes, only with a sweetness to them. White ones are sweeter than the yellow ones. Yellow ones seem more substantial.

The only downside to daylilies is a certain digestive uncertainty. A small number of people who eat daylily flowers get farty and nauseous afterward; I hear "less than 5 percent" a lot, but I can't verify it. Suffice it to say you should eat only a little at first, then, if your digestive system doesn't react unpleasantly, have at it.

According to the USDA, the daylily has gone feral in every state except Alaska, Hawaii, Oklahoma, North Dakota, New Mexico, Arizona, Nevada, and, um, my own state of California. Sigh. That said, you can't swing a dead cat without seeing a planting of daylilies in a parking lot or person's yard, and they are so common in urban settings that Charlotte Bringle Clarke writes about them in her *Edible and Useful Plants of California*.

CHICORY AND DANDELION ROOT

For a time, my favorite coffee was New Orleans style, which is cut with roasted, ground chicory root. The result is smooth, a little more acidic than normal coffee, with a taste and aroma similar to a mocha but darker than the inside of a cow. I used to Ozark it up even more by drinking it black and sweetened with molasses, not sugar. Definitely a manly drink and probably the reason I have so much hair on my chest. I imagine lumberjacks or pioneers drinking chicory coffee with molasses in between cutting wood or fording wild rivers.

Ultimately, however, I switched back to straight coffee because the canned chicory coffee I'd been buying grew pretty grim on my tastebuds over time, stale and dusty tasting. I never found anyone who made a premium version, so I left chicory root by the wayside.

For some reason, I never bothered to make my own, even though I knew I could dig up the raggedy sailors. Chicory is easily spotted as a weedy azure-blue flower that probably grows on a roadside near you. You should dig it in fall, but you only really notice this plant in summer when it's flowering or in early spring when you look for the greens.

Then, one day, I bought some "root chicory" seeds and planted them with the intention of cooking the roots like parsnips. Then, as typically happens, life got in the way. I looked up and it was May already—while the chicory roots had not yet sent up flower stalks (except for one), they would be far too bitter and "hot" to eat as a veggie. Damn.

What to do with these things? I pulled one out and was astounded at how large it

was: a good 30 inches, with a base about 2 inches across. Damn big root. Then I remembered my lumberjack coffee. Maybe I could make a homemade batch? Most instructions for homemade chicory coffee sounded dubious to me. Then I red some instructions for making dandelion coffee (dandelions are cousins of chicories) that call for slicing the roots into thin discs, drying them, roasting them, and *then* grinding them. This sounded saner.

As I was slicing, it was 104°F outside. Perfect weather to dry things. When our weather warms, my "drying rack" of choice happens to be the hood of my pickup. So I set the sliced roots in a tray out in the sun, and they dried nicely in 2 days. You could use an oven set on Warm, which should dry the roots sufficiently in half a day. Then turn the oven off and leave the roots in the oven until morning.

When it came time to roast the chicory, I found even more misleading instructions. Everyone said to roast dandelion or chicory root in a 350°F oven for 10 to 15 minutes. Uh, yeah. You then have slightly warmer dried chicory roots. Instead of 15 minutes, try 90 minutes, or even 2 hours. Incidentally, even if you have no intention of actually drinking chicory coffee, it is worth roasting the roots this way. Your whole house will smell wonderfully malty, chocolatey, and feel warm. So lovely. I had let the roots cool overnight before I ground them. Unfortunately, they didn't grind evenly, so I had powder mixed with chunks.

But I make coffee with a press pot (French press), whose filter can strain it all out.

I later learned that even though the roots will have a heavy stalk running through them, flowering chicory roots can be dug for coffee, too. They will not be as good as late fall roots, however, because the plant is spending more energy producing flowers and, later, seeds. I also learned that everything about chicory applies to dandelion roots. Their flavor is a little different, but not so much that you could not combine the two in the same pot of grounds.

To make the "coffee," put 2 tablespoons of ground chicory or dandelion into a single-serving press pot—less than you use for coffee—boil some water, and steep the inky brew for 5 to 8 minutes. Straight chicory coffee is some powerful stuff. It tastes like it is loaded with caffeine, but it isn't. It looks a lot like motor oil but has a malty-chocolate aroma, a brighter acidity than coffee, and a flavor that really is "earthy."

BLACK WALNUTS

Wild walnuts live in most of the United States and differ from the cultivated English walnut in size and flavor. Being wild, they are smaller and have a stronger flavor than the cultivated varieties. In all other respects, however, wild walnuts are similar to the ones you buy in the supermarket. So why put them in this book? Wild walnuts can be surprisingly difficult to identify and process if you are used to store-bought walnuts.

Several nuts in North America are easily confused: walnuts, pecans, butternuts, and hickory nuts chief among them. All have husks and all grow on stately trees, unless you happen to live in the southern United States from Texas to Los Angeles, where the native desert walnuts are shrubbier. Walnuts have skinny leaves opposing each other on long stalks, a little like a sumac bush or that hideous, invasive tree-of-heaven, which is a plague on eastern cities. But you'll know a good nut tree by the green balls on the tree itself and the remnants of last year's nuts surrounding it. Walnut husks, unlike those of the hickory, do not split when the nut is ripe. Walnut husks turn from green to beige to black and then fall off the tree. There are no poisonous look-alikes to any of these trees.

If you're looking for walnuts and happen upon a hickory or pecan, no big deal. The nuts are interchangeable in the kitchen, although they have different flavors and shapes.

Look for butternuts in September, and hickory nuts, pecans, and walnuts in October through the beginning of December. Harvesting the nuts is as easy as picking them up off the ground. But don't bother with these nuts unless you are willing to deal with at least a gallon bucket's worth. The husk is large, and you will need to crack the meats, so a gallon bucket will yield you about a quarter pound of nutmeats, depending on species and the size of the nuts. Some trees bear larger nuts than others; the Southern California, Arizona, and Texas walnuts bear the smallest of all.

Take the husks off by stomping on them or by slicing them off with a pocketknife. Wear heavy gloves when you do this so you don't cut yourself. Some people advocate driving over them with your car, but I am not a fan, as this will crack the nutshells in many cases, causing the nutmeats inside to go rancid, and will stain your driveway black. I am serious about the stain. Nothing stains like walnut, which is another reason to wear gloves. Trust me, it does not wash off. So stomp and pull off the husk as best you can, or whack the husks with a hammer. Do not, as some sources suggest, simply let the husks rot off, as this will ruin the flavor of the walnuts.

Once you have the walnuts out of the husk, dry them in the sun or the garage for a couple of days, or in an oven set on Warm for a couple of hours. Do not let the nuts get wet at this point, or you will need to dry them again. Once dried, you can store the nuts for several months at room temperature.

To crack black walnut (or hickory) shells, start by wearing gloves to remove any husk residue, unless you want Walnut Hand for several weeks. Since these shells are legendary in their reluctance to break open, cover the nut with a terrycloth rag and use a hammer to whack the shell on the side, away from the seam. And if you whack it on top like an English walnut, you will get two halves of black walnut with an impervious shell separating you from the nutmeat. It's like looking into the display case of a candy store with no money. Frustrating.

Forget about perfect halves. It can happen occasionally, but more likely you will get lots of bits. Black walnuts are all about flavor, not looks. Use a pair of wire cutters to clip away parts of the shells to extract larger pieces. It's persnickety, but worth it.

Roast the shelled walnuts, if you like, at 300°F for a few minutes. The exact time will depend on how old your walnuts are and how rainy it was that year. Check them after 5 to 10 minutes. Inhale, and if you smell a deep nutty aroma, you're done. Store the shelled nuts in the fridge or freezer, as they will go rancid easily.

Use as you would any walnut. Black walnuts are especially tasty in ice cream and in baked goods.

SASSAFRAS

The aromatic bark, leaves, and roots of this pretty little tree were believed to be the first exports from North America to Europe, back in the late 1500s. All parts of the sassafras make for delicious—and different—teas, sweets, and other confections. It commanded exorbitant prices in Europe, until everyone started drinking sassafras tea believing it would cure their syphilis. Soon no one wanted to be seen sipping their syphilis cure in public, and the sassafras trade went limp. So to speak.

More recently, sassafras has been getting a bad rap by the folks at the USDA, who say that the active component of sassafras, safrole, is a "known carcinogen." Why? They gave tons of pure safrole to rats, and the rodents got cancer. Later researchers noted that, like the saccharine scare of the late 1970s, safrole seems to cause cancer in rats but not people.

And yet, many people still think that sipping sassafras tea or eating sassafras ice cream will doom you to a date with an oncologist. Just know that there are many more "known carcinogens" in a bottle of beer than in any homemade sassafras product you might make. By one calculation, you'd need to drink 24 gallons of sassafras root beer a day for months to get the amount of safrole fed to those rats. And if you drank that much soda, you'd have lots of other problems to deal with.

Sassafras is unmistakable. It is a spindly, shrubby tree that lives beneath larger trees. Its upper bark is green, and the leaves come in three varieties, often on the same branch: a mitten, a three-lobed leaf, and a simple spear-shaped leaf.

To collect sassafras, you'll need to pull young trees right out of the ground. I know, it sounds destructive, but it isn't. Sassafras grows in clumps, and the parent tree sends out suckers under the ground, which then become little trees. It's a lot like mulberry. Find a clump—look for at least 8 to 10 treelings scattered about—choose one about 2 to 3 feet tall, grasp the very base of the tree, and yank it straight up. You should come away with the seedling and about 10 inches' worth of the root.

The bottom of the root will remain in the ground and will regrow later. So what seems a little wanton is actually good for the sassafras cluster. It lets the surrounding seedlings grow with less competition.

All parts of this tree are useful. Notice I did not say "edible," because the leaves are the only part you actually eat. You may know them as filé powder, and without sassafras leaves your gumbo would not be gumbo. The twigs and roots make very different teas. The twigs have a lemony-gingery flavor and aroma that New England forager Russ Cohen has compared to Froot Loops cereal—not exactly a selling point to my mind, but they are lovely. The roots, however, are the "root" in root beer.

I am not a tea drinker. But I do like using flavored syrups from wild ingredients to use as glazes for meats, homemade sodas, sorbets, or ice creams. Sassafras is a prime candidate for this treatment.

After gathering two to three sassafras seedlings, you should chop some twigs, peel the green bark to expose it to water—the bark has most of the flavor—then simmer the twigs for 10 minutes or so. A good ratio is six to eight twigs about 4 to 5 inches long to 1 quart of water. The brew quickly turns a pretty amber, a little like cola. I let it steep overnight and then strain it through cheesecloth. Pour it into a pot, bring to a simmer, and stir in an equal volume of sugar to make a simple syrup. It is outstanding. I mean, really outstanding. Think cola with a lot of lemon in it.

You can also make homemade root beer. Root beer is my soda of choice, although I am also a big fan of good ginger ale. Making traditional root beer at home normally involves yeast and a small amount of alcohol—that's the "beer" in root beer. But root beers made with fermentation are tricky and have a bad habit of exploding. I prefer a stable, nonalcoholic base flavoring that you can make into a soda by adding seltzer water.

Root beer is not just sassafras, it is a concoction of many things. Recipes differ on exact ingredients, but mine, which is at the end of this chapter, goes heavy on the sassafras roots and adds some burdock root, molasses for color, clove, star anise, coriander seed, and 2 to 3 drops of peppermint extract.

If you live near sassafras trees—and you do if you live east of the Great Plains, south of Quebec, and north of Orlando—by all means make this syrup. If you don't live there, or don't feel like foraging, you can buy sassafras root bark online. You'll never go back to store-bought root beer again.

RECIPES

MADRONE BARK TEA EGGS

This is one of the cooler dishes I've ever made. Cracking the egg after an initial boil gives it a spiderweb-like lattice of madrone tea stain. The subtle flavor of the bark seeps into the egg, too. These tea eggs will last in the fridge for 10 days, but they are best within 3 days. Make a lot of them—they're great snacks.

Makes 12 eggs

6–7 cups water

15–25 madrone bark curls

1 dozen eggs

2 bay leaves

1 star anise

Peel of 1 lemon

10 crushed juniper berries

3 tablespoons kosher salt

Bring the water to a boil, then add the madrone bark curls. Cover and turn off the heat. Let steep overnight. Strain the tea through a paper towel.

Put the eggs in a pot, cover with cool water, and bring to a boil. Turn the heat down and simmer for 2 to 3 minutes, then turn off the heat. When the water is cool enough to touch, pull the eggs out and submerge in a bowl of ice water.

Meanwhile, add 6 cups of the madrone tea, the bay leaves, star anise, lemon peel, juniper berries, and salt to a large pot set over medium heat. Bring to a simmer.

Take each egg and tap it on the counter to crack the shell gently all around the egg. You want it to stay intact, but be covered in tiny cracks (think cracked porcelain). Place the eggs in the pot and simmer for 2 to 3 hours. Turn off the heat, cover, and steep overnight in the refrigerator. Eat cold or at room temperature.

BLACK WALNUT ICE CREAM

There is absolutely nothing like this ice cream. First you infuse the cream with the nuts, for flavor and a little color, and then you add those walnuts back to the finished ice cream, which is itself enriched by several egg yolks. It's roll-your-eyes-back-in-your-head good. Can you use regular walnuts to make this ice cream? Yes, but it will not be the same. Nothing beats wild walnuts.

Makes about 1 quart

2 cups cream

2 cups milk

⅔ cup roughly chopped black walnuts

⅔ cup sugar

½ vanilla bean, scraped

4–5 egg yolks

Heat the cream, milk, walnut pieces, and sugar in a large heavy-bottomed pot to 170°F, or to the point at which it steams but does not simmer. Turn off the heat and add the vanilla bean and the scraped insides of the bean. Stir well, cover, and let cool for 1 hour. Move the mixture to a container and refrigerate for at least 4 hours, or up to overnight.

Strain the mixture, reserving the walnut pieces in the fridge. Return the strained mixture to the heavy-bottomed pot and heat to 160°F. As it is heating, beat the egg yolks in a medium bowl to combine. When the cream has hit its temperature, you will need to temper the eggs so they don't scramble when added to the pot. Hold a ladle in one hand and a whisk in the other. Ladle a little hot cream into the bowl while whisking the eggs vigorously. Whisk in 2 full ladles, then pour the egg-cream mixture into the pot and stir well. Cook gently, stirring often, for 5 minutes. Do not let it simmer.

Strain this one more time before putting into the ice cream maker. Churn it until it has the consistency of soft-serve ice cream, then remove to a large bowl and gently fold in the reserved black walnut pieces. Freeze and eat!

HOMEMADE ROOT BEER SYRUP

Traditional root beer is brewed with yeast, which makes it mildly alcoholic, and can be tricky to make. This recipe will give you a wonderful root beer–flavored syrup; add 1 tablespoon to a pint of seltzer water or club soda for amazing homemade root beer.

You will need some unusual ingredients to make this, notably sassafras roots. Burdock, or at least its cousin curly dock, grows all around you, or buy the long, pale, skinny roots under their Japanese name, *gobo*. If you absolutely cannot get your hands on burdock, skip it. The root beer will still be fine. If you can't find wintergreen extract, peppermint extract is a good substitute.

Makes 2 quarts

2–3 ounces fresh sassafras roots, or 4–5 ounces dried

1 ounce burdock root

1 clove

1 star anise

1 teaspoon coriander seeds

6 cups water

¼ cup molasses

2–3 drops wintergreen or peppermint extract

6 cups sugar

Chop the sassafras and burdock roots into small pieces, about ½ inch or smaller. Put the roots in a medium-size heavy pot with the clove, star anise, and coriander seeds and cover with the water. Cover the pot and bring to a boil. Turn the heat down to a simmer and cook for 15 minutes. Add the molasses and simmer another 5 minutes. Turn off the heat, stir in the extract, and cover.

When the mixture is cool, strain it through cheesecloth to remove any debris. Return it to the pot and add the sugar. Stir to combine. Bring to a simmer and cook for 5 minutes, uncovered. Pour into 1-quart Mason jars and seal. It keeps for a year in the fridge.

6

WINES FROM FRUIT AND FLOWER

One morning, I found myself looking out the window of my kitchen, staring at a sea of yellow flowers in the vacant lot next door. Dandelions. Nearly a quarter acre of them. They were beautiful, but once they flower they're no good for salads or the sauté pan. Seemed like a waste to just let them go. Then I remembered something. You can make dandelion wine, can't you?

I'd already made a few batches of homemade wine, but only a couple had even been drinkable. This time I was determined to take my time and do this right. So I read several books on making wine at home and visited the local brew shop.

The proper way to make a fruit wine, the brew shop folks explained, was to basically ignore all the "country wine" recipes you normally see in books. Instead, take your cue from professionals who deal exclusively in grape wines. Enology is a science, and wine making is an art, so trust the grape guys—they know what they're doing.

So I did. Before picking the first dandelion, I bought equipment and powdered things with strange names like diammonium phosphate, and actually wrote out a "wine plan," something only professional winemakers do. The country recipes, however, taught me about the idiosyncrasies of dandelions. Like the fact that you must not let any green parts into your wine, only petals. And that you should pick in late morning, after the dew has dried.

Armed with knowledge, I set to picking, bucket in hand. In retrospect, I should have bought a blueberry rake for the job and just skimmed along the Yellow Sea, snipping dandy heads as I went. As I picked, I couldn't stop myself from humming the little song my friends and I used to sing as boys when we found dandelion heads: "Your momma had a baby and his head popped off!" When you get to the head-popping-off part, you flick the flower head with your thumb at the person you're singing to. Charming, I know.

Back in my kitchen with a bucket of dandelion flowers, I set to separating the petals from any green parts. I immediately discovered why there is no commercial dandelion wine: Petal-picking is tedious, persnickety, repetitive work. It took me an entire football game (I had to watch something to relieve the drudgery) to remove all the green parts.

I was left with about 2 quarts of flowers, enough for just 1 gallon of wine. I looked out at the largely untouched lot, with plenty of flowers grinning at me. Sorry, man, I ain't going there. One gallon was all I had energy for.

I fermented the wine with a light honey to give it some body, adding enough to get the alcohol level to approximately 14 percent; accurately gauging alcohol levels is impossible without special instruments. I then broke out some of the stuff I'd bought from the brew shop: diammonium phosphate (which is a yeast nutrient), champagne yeast, a little grape tannin, and some tartaric acid to brighten the flavor. Once it fermented and aged a little in a glass jug, I set to bottling. That's when I learned that a gallon, which seemed like a lot at the time, makes only five bottles. Now the full impact of my laziness hit me: What if this wine was good? Five bottles is not a lot.

Every source I'd read said that dandelion wine needed a long time to mature, so I waited 6 months before opening the first bottle. It smelled like the first warm day of spring, clean, like the air smells after a cool rain. Sweet and, yes, floral. No yeasty aroma, no cloudiness, and it tasted dry. It still had a little of that fizziness a young wine will have, like weak champagne. The aroma was intense. I'd never really smelled a dandelion before—hell, I didn't even know they *had* an aroma.

Two years later, I stared at the last bottle. I was living in a different state, under very different circumstances, and that vacant lot was but a memory. I'd shown what I thought had been remarkable restraint by hanging on to this last bottle, but now was the time. It was a cold, snowy day in Minnesota, and I wanted to smell the sunshine. I opened the bottle, hoping it had not gone bad or become tainted by the cheap cork I'd used. I poured a glass. The wine was still a lovely light canary color. I swirled it, inhaled deeply, and shut my eyes. I had to. The sun was too bright.

FRUIT (OR FLOWER) WINES VERSUS GRAPE WINES

A caste system exists in wine making between those who work with *Vitis vinifera* and those who do not. You know *vinifera* grapes: They're called Merlot, or Chardonnay, or Sangiovese.

This is where 99 percent of all wine-making research goes, and much of the rest goes into those non-*vinifera* grapes considered suitable for professional wine making, like the hybrids Norton or Marechal Foch. Winemakers who work with honey or fruits are largely left to their own devices.

I work with both *vinifera* grapes and other fruits. My Northern California home is surrounded by excellent wine grape–growing regions: Lodi, the Sierra Foothills, Napa. I grow several wine grape varieties in my backyard, notably a rare Spanish red varietal called Graciano. But I also make meads, which are honey-based white wines, as well as other fruit wines such as blackberry, plum, and elderberry.

What you most need to know about making wines is that if you take the basic principles of wine grape wine making to heart, almost anything can be made into a decent table wine. At its essence, wine making is how well you extract the flavor and aroma of the ingredients you use. Wine grapes are so popular because they have excellent aroma and flavor, bear heavy crops that are relatively easy to harvest, and can, without too much outside help, be brought into a sugar-acid balance to make a beautiful, stable wine that can mature for decades.

It is the sugar-acid balance that is the most important starting point for making wine. Good wine grapes possess enough inherent acidity and natural sugars to make a wine with bright flavor and an alcohol level high enough to preserve the wine for years. Most other fruits lack either the acidity or natural sweetness of wine grapes. That's where your friends sugar (or honey) and the various acids come in.

My dandelion wine had no sugar at all until I added the honey. Nor did it have any acid until I added the tartaric acid. Tartaric acid is derived from grapes and is used in professional wine making. That meant the bones of my dandelion wine were generic—I could make almost any sort of wine from that honey-acid base, or I could have left it alone and made mead. What made the dandelion wine special was the aroma from the flower petals.

What follows is a primer on wine making, using two recipes as models. The first is dandelion wine, to represent a generic white wine boosted with an aromatic, usually a flower. The second is elderberry wine, one of the best fruit wines in the world and a wine that can stand in for most other fruit wines.

Bear with me as you read this chapter. Making wine that is worthy of aging and of serving serious wine people requires some science and—dare I say it?—some math. But you can do it. Just follow these instructions step by step.

GETTING STARTED

Wine is juice transformed. Alcohol forms as a by-product of yeasts consuming sugar in juice (or honey). Once the alcohol level reaches a certain point, which is different depending on the yeast involved, the wee yeasties die. Ideally, your juice has enough sugar in it to eventually produce an alcohol level between 12 and 15 percent. Most wild yeasts—those that live in the air around us—will die below that level, leaving some sugar remaining. This is why most winemakers use special wine yeasts that won't die until they eat up all the sugars in grapes, which results in a dry wine with that magic 12 to 15 percent alcohol level. This is enough to preserve the wine without making the drink so strong it tastes like hard liquor. These wine yeasts also work well with fruit juice or honey.

Once the yeasts have turned the sugar into alcohol, you technically have wine. But your wine is still biologically active, which is why you need to strain the solids from your new wine and then age it. Even then, wine will change over time. In general, older wine is better. There are exceptions.

Proper wine making requires special equipment. Can you make an alcoholic beverage with nothing more than a bucket, a kettle, and a cork? Yeah, but if prison hooch is your aim, this is the wrong book. If your goal is to make a non-grape wine that will make a wine snob rethink his opinions, then read on. Most of this equipment is readily available at your local home-brew store or online. Here is what you need.

- A 5-gallon bucket with a cover, available at most hardware stores.

- A kitchen scale that can measure in metric units. Gram measures are important in wine making.

- Two 3-gallon carboys (large glass bottles) and a 1-gallon carboy. You will need airlocks and rubber stoppers for each carboy.

- A hydrometer, which is a glass thermometer–looking thing used to check sugar levels in juice or wine. You stick the hydrometer into a beaker filled with your juice or honey. It is vital to have this for two reasons: first, to see how much sugar or honey you will need to add to your juice, to bring the sugars to a proper level; and second, to see when the fermentation is done.

- An acid test kit. You want to test what's called the total acidity (TA) of your juice.

Juice that's too low in acid makes a flat-tasting wine. Shoot for a TA of no lower than 6 grams per liter. Don't worry; the test kit has easy instructions on how to use it.

❧ A press bag, which is essentially a giant jelly bag.

❧ A siphon tube, at least 3 feet long, to get your wine from the carboy into bottles.

❧ A special carboy funnel for pouring freshly fermented wine.

❧ A thermometer. You want to check the temperature of your juice. It matters when you are gauging your sugar levels.

❧ Wine yeast. Do not, under any circumstances, ever, ever, ever use baking yeast to make wine. Your wine will taste like bread. It will be nasty. And don't try to get all French and use "wild yeasts," either. Unless you live near a winery in Napa, you don't have the right wild yeasts in your area. I buy a variety of yeasts, but good standbys are Pasteur Red and EC-1118.

❧ Potassium metabisulfite, also known as K-meta. This is your cleaner and disinfectant. Use it sparingly, or you will wind up with that fun, cheap jug wine headache we all know so well.

❧ Tartaric acid. Don't use lemon juice and don't use citric acid. You are making wine here, not lemonade.

❧ Grape tannin. Tannin builds "structure" to a wine, making it taste and feel a little felty at first. But tannin also gives wine a foundation upon which to age. Not every wine will need it. Elderberries and some plums have lots of tannin, but you'd need to add tannin if you made blackberry wine.

❧ Diammonium phosphate (DAP), also known simply as yeast nutrient. This is vital when making honey-based wines. Honey is a terrible environment for yeast, and without DAP, fermentations can stop halfway without fully converting all that sugar into alcohol.

❧ Oak cubes. You can buy these in wine shops and they add a lot of flavor to red fruit wines such as elderberry, blackberry, blueberry, or plum. Want to make your wine taste like a "real" wine from Napa or Europe? Use oak cubes.

❧ A bottler. I recommend finding a friend with a bottler or asking the brew shop to rent theirs rather than buying a cheap handheld bottler. I hated my handheld bottler, and you need arms of steel to work it correctly. My current bottler is a large Italian contraption that works like a dream but cost me $125.

❧ Ultimately, you will need bottles and corks. You can start by saving your store-bought wine bottles (soak the labels off in warm water). Depending on which wine you are making, I suggest using real corks or plastic, not the cheap composite corks. Plastic closures are great for wines you don't intend to age for more than a year or two, while real corks are vital for long-aging wines, like raisin wine.

KNOWING YOUR FRUIT

While nearly any fruit, flower, or even vegetable can be fermented into wine, different ingredients have different needs. Here are a few pointers.

❧ Elderberries are nearly perfect for wine making, except they will need some additional sugar and sometimes additional acid. They mature into wonderfully aromatic reds reminiscent of Mourvedre or Malbec. Elderberries will not need extra tannin.

❧ Elderflowers—indeed all flowers—should be picked before 11 a.m. and need to be made into wine immediately, or else you will lose the aroma you are seeking. Always use a light honey when making flower wines. Light honey adds body without overpowering the flower itself. You will also need to add tartaric acid. Other good flowers for wine making include roses, lavender, chamomile, citrus blossoms, almond blossoms, and honeysuckle. When making rose petal wine, be sure to cut off the white part at the base of each petal. It is bitter.

❧ Strawberries make a wonderful blush wine, but the strong strawberry aroma seems weird if you ferment this wine dry. A little sweetness, like a commercial Gewürztraminer wine, will make your strawberry wine taste better. Ferment the wine dry first, then add sugar a little at a time until you are pleased with the taste.

❧ Raisins make a wonderful, sherrylike wine, but it really needs to be aged a long, long time. Don't even think about opening a bottle for at least 18 months.

❧ Blueberries and blackberries make ideal red wines, but they will need tannin. They often have nearly enough sugar and more than enough acid. Domestic blueberries might need a little extra tartaric acid, though. Wine from both fruits ages well.

❧ Plums make wonderful wines, but try to find damsons or another plum that has a strong bloom—that foglike coating over the skin of the fruit. The very best fruit wine I ever made was from damson plums, which can be hard to find.

FROM FIELD TO GLASS

So you have all your equipment and you are ready to make wine. What now? Think about what sort of wine you want to make. A big, bold red? A light rosé? A white? What's around you? Do you have elderflowers in bloom? Blueberries everywhere? I highly recommend that you make your wines from local ingredients, including local honey if you can find it.

Why? The way I see it, if you just want a drinkable wine, buy one. But if you are going to go through the yearlong effort of making your own creations, they ought to be special to you and your region. Not everyone has easy access to *vinifera* wine grapes, and, I would argue, if you live where they cannot grow, you should not try to make wines from these grapes. If I lived in Tucson, I'd make wine from prickly pears, and if I lived in northern Minnesota, I'd use blueberries and highbush cranberries. Anyone can buy a Merlot. Not everyone can make a prickly pear rosé.

Your first decision in a fruit wine is, wild or domestic? I make *vinifera* wines from grapes in my garden, and I rarely buy other fruit to make wines with; damson plums would be an exception. But I get a rush from a foraged wine, especially those made from elderberries and blackberries, which are common where I live. Foraged wines have an added "wow" factor, but you might want to start with a domestic fruit first. Harvesting enough wild fruit to make a batch of wine takes a lot of time. Maybe go halfway and make wine from fruit you gathered at a U-pick orchard or farm. Came home with 30 pounds of blueberries from a day at the blueberry farm? Make wine.

You will need a lot of fruit to make a proper wine. For wine grapes, the ratio is roughly 12 pounds of grapes for each gallon of wine. That's a lot of fruit, but you add no sugar or water to *vinifera* wines. With other fruits, you can get away with as little as a pound per gallon and still get some of the fruit's character in the finished wine, but it will taste thin. Shoot for 3 to 5 pounds of fruit per gallon and boost the sugar and liquid levels with sugar and water. Why not go for the whole dozen pounds? Well, first off you'll have a tough time gathering that much. And ever take the stems off that many elderberries? You'll go insane. More importantly, a lot of fruits have too much acid or tannin that you will need to mitigate.

THE CRUSH

You will need to destem and juice or crush your fruit first. I normally do this in a clean 5-gallon bucket. You can do it all by hand, or crush it with a potato masher, a blender, or your very clean feet (watch out, though, lots of fruits will stain your skin for days). Be careful with blenders or food processors, as you will want to avoid crushing too many seeds. Seeds contain bitter elements that can overwhelm your wine. Crush just enough to get broken-up fruit.

Many fruits contain a lot of pectin, which is great for setting jam but not for wine. To prevent your wine from jelling, buy pectic enzyme for these fruits. The enzyme eats up the pectin, and using it also extracts more flavor and color from the fruit skins. Fruits high in pectin include citrus, blackberries, apples, cranberries, gooseberries, and plums. Low-pectin fruits include apricots, blueberries, cherries, elderberries, peaches, pears, raspberries, and strawberries.

Once you've crushed your fruit, you will need to add water for volume. My recipes are for 3 gallons, which is a good starter volume. Three gallons makes 15 bottles. For experienced winemakers, 5 gallons is better. Once you have added water, it is time to break out your hydrometer and acid test kit.

Mix the juice and water and pour a little into your hydrometer's test tube. Drop the

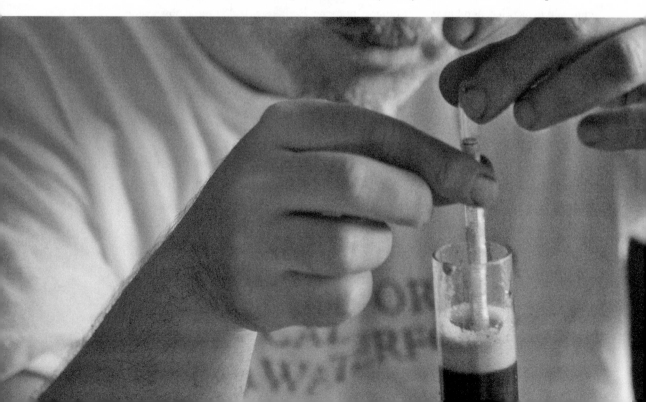

hydrometer into the tube and read the scale. Most hydrometers have several ways to measure sugar levels on them, and I prefer Brix (pronounced "bricks"), which is the scale professional winemakers use. An ideal red grape juice being made into wine will have a Brix rating of about 24.5; an ideal white grape juice is about 22.5. You want your sugar levels above 20 and below 28 Brix.

What if your juice is not in that window? "Fixing" your juice requires some math. The following formula is adapted from one I found in *Making Table Wine at Home*, by George Cooke and James Lapsley.

$$\textbf{(Target Brix – Initial Brix reading)} \times \textbf{0.125} \times \textbf{gallons of juice}$$
$$= \textbf{pounds of sugar to add}$$

Let's say you've crushed 12 pounds of elderberries and added water up to the 3-gallon mark. You check the sugar level, and it comes out to 17 Brix. You want it higher, around 24 Brix, meaning the difference between your target and your initial Brix is 7 points. Following the formula, you multiply $7 \times 0.125 \times 3$, and you find you need about 2.6 pounds of sugar to hit your target. Easy, right?

Not so fast. Sugar acts weird, so once you have determined your target sugar level, dissolve the amount you think you need in a little water and add in four batches. After each batch, stir the juice, wait 5 minutes or so, and take another reading. Keep adding until you are within 1 to 2 Brix of your target. A rule of thumb is to shoot low with fruit wines, and here's why: They will often pick up sugar overnight, so your initial Brix reading can be artificially low. Flower wines will not do this.

Temperature adds another wrinkle. Your Brix reading will be skewed if your juice is really cold or warm. Hydrometers assume your juice is 60°F. If the juice is instead, say, 45°F, you need to subtract a half Brix from what your hydrometer reads. If your juice is 75°F, you need to add about a half Brix. You don't need to alter the temperature of your wine to do the hydrometer test, but you do need to know it.

Phew. Okay, now you have enough sugar to ferment a wine with roughly 12 to 14.5 percent alcohol, perfect for table wines. But what about this crazy acid thing?

The acid test confirms that your juice has enough acid to withstand aging without going bad. Acid also makes the drink taste bright, not dull. There are several ways to measure total acidity. I use a test kit where you take some juice, put a few drops of one chemical in it, then add another chemical drop by drop until the juice changes color. The number of drops you use of the second chemical corresponds to the total acidity of the juice. Fruit wines, and especially flower wines, can be all over the map on acidity. You want the total acidity (TA) to be between 6 and 10 grams per liter. In most cases, you will need to add tartaric acid, although blackberries, blueberries, cherries, cranberries, plums, and strawberries are generally high enough in acid already.

Always test your acidity, even with high-acid fruits. You might not need to adjust it, but it is good information to know. If you find your acidity is too low, use this formula: To increase the TA by 1 gram per liter, add 4 grams of tartaric acid for every gallon—yeah, I know I just gave you a formula in both metric and English measurements. Sue me. Always recheck your TA after each 4-gram batch you add so that you don't add too much. Too much acidity makes an unpleasantly tart wine. More water and sugar will offset this.

Still with me? Just remember, this is the hard part. Do this and you've gone a long way toward making a drinkable wine that has the potential to age well—and this is a helluva lot more than many fruit winemakers can say.

Now, ready for the yeast? Hold your horses. First, I advise adding into the juice a pinch—less than 1 gram—of your K-meta, the potassium metabisulfite. This is your insurance that wild yeasts will not jump on your sweet, lovely juice until you are ready to add the good yeast. Simply sprinkle it on and stir the juice.

This next part is optional. I recommend "cold soaking" your red wines for up to 3 days (honey-based white wines don't need this). It extracts more color and body from the skins of the fruit, notably blueberries, elderberries, and plums. You know those big, burly Cabernet Sauvignons from Napa? Almost all of those wineries do this. Here's how you cold soak.

➤ Cool your juice to below 50°F, by any means necessary. Put it in the fridge, or drop either a sealed ice pack or a plastic soda or milk carton filled with ice into the juice. Don't let the juice climb above 50°F or it might begin to ferment. Keep changing the ice cartons as they melt to keep your juice cool.

➤ Cover the juice. Lay a sheet of plastic wrap over it—right on the top of the juice and crushed fruit. You want no air touching the juice, if at all possible. Advanced winemakers pump carbon dioxide over the juice, which is heavier than air, forming a gas seal. Gas canisters are available at brew shops.

❧ Be sure to add any pectic enzyme when you start this process. You want it to get to work before you add your yeast.

Even if you don't cold soak, you will need to add pectic enzyme and any tannin into your juice on the first day, about 12 hours after you put in the K-meta. Cold soaking or no, once you've added any pectic enzyme or tannin, cover the bucket and walk away until tomorrow.

THE FERMENT

Day 2 (if you are not cold soaking) begins with your yeast. Start by mixing into the juice half the amount of yeast nutrient, the diammonium phosphate, that you intend to use for the whole wine-making process. Now get your tap water hot, measuring it with a thermometer

BOTTLING AND BEYOND

When can I drink my wine, you ask? No earlier than 6 months, if you want decent wine. Some, like raisin or dandelion wine, need at least a year or more. Wine ages differently in the carboy than in the bottle, and both steps are necessary. I typically bottle my red wines after a year or so, and whites after about 9 months. I then age them in the bottle for several more months before drinking. But that's just me. You can bottle anytime after 4 months or so.

When you bottle, be sure to use real cork if you plan on aging your wine a long time. Synthetic corks do not allow a wine to breathe, so they're fine for whites and rosés, but not for your big elderberry, damson, blackberry, or blueberry reds. Do yourself a favor and label your bottles. You will forget which is which if you do not.

What if, after all this, you make a bad batch? It happens, after all, even to me—and I have been making wines for more than 20 years. If it is okay, just not really worth drinking, go back to the brew shop and buy a "mother" to make wine vinegar out of it; a mother is a starter culture for making vinegar. Pour all the iffy wine into a big crock or pail, and drop the mother in. Keep the crock covered (but let air get in), and within a few weeks you should have vinegar. What if it is *really* bad? Well, it is no sin to chuck it. And the great thing about making fruit wines is that, unlike the grape harvest, which comes but once a year, you can make a fruit or flower wine anytime. Salud!

until it hits 100°F. Pour one-half cup of the hot water into a measuring cup and then add the yeast. Just sprinkle the yeast on top of the water. Wait 5 minutes before stirring it in gently. Wait another 15 minutes. Now you can add your yeast to the juice.

If your juice is colder than 70°F, let the yeast sit on top of the juice for 30 minutes. This lets it acclimate to the colder juice. Shocked yeast can die or delay fermentation. If you are cold soaking, you will want to let your juice come up to temperature early in the day, and add the yeast when it has warmed to at least 60°F. After the yeast has acclimated, stir it in and put the bucket cover on. Now walk away.

Yeast will take a day or so to get rolling, but by morning you should see it bubbling, and the temperature of the juice should have risen. Now your job is easy. Take the juice's temperature every day. This helps you track fermentation. It will rise steadily as fermentation gets started, then drop as the initial fermentation finishes, usually after 3 to 6 days.

If you are making red wine, during the fermentation you will also need to churn the juice at least twice a day and up to four times a day. Simply stick your clean arm in the juice and swish it around. This aerates your yeast and blows off any hydrogen sulfide (an unwanted by-product of yeast fermentation), and will result in a wine with more color and body. If you are making white fruit wine, aerate the juice no more than once a day. Skip it altogether if you have nothing floating on the top of the juice.

On Day 2 of the fermentation, add the rest of your yeast nutrient. This will help the yeasts eat up the last of the sugar.

THE PRESS

The initial fermentation should be done in 3 to 6 days; 5 days is normal. After the temperature tops out, ideally at about 80°F for reds and 70°F for whites, the temperature should drop toward room temperature. When it does hit room temperature, that's a good sign the initial ferment is done. Now you'll need to separate your wine—because that's what it is now—from the solids. Serious winemakers use a grape press. I'd suggest something called a press bag, which is essentially a giant jelly bag. Get ready to be messy.

First, ladle off the "free run" juice into the 3-gallon carboy—this is what looks like wine in the bucket, not mushy fruit. Try not to get any debris in there. If this is impossible, pour a bit of the debris-laden juice though a fine-mesh sieve into another bucket or a large bowl. Using the big carboy funnel, pour the strained juice from the bowl into the 3-gallon carboy.

Now you will want to get all the wine locked in the skins into the carboy. Scoop the skins into the press bag (you can use a standard jelly bag, too) and squeeze it over that fine-mesh sieve—with a layer of cheesecloth over the mesh—into a bowl. It will get gunked up frequently, so you will have to rinse the cheesecloth from time to time. Pour the strained juice into the carboy. This step will result in a cleaner, clearer wine down the road.

It is vital that you fill your carboys to within an inch or so of the bottom of the airlock stopper. This prevents your wine from oxidizing and protects it from wild yeasts or bacteria. After filling, you may have more than 3 gallons. If so, pour any excess into a glass container that will just about hold the amount of excess; you want to minimize air in the containers. If you find yourself short of the 3 gallons for some reason, top off the new wine with a comparable wine: If you are making a red, use red wine; if you are making a white, use a white wine. You want the wine to come up to about one-half inch below where your rubber stopper will be. Don't worry about this no longer being "your wine." The amount of commercial wine you add in the entire process will be less than 5 percent.

MOPPING UP

Top the carboys with their airlocks and stoppers, and put them in a cool, dark place. This is especially important with white wines, which can oxidize and turn amber if left in the light too long. You will soon notice two things: First, the suspended solids in the juice should be settling to the bottom. Second, the wine will be bubbling slightly. This is called secondary fermentation, and it is important that this step be done before you bottle, unless you like exploding bottles.

I let my wines age in the carboys like this for several months before I begin to mess with them. A good rule of thumb is to wait 2 months for reds, 1 month for whites. After this time elapses, you will need to "rack" your wines. This is where that second 3-gallon carboy comes in, as well as the siphon.

Clean the inside of the new carboy by adding a pinch of K-meta to it, then swishing around a lot of water. Pour out and rinse well. Now add 1 gram more of K-meta. This will help the wine age safely. If you fail to use sulfites, your wine can develop "off" flavors or aromas or even turn to vinegar.

To rack your wine, use the flexible tubing to siphon it from the old carboy into the new one, making sure you get as little of the sediment that has fallen to the bottom as possible. To do this, set the full carboy higher than the empty one. Now put one end of the tubing midway into the full carboy and get yourself close to the other carboy. You will need to be quick on this next step: Suck the air from the tube, pulling the wine with it. The moment you get a splash of new wine on your lips, stick the tubing into the new carboy. Suction should siphon the wine from one carboy into another. It is better to leave some wine in the carboy than to transfer too much sediment.

Due to the sediment, you will have a lower volume of wine than you thought. What to do? You have a choice: Add some more commercial wine, or add oak cubes. Oak cubes simulate aging wine in oak barrels. I add oak cubes for most of my wines. How many? Depends. I buy French oak, toasted medium, which are pretty mild. A heavy-toasted American oak will be stronger. The more powerful the oak flavor, the shorter the time it should stay in the wine. In no case would I use more than a handful in a 3-gallon batch.

If you do add oak cubes, taste your new wine after 3 months to see if it is getting oaky. If it is, siphon the wine off the oak cubes into a clean carboy and replace the lost volume with table wine.

RECIPES

DANDELION WINE

This is your basic aromatic white wine that will work with the flowers (page 80) or another aromatic element such as sassafras bark, bayberry, or spicebush. Remember when using flowers to use only the flowers, not bitter stems or green parts. And do your best to find a light-colored local honey for this. It will make your wine more special.

When gathering dandelion flowers, you will need a lot of them—5 gallons, to be exact. It sounds like a lot, and it is, but gathering this many is easy if you find a place overrun with the weeds. Remember while you're picking that this is a wonderful wine that ages well for years.

Makes 3 gallons

> 6 quarts dandelion flower petals, loosely packed
>
> 3 gallons water (spring water is best)
>
> 9 pounds honey or sugar
>
> 1 teaspoon grape tannin
>
> 6 teaspoons or more tartaric acid (see page 90 for exact amount)
>
> 3 teaspoons yeast nutrient
>
> Wine yeast

Pick your flowers early in the day and remove all green bits. Bring 1 gallon of the water to a boil and add the flowers. Turn off the heat and cover the pot. Let this steep until it returns to room temperature, or 6 hours, whichever is longer.

Meanwhile, boil the remaining 2 gallons water and stir in the honey or sugar. Skim any foam that surfaces, and simmer for 5 minutes. Turn off the heat and let it cool.

Pour the dandelion tea through a strainer set over a large bowl, pressing on the petals to get all the juices you can. Pour the strained tea through a fine-mesh sieve lined with cheesecloth. Add the tea to the honey water.

Pour the mixture into a freshly cleaned 5-gallon bucket. (Clean the bucket with 2 teaspoons of K-meta diluted in a gallon of water and rinse well.) Add the grape tannin and 4 teaspoons of the tartaric acid. Test for both Brix and acid levels. You may need to add more acid or increase sugar levels. If you need to increase the Brix, use table sugar this time, dissolved in a little lukewarm water.

Add half the yeast nutrient to the juice and mix well. Wait 1 hour. Hydrate the wine yeast and add it to the juice. Cover and ferment away. Follow the directions on page 85 from here.

ELDERBERRY WINE

This is the basic recipe for red fruit wines. It will work with blackberries, blueberries, plums, or any other dark fruit or berry. All these wines age very well and do well with added oak. If you make them correctly and age them a few years, you can shock your wine snob friends. Serve it first, and tell them what it is later.

Makes 3 gallons

9–15 pounds elderberries, stems removed

10 quarts water (spring water is best)

3–6 pounds sugar (see opposite page for exact amount)

Tartaric acid (see opposite page for exact amount)

1½ teaspoons pectic enzyme

1 teaspoon grape tannin (only for blueberries and blackberries)

3 teaspoons yeast nutrient

Wine yeast

Crush the berries by hand, or pulse them in a food processor in batches just enough to break up the berries. Do not liquefy them.

Pour the crushed berries into a large pot with the water. Add 3 pounds of the sugar.

Bring to a simmer, then turn off the heat. Heating elderberries makes them easier to digest and helps set the color of the wine. This step is not essential for other fruit wines, and your finished wine, while dark in color, will have a "cooked fruit" character to it. I get good color and more fresh fruit flavor by heating other fruit wines just to the steaming point, about 180°F.

Pour the juice into a freshly cleaned 5-gallon bucket. (Clean the bucket with 2 teaspoons of K-meta diluted in a gallon of water and rinse well.) Let it cool to room temperature, then test the juice for acid and sugar. Both may be a little low, so be prepared to add another 1 to 3 pounds of sugar and possibly tartaric acid. Add tartaric acid to get the juice to about 7 grams per liter. You might not need to add any—I've had elderberry batches that needed no additional acid and others that needed a lot. We're dealing with a wild food, and wild foods are variable.

Add the pectic enzyme (and tannin, for blueberries and blackberries) and chill to below 50°F in the fridge or with ice packs. Lay a sheet of plastic wrap on the juice to keep out air. Keep the juice covered and at this temperature for up to 3 days. The longer you cold soak, the more flavor you extract. (But you run a higher risk of oxidation—which will turn the wine an unappetizing brown—or spontaneous fermentation, which can ruin the whole batch.)

On the third day, bring the juice up to room temperature. Add half the yeast nutrient as the juice warms. Once the juice is at room temperature, hydrate the wine yeast and add it in, then follow the directions on page 85 from here.

PART II

FISHING AND FEASTING FROM STREAMS TO THE SEA

7

WHY FISH?

Not long ago, I was asked by a friend why she should ever want to go fishing. I was taken aback at the question. It had never occurred to me that someone had never been fishing or, if not, why she wouldn't want to. It's a naïve notion, I know, but fishing, clamming, and crabbing are as much a part of me as are my arms or eyes. I've fished, gathered clams, and collected crabs since I could walk, and even before that was carried by my mother and sisters along shorelines and in the cabins of boats as they caught fish or dug for the delicacies of the beach.

My friend's question made me sit down and think about what it is that drives me to the sea, the rivers, lakes, and ponds in search of fish. For me, it starts with the sea. The sea is a place of calm for me, an endless expanse where I can fully appreciate how small I really am in this world. At sea, any hubris or airs I've accumulated on land are stripped away by the majesty of an ocean more powerful than us all. The sea is one of God's great cathedrals, and it is the one that most stirs me within.

Most of us are drawn to water. The smell of the salt air, the burble of a wooded stream, the sullen murmur of a great river—or the crushing silence of a lake robed in fog—all of these awaken something within us. We want to be in that setting, often for reasons we don't fully understand.

Mystery grips the water. What lies beneath the waves? Fishing taps that feeling to the utmost. Hunters and foragers can see the habitat where their quarry lives, but casting a line into the water is an act of faith. Yes, experienced anglers know where fish ought to be, but, for the most part, you cannot see them. Fishing is a blind man's pursuit. When I am fishing, really fishing, my eyes lose their focus and all my energy runs through that rod, down through the fishing line and onto the sinker and the hook. I fish by feel. Tap, tap, tap goes the sinker on the bottom. Is that mud, rock, or the deck of a sunken ship? A twitch on the line! A fish? Or just the hook brushing against an unseen object? Fishing awakens my senses the way no other pursuit does.

And when a fish finally strikes my line, the jolt of adrenaline rippling through me never gets old. Fish on! I find myself grinning as I set the hook and the battle begins. The fish, still unseen, darting, shaking, pulling, pulling, pulling. Big fish can wrench you so hard you sometimes wonder who is the hunter and who is the prey. Many fish will play dead on the way up to the surface, making it feel as if you've lost them. That feels like a punch to the gut. Oh no! Did I lose it? It's a little boy's loss—for a split second, you feel like you will never be happy again. And then the fish runs, ripping a hundred yards of line off your reel. Adrenaline rushes through you, and you crank the reel some more.

In a flash of metallic wonder, you snatch your first glimpse of the fish: It is the most beautiful thing in the world, and you feel yourself wanting it more than diamonds, power, or money. You are not a rational person at this moment. The fish breaks the surface of the water with a thrash. A large fish will douse you with its fury. "Net! Net!" You hear yourself shouting for your friends to help bring this gift from an alien world into your possession— for this is now *your* fish.

And there it is, a silvery, brightly colored, dazzling thing. It is gasping for air. With a shock, you awaken from your trance and feel a wash of sadness seeping through you. This fish, staring up at you and gasping, wants to live as much as you do. Sometimes the feeling overcomes you, and you return the fish to the water. Sometimes your sadness is overtaken by thoughts that come from another place within you, thoughts of fried fish and seviche and sushi. And that's when you toss the fish into a cooler or a bucket.

This is fishing, a primal soup of emotions that may or may not end in a wonderful meal, but will most certainly end with a powerful memory. For an angler, the act of fishing is as affirming as a blessing, as calming as longtime love, and as addictive as any drug.

BASICS

Most people know what a rod and reel are, what a net is, and that you need some sort of bait to catch a fish. But beyond that, the world of fishing can be confusing to an outsider. River fishing requires different equipment and skills than does pond fishing. Ocean fishing is a world away from casting a line for trout in a mountain stream, but fishing the Great Lakes is a close approximation. Then there is the chasm between the freshwater anglers and the saltwater anglers. I fished nothing but saltwater until I was in my late twenties. Some fishing is finesse; some fishing requires brute strength and the stamina of a prizefighter. Most kinds of fishing are somewhere in between.

What follows is a very short, very incomplete primer on what you need to know when you try to catch the critters in this section. You'll find more details in each chapter.

If you've never done any fishing before, here are the very basics. First, to fish you generally need a rod and reel. On the reel will be fishing line. At the end of the line will be what's called terminal tackle, which includes a length of stouter line called the leader, some sort of weight (typically a lead sinker), the hook, and some kind of bait.

To get the bait in front of a fish, you either cast the line out into the water or just drop it straight to the bottom. This brings me to reels. There are all sorts of types, but the most basic you need to know about are the spinning reel, the boat reel, and the fly reel. I recommend anyone serious about becoming an angler buy a spinning reel and a boat reel, each with different rods.

Spinning reels and fly reels allow you to cast to a spot in the water. Highly useful from shore, in rivers or in ponds, they can also be used from a boat to work your bait along the bottom to cover more area or to cast and retrieve lures. A disadvantage to a spinning reel is that it generally cannot handle a lot of weight, so it is ineffective for deepwater fishing or if you need to fish the bottom where the currents are very strong. Casting also takes practice to perfect.

Boat reels can be cast a short distance by experts, but normally you just open the bail (the lever that keeps the line from tumbling out of the reel) and let the line unwind from the reel, all the way to the bottom. This is what you normally do in the ocean and in large lakes. Boat reels are easy to use and are the rig of choice in deep water, especially the ocean.

A word on bait. Bait can be anything from worms to live fish to dead fish to artificial lures. These artificial lures come in a bewildering array of shapes and sizes. My advice is to go to an independent sporting goods store, or one with an expert angler who fishes the area, and ask what you should buy for the fish you are seeking. The same species of fish will not eat the same thing in different places. Crickets and curly-tail jig heads work great for panfish in some ponds but are useless in others. It pays to ask.

If you plan to fish on your own, get yourself set up in a sporting goods store with a basic rod and reel combo, which means the two come packaged together. Get your reel spooled with the proper line. Line is measured in "test," meaning you should reasonably be able to catch a fish of "x" weight on "x" test—i.e., you ought to be able to catch a 10-pound fish on 10-pound test line. Other things you need for on-your-own fishing:

- A net appropriate for what you are catching.

- An inexpensive tackle box to carry your hooks, lures, weights, and extra line.

- A variety of weights, sinkers, as well as split shot, which looks like a lead Pac-Man.

- Hooks of various sizes—buy ones with leaders already attached.

- A pair of nail clippers to clip the ends of the line after you tie knots.

- Artificial lures. I recommend several sizes of a lure called a Kastmaster, a supply of lead jig heads, and different colors of curly tails. The tails go on the jig heads, and you fish them by gently twitching the line to "jig" the lure (as in dancing a jig). Also get several Rapala lures, which look like fake fish and have various sizes of plastic lips where the fish's mouth should be. A Rapala lure is a casting or trolling bait.

- Barrel swivels. These are invaluable when you are attaching your leader to the main fishing line. They prevent the line from twisting too much.

OCEAN FISHING

Ocean fishing is one of the few areas where being a do-it-yourselfer isn't always the best idea. Unless you want to learn navigation and boater safety—and have lots of money to flush into the briny deep—don't bother buying a boat if you don't live within sight of the water. And even if you do live in sight of the water, think hard before plunking down dollars for your own vessel. It is far cheaper and far easier to do your ocean fishing from someone else's boat or from shore. That means either tagging along with friends or chartering a boat.

Chartering generally comes in three categories.

1. A true charter, where you pay big bucks to rent a whole boat for you and up to five of your friends; most small charter vessels can take a maximum of six passengers

and are known as "six-pack" charters. These charters will typically include all bait and tackle, as well as fish cleaning.

2. An open charter, which is aboard the same sort of boat as a true charter, but in this case the captain allows you to tag along on someone else's charter. The price will be a lot lower than a true charter, you get personal service from the captain and mates, and there's lots of room to fish. It is my preferred method of ocean fishing.

3. A party or "head" boat, which is a larger vessel that typically lets between 15 and 40 anglers aboard. It is often first come, first served to get a spot and will be a lot cheaper, often less than $50 per head. Fish cleaning and rod and reel rentals are usually extra, however.

Another rule: The larger the fish you are after, the smaller the boat you want to be on. Think about it. Do you really want to fight a 150-pound tuna on a boat with forty other guys lined up on the rail? In case you cannot picture this mayhem in your head, trust me, you don't. It's a nightmare, unless everyone on the boat is an experienced angler. I once had a 60-plus-pound grouper on the line that was taking me for a ride when a newbie angler next to me freaked out when she caught a tiny sea bass. Instead of simply lifting her microfish over the rail, she let it swim around at the surface. The fish circled my line—despite me screaming at her to hoist up her fish—and when it completed the circle, the added tension snapped my line and off swam my grouper. I am pretty sure I've never come closer to committing a felony than on that day.

Party boats are great where no one fish will make or break your trip. Stick to smaller, more intimate settings when you are seeking larger fish such as striped bass, tuna, sturgeon, halibut, and the like.

If you are still lost, I've included several book-length primers on how to fish in the Resources section at the end of the book.

8

CLAMS
AND THEIR COUSINS

I've been clamming a long, long time. I remember being about 6 years old, on Block Island, standing in water up to my chest. I was dancing the twist, screwing my feet into the sand hoping my toes would bump up against the hard, smooth shell of *Mercenaria mercenaria*, a hard-shell clam.

I'd squeal in pain when a crab would grab my toes, and yip in fright when stingrays or horseshoe crabs would scuttle through my legs. It was an early lesson that foraging has its dangers, no matter how trivial. That element of danger made the whole thing thrilling, though. And every step became Christmas morning. Would I find a clam that was too small? Maybe it would be one of those giants, so huge their shells would gape and squirt seawater at you when you looked at them. Mom called them "piss clams." They were for the night's chowder.

Like a monkey, I could find a clam with my feet, grab it in my toes, and bring it up to my hands—that way, I never had to dip my head in the water. Each clam I brought up would need to pass the ring test: If it was too big to fit through a neon green or orange plastic ring given to us by the harbormaster, the clam would go into a floating bucket I had tied to my arm. If it was too small, we had to toss it. I took great pleasure in seeing how far I could throw the clams down the beach. Mom told me not to throw them in too deep or they would not be able to rebury themselves; we wanted to catch them again on next year's vacation. It was an early lesson in the forager's code.

My family would spread out in what I'd later recognize was a squad pattern the army uses on patrol: Everyone more or less evenly spaced, working the submerged sand in roughly the same direction. Sisters Lizz and Laura and Mom and my stepfather, Frank, would be in the deepest water, while I would tend the shallows. After a few hours, we would collect our haul and pour it out on the beach. I remember seeing a sea of clams, enough to cover our dining room table at home. Who knows how many we really had.

Back at the cottage we rented, Mom and Frank would open the piss clams and run them through an old grinder for the chowder. The kids' job was to sort the smaller ones. Littlenecks, the smallest, would go in one pile, while cherrystones, slightly larger, would go into another. Cherrystones were to be eaten on the grill, or roughly chopped and served in a shell with bread crumbs, as a variation on clams casino; Mom called them "clam things." I still love them.

The littlenecks met their fate on the back porch, where a curious contraption stood on a picnic table. In my young mind, it was a clam guillotine; I think the makers call it a clam shucker. You take a clam and line up the seam between the two halves of the shell and lever down a dull steel blade through the shells, severing the clam's adductor muscle to open it. It is an ingenious device, so easy a 6-year-old could use it. Once open, we would feast on the clams raw, with lemon or cocktail sauce and lots of horseradish. I couldn't get enough of them: salty, chewy, a little sweet from the cocktail sauce, then that sinus-clearing rush from the horseradish.

This lifelong relationship with clams has colored my tastes. I like oysters, especially the tiny Olympia oysters, but I'll still take a plate of littlenecks on the half shell over a plate of oysters any time; besides, it's cheaper. Chefs rhapsodize over the delicate differences between a plump Wellfleet oyster and a briny Watch Hill. But a quahog is a quahog. Clams are the people's bivalve.

Mom's clam chowder was a constant growing up, as were her "clam things." We ate clam fritters on Block Island and fried clams whenever we were within sight of the sea. Back home in New Jersey, raw clams became a treat at restaurants, where I'd have to settle for a mere dozen.

I went to college on the East End of Long Island, at the State University of New York at Stony Brook. Long Island has legendary clam beds, and I was drawn away from the dorms by my college girlfriend, who worked at a clam hatchery in a town called Islip. Clams are king there—they once paved the streets with the shells. But generations of overfishing crippled the beds, forcing the town to open a hatchery to restore the stock. The big clam dredgers were all but gone, leaving a motley band of individual clam diggers to provide the Island with its favorite shellfish.

For a time, I became a member of that motley crew. A friend took me out several times on his boat on the island's North Shore and showed me how it's done. Clammers know their spots and guard them well; not being terribly mobile, clams can be easily wiped out by the greedy. The trick is to hit one spot one day, then another, then another, and so on, rotating around your areas over the course of the year.

We collected the clams with an iron rake attached to lengths of aluminum pole; the deeper the water, the more lengths you put on. At the end of the pole is a T-shaped handle used to make the rake scour the bottom. It is hard work. Once the rake is at the bottom, you repeatedly jerk the handle up and back to just under your chin. It is a lot like weight lifting, and longtime clammers develop massive shoulders and back muscles. Clams and stones will rattle around in the rake as you dredge, and when you think you have enough, you haul up the pole. Once the rake is just under the surface of the water, you must rotate it so the clams don't fall out, then shake it back and forth to dislodge the mud you brought up. You dump the contents of the rake into a cull box with a grate set by law to allow undersized clams to fall back into the water.

On a good day, I could earn several hundred dollars in 4 hours. On a bad day, I'd barely earn my gas money. Most days brought enough for gas, beer, food, and rent money. Not a bad existence while on break from college.

COLLECTING SHELLFISH

Digging your own clams follows that old saw "location, location, location." Clams are not evenly scattered underneath the sand, and there are all sorts of varieties to hunt, depending on where you live.

Most of my experience with clamming is in the Northeast with hard-shell clams, but that only scratches the surface. I've dug eastern razor clams and the soft-shell clams known as steamers. I've collected surf clams on open beaches and even freshwater clams in Minnesota rivers; these taste like snot, so unless you're a big fan of eating snot, I'd avoid freshwater clams for everything but bait.

In the West, clamming is tougher, as many places south of Washington have been fished out. There is a native variant of the eastern hard-shell clam, but more abundant are butter clams and the imported Manila clam. In Southern California, you can still find some Pismo clams, which are similar to the Manilas only larger, and up in the Pacific Northwest, there are huge horse clams and enormous geoducks, one of which can feed a family.

What's more, you can find a host of other tasty bivalves in the tidal zones, notably oysters and mussels. Add little snails called periwinkles, turban shells, limpets, and the giant whelks and conchs, and a molluscular feast awaits the intrepid.

Before you begin, check your state's fish and game department to see if you need a license. In many states, the shellfishing license is given through the town or county where you intend to clam. Licenses are rarely expensive. Also check with the state or local authorities to see which beds are safe to dig. Some places close from time to time, often in high summer, due to pollution or poisonous algae.

Once you're licensed, start with the easiest critters. By far the easiest tidbits to gather on any shore are periwinkles, limpets, and mussels. They attach themselves to rocky shorelines and can be plucked off—yanked off in the case of mussels, which attach themselves with stiff fibers called the beard. Periwinkles are a cute little snail, and they wander around the rocks eating algae and other tiny yummy bits. The West Coast equivalent is a turban shell.

Gather mussels in cold weather along ocean beaches. November to April are the best months. You want the blue mussel, which has a smooth shell and is what you buy in the store. In the Pacific, there is a California mussel that looks like a store-bought mussel but is brown, not indigo. In the East, avoid the ribbed or striated mussel that lives in back bays. These taste nasty but are fantastic flounder bait. Mussels prefer cold water and, because they filter food from the surrounding seawater, can accumulate toxins in warmer months or when they live at the southern end of their range, which in the Atlantic is about North Carolina. If you plan on collecting mussels, check online or with your local harbormaster for closures in your area. The state of California posts this information on the Department of Fish and Game's Web site.

To collect mussels, don rubber boots and prepare to get wet: The best mussels are a few feet into the surf, clinging in clusters on rocks. Bring a mesh bag with a shoulder strap to put them in, and be careful! I've been knocked over by waves while fixated on prying a clump of blue mussels off a rock. Mussel collecting is by no means a dangerous activity, but use common sense.

Even easier to collect are periwinkles. Periwinkles are little gray-and-black snails with either smooth or corduroy shells. Winkles can be so abundant they coat whole rocks at low tide. You can collect them all year long, too. Just pluck them off and pop them into a container with a lid, and you are good to go. Count on at least a dozen per person for an appetizer, but I've eaten 50 or more when I'm very hungry. Cook them as you would mussels, steamed in white wine and garlic butter. To eat them, you stab the end of the snail with a toothpick, then corkscrew out the meat. After a few

snails, you'll get the hang of it. A periwinkle has a hard cap on the outer side of the meat called an operculum, which feels a little like a fingernail. It comes right off after you've cooked the winkles.

On to clams. A few generalities first. Most hard-shell and soft-shell clams prefer to live in calm backwaters with a mixture of sand and mud. That said, some species love crashing waves, rocks, or pure sand, while others lurk in solid mud.

It's best to dig clams from cold water. Clams dug from warm water go bad more easily—they fall into shock when they sit in the car or basket, then again when they are put in the fridge. They also tend to be tougher.

Washington state is the undisputed center of West Coast clamming. If you're looking for a sweet spot in Atlantic clamdom, it's the waters in and around Rhode Island, because along this portion of the Atlantic coast, water temperatures are cool enough to prevent clams from falling into shock when they're taken from the water and stored in a refrigerator; the quahogs last longer and taste fresher, at least to me. Northern quahogs are also more likely to be free of the toxin vibrio, a warm-water bacterium that makes it risky to eat a southern clam on the half shell, especially in summer.

I still do most of my recreational clamming with my feet. I have a few more scars on my toes and I can stand in deeper water, but the method hasn't changed much since I was 5. It's more fun than the more civilized raking method. Treading clams should only be done in the north, however, because the combination of warmish air and cool water makes the exercise more comfortable. In southern waters, I'd be worried about vibrio and about bull sharks, which love this sort of water. Bathers do die every year from bull shark attacks, although the chance it will be you is minuscule. Still, I have been around too many sharks to stand waist-deep in murky, warm water around an estuary in summer. This is exactly the combination of factors in which most bull shark attacks occur. Thankfully, these sharks rarely venture north of New Jersey.

Most people dig clams in less than a foot of water using rakes, which you can buy at seaside sporting goods stores. Basically, you don rubber boots and march out into the mud, using the metal rake the same way I did from the boat in the bays around Long Island. It is a cleaner, slightly safer way to catch your clams.

As for where to look, bait shops can point you in a general direction. If you are within scouting distance of the shore, start looking at back bays at low tide. Timing is critical. You can only collect clams or any other mollusk at low tide. Check your local tides online at places like Weather Underground (www.wunderground.com), local newspapers, or at the source: the National Oceanic and Atmospheric Administration (www.tidesandcurrents.noaa.gov), which has tide tables online.

Start scouting or clamming in the last two or three hours of a falling tide. That way, you have enough time to find a good spot to dig during the last hour of the outgoing tide, the slack water, then the first good hour of the incoming tide. If you go wandering while you're clamming, watch your surroundings and be careful to have escape routes—nice sandy beaches lying next to cliffs at low tide can flood and cut off your return when the tide is high. Keep your wits about you.

I have found that soft-shell clams, the steamers, live closer to shore in areas that are more mud than sand. Look near sources of running freshwater, like little springs. They also seem to like muddy areas where saltwater drains out of trapped pools created during high tides. Soft-shell clams are generally smaller than quahogs, typically only about 4 inches long, although I've seen them as long as 8 inches across. The clam doesn't entirely fit inside its shell, and it will have a brown siphon tube sticking out one end. The shell will be ivory with caramel-colored striations on it.

Be careful digging soft-shell clams, as they have very brittle shells and, once broken, will be hopelessly full of sand. You'll probably break one or two when you first discover them, but don't worry—they live in colonies, so there will be more nearby. Slow down and use your fingers to grab them gently but firmly while digging them out with the other hand. Another reason to be careful: In many states you must keep the broken clams as part of your bag limit, which is good conservation but a major bummer, as it's tough to remove the sand from a broken steamer. You'll need at least a half dozen per person for a good appetizer, and a dozen makes a good meal with bread and white wine.

Hard-shell clams like the eastern quahog, the western littlenecks, and butter clams—as well as cockles, bean clams, and Pismo clams—are often in deeper water. I've found them as deep as 15 feet while digging from a boat. As with steamers, they live in vast colonies. A good place to start looking is in the debris lining the beach, where storms and unusual high tides deposit a band of seaweed, driftwood, and dead things. If you see broken clam shells in that debris line or all over the beach, you know you are in business. Broken clam shells indicate that there are clam predators around, which means live clams are near.

The next step is to look for little holes along the sand or mud where the tide has receded. Now holes don't always mean clams—ghost shrimp and crabs will also bury themselves in sand, leaving an air hole behind them—but it's a good bet that if you start raking the area you will come up with a clam. If you see little geysers spurt out of the holes, you definitely have a clam. The geysers are the clams' siphons retracting. It also means they're on to you and could be burrowing deeper. Best to sit tight for 10 minutes or so and wait for them to think the coast is clear. Clams can live for a decade or more, and the giant geoducks of the Pacific Northwest can live to be more than 100, so they are more clever than you might think.

How deep to rake or dig? A spade's depth for most clams, which have short siphons and are usually just below the sand. When you come across the holes, plunge the shovel directly into the sand next to the hole and lever out a spade's worth. With luck you will have a clam. This can be risky, however, because if you are in a steamer or razor clam area, you could have just broken one. And if you are hunting Western razor clams, you just gave the critter a head start, and he can dig faster than you. But the shovel method works great—as would a standard garden rake (not a lawn rake) or pitchfork— for Pismo, Manila, hard-shell, and bean clams, as well as surf clams and cockles.

A word on surf clams. These are the only clams I know of that really enjoy the pounding surf along the open ocean. They look like giant hard-shell clams, although a little more triangular, and they don't burrow too deep. Some live in deep water though, which can make them tough to reach. If you find them in shallower water, such as an exposed sandbar at low tide, you can find dozens in one foray. Surf clams will always be gritty and sandy, however, so you will need to purge them (more on that later) and mince or grind them. Except for their adductor muscle, which looks and tastes exactly like a bay scallop, surf clams are tougher than the leather on your boots.

STORING SHELLFISH

I've eaten virtually all of the clams I've dug within a day. But sometimes I bring home a bucket of seawater with my clams, empty the vegetable drawer of the fridge, coat the bottom of the drawer with cornmeal, fill it with the seawater, and drop the clams in. After a day or two, the clams filter in the cornmeal and filter out the grit. Even a warm-water clam dug in summer will last more than a week this way. I've done this successfully with hard-shell clams and steamers, and it is the only way I know of to eat a whole surf clam.

Mussels and oysters should be kept in a net bag in the fridge, where they will last up to a week, although if you wait that long you will get some die-off. Never eat dead shellfish, as they rot fast. Clams, oysters, mussels, snails, and even crabs and lobsters need to be alive when you begin cooking. A good way to tell if a clam or mussel is dead is to set it on a counter and leave it alone for a while. Most will loosen their shells visibly, and when you touch the shell again, it will clamp down tight. While it is not entirely true that clams, mussels, and oysters that don't open after cooking are rotten, it is still a safe practice.

Periwinkles should be kept in something that allows them to breathe but prevents them from wandering all over your refrigerator. The setup I use is a bowl with a damp cloth in it—to keep them moist—covered with some cheesecloth and secured with a rubber band.

For longer storage, steam the critters gently to get them out of their shells. Different shellfish require different cooking times, and each batch is variable, so you will need to check on them every couple of minutes. Once out of their shells, vacuum-seal your shellfish and freeze. When you use them again, make sure to add the shellfish at the very last minute, just to heat through. If you cook precooked shellfish too long, they will get tough and rubbery.

EATING SHELLFISH

Shellfish may not look tasty, but they are. And they're full of nutrients and minerals, and are high in protein. Ancient peoples all over the world ate them with such gusto that they left behind huge middens of shells, some as large as a city block.

Every shellfish has its own flavor and texture. Oysters are dainty and minerally, and often have a floral aroma under a stronger metallic, briny smell. Scallops and the adductor muscle of a surf clam are all about the meat: chewy and sweet. A good hard-shell clam is denser, as its "foot" muscle is the main event when eating one. Razor clams and butter clams are uncommonly sweet, while cockles and any large bivalve tend toward toughness. Mussels are very tender and minerally, while periwinkles are super savory and a little chewy. To eat shellfish, you must first extract them from their shells. In many cases, the easiest method is heat. Toss the shellfish into a pan with some liquid to steam, which kills them and opens their shells. Sometimes, however, you will want clams or oysters shucked before they are cooked—or, better yet, you will want to eat them raw, on the half shell. This is my favorite way to eat clams and oysters.

Which shellfish are good to eat raw? Not mussels, in my opinion, although I have heard of people who like eating them raw. Not large oysters or clams, either. While perfectly edible, who wants a mass of amorphous protein filling his mouth? Not I. Your best bets are small hard-shell clams and small oysters. My favorites are Olympia oysters from Washington and littleneck clams from New England.

To get shellfish open, you need a clam or oyster knife, which is a primitive thing with a stout, blunt blade about 3 inches long. To open a clam, I wedge the blade into its hinge, holding the clam securely in the pit of my palm. You might want to wear a sturdy glove to protect your hand from the knife until you get the hang of things. Do this over a bowl. A quick twist, and your hand will be doused with the brine from inside the clam. Slip the blade above and below the meat to free it from the shell, then slurp it down. It'll be cool, a bit metallic, slippery, and salty. You will get a little mouthful of pleasing chewiness, and yes, an inevitable bit of grit. Clams feed by filtering plankton from their surroundings and often have sand lodged within them. It's part of the deal.

Open an oyster with the same method. Put the point of the knife into the hinge while holding the oyster in your hand. A quick twist and the hinge should pop. Slice the oyster free from the shell, and you're done. Keep either heavy gloves or a kitchen towel around your hand because the knife slips from time to time and you don't want to stab yourself. Oysters have a thick heavy side to their shells and a lighter flat side. Hold the oyster with the heavier bowl-shaped side of the shell in your palm and pry off the light side, leaving the oyster in its own bowl.

Shellfish can be cooked in all sorts of ways. I love them steamed in wine and seawater, chopped and fried, made into fritters, barbecued, wrapped in bacon, or bathed in pasta sauce. The general rule is that small clams and oysters are best raw, although small Manila clams are excellent in Italian red sauces. Mussels are also good in red sauces, and are unsurpassed steamed with wine and garlic butter; periwinkles are best this way, too. Larger oysters are wonderful wrapped in bacon, grilled, and served with citrus.

No shellfish need to be cooked for very long. Always add them at the last minute to a longer-cooking dish, and serve them as soon as all the shells open. The longer they cook, the tougher they get. This is especially true with clams. Overcooked oysters get chalky, and overcooked mussels disintegrate. And you want to talk rubbery? Try an overcooked snail. You will chew for hours.

Acid and fat are keys to a good shellfish dish. Clams, mussels, and oysters are not high in fat and, while briny, are not acidic. That's why fried clams are so wonderful, or why you need so much butter with your steamed mussels. As I am no longer a fan of the cocktail sauces I loved as a child, I require only a squeeze of lemon on my raw clams and oysters now, though a classic mignonette is still nice.

RECIPES

MY MUM'S CLAM CHOWDER

This is my mother's recipe for a Maine-style clam chowder, which is lighter and brothier than a typical Massachusetts chowder. Serve with good bread and a green salad.

Serves 8–12

   4 cans clams (save the juice), or 1 dozen large clams

   2 tablespoons unsalted butter

   1 large onion, chopped

   ¼ pound salt pork or slab bacon, chopped into small cubes

   3–5 large Yukon Gold potatoes, chopped into ½-inch cubes

   1 can (8 ounces) evaporated milk

   1 quart whole milk

   Salt and freshly ground black pepper

If you are using fresh clams, shuck them over a bowl to collect the juices. Strain the juice through cheesecloth to remove any debris. Chop the clams roughly and set aside.

In a large pot or Dutch oven, melt the butter over medium heat. Cook the onion with the salt pork, stirring frequently, for 6 to 8 minutes, or until the onion is translucent but not browned.

Pour in the juice from the fresh or canned clams. Add the potatoes and bring to a simmer. If there is not enough clam juice to cover the potatoes, add a little water or fish stock. Simmer gently for at least 25 minutes.

When the potatoes are fork-tender, add the clams, the evaporated and fresh milk, and bring to a bare simmer. Do not let it boil or the chowder will separate. Season with salt and pepper to taste.

SARDINIAN MUSSEL OR PERIWINKLE SOUP

Fregula kin arsellas, or fregula pasta with baby clams, is a Sardinian classic. You can use small clams, but my version of the dish uses mussels or periwinkles. The Sardinians use San Marzano tomatoes, but in winter you can use preserved roasted red pepper instead. My secret? Much of the water in the broth is seawater, which I boil first and then strain to rid it of impurities. Seawater makes this soup powerful, briny, and achingly perfect with a crisp Vermentino, one of Sardinia's best white wines. If you aren't near the ocean, just salt your water liberally.

You need fregula pasta or Israeli couscous to make this soup correctly. You can buy fregula online or in specialty Italian grocery stores. If you must, substitute orzo, but it won't be the same.

Serves 4

2–3 pounds mussels, small clams,
   or periwinkles, in their shells

2 cups seawater or salty tap water

¼ cup olive oil

A healthy pinch of saffron, or
   1 packet saffron powder

5 cloves garlic, thinly sliced

½ cup chopped parsley

½ teaspoon Calabrian hot pepper or ground red pepper

½ pound fregula pasta

½ cup coarsely chopped roasted red pepper

Grated peel of a lemon

If you are using wild mussels, scrub their shells and pull off their beards. If using clams or periwinkles, wash them in cold water.

Pour the seawater or salty tap water into a large wide pot with a cover and bring it to a boil. Add the mussels, clams, or periwinkles and steam for 3 to 5 minutes, or until they open. Remove the shellfish from the water and pick out most of the meats. Put them in a bowl and toss with 1 tablespoon of the oil. Set aside. Leave a few clams or mussels in the shell—it makes the soup look more interesting.

Strain the remaining broth though cheesecloth or a paper towel into a bowl and set aside. Crumble the saffron into it while it is still hot.

In a large soup pot, heat the remaining olive oil over medium-high heat and cook the garlic, stirring frequently, for 1 or 2 minutes. Add the parsley, hot pepper, and broth and mix to combine. Bring it to a boil and add the fregula. Simmer for 10 minutes, or until the pasta is nearly done. Add the roasted red pepper and the reserved mussels and cook for 3 minutes longer.

Right before you serve, add the lemon peel. Serve with crusty bread and a crisp white wine.

CLAM THINGS

This is really just a version of the classic "clams casino," but for whatever reason my mom called them "clam things." An old recipe, originally made in ceramic clam shells handed down from her mother, it works fine in real clam shells, ramekins, or small bowls. It is also one of the few recipes in this book that requires a specific store-bought product: Ritz crackers. There just isn't a proper substitute for them. Use bread crumbs if you hate Ritz crackers, but it will not be the same.

This is an ideal recipe for the innards of horse clams or geoducks, large hard-shell clams, surf clams, or big Pismo clams. Mom used large quahogs.

Serves 6

5 tablespoons butter

1½ cups finely chopped onion

1½ cups finely chopped celery

¾ cup finely chopped green pepper

Salt

3 cups chopped clams, or 3 cans minced clams with juice

Dash of Tabasco sauce

Dash of Worcestershire sauce

3 tablespoons grated Parmesan cheese

1 package Ritz crackers, pounded fine

Freshly ground black pepper

Preheat the oven to 350°F.

In a large pan, melt 2 tablespoons of the butter over medium-high heat. Cook the onion, celery, and green pepper with a sprinkling of salt, stirring frequently, until the vegetables just start to brown.

Remove the vegetables to a large bowl and mix in the clams (without their juice), Tabasco, Worcestershire, cheese, and half of the crushed crackers. Pour in enough clam juice to moisten the mixture into a thick paste. Stuff into 4-inch ramekin dishes or large clam shells.

Melt the remaining 3 tablespoons butter in the pan and mix with the remaining Ritz crackers. Turn off the heat and sprinkle the buttered crumbs on top of each clam thing. Grind some black pepper over them.

Put the ramekins or clam shells on a rimmed baking sheet and bake for 20 minutes, or until bubbling. Check after 15 minutes and don't overcook. Serve hot.

9

BLUEGILLS AND OTHER PANFISH

Whether they're called sunfish, sunnies, pumpkinseeds, or brim, bluegills and other panfish are often the first fish children learn to catch, usually shortly after they learn to walk, talk, and carry those brightly colored fishing poles meant for little hands. Bluegills live alongside other panfish—so called because a whole fish will fit into a frying pan—such as spotted bass, white bass, yellow perch, and crappies. One species or another will be in most rivers as well as in nearly every pond and lake in every municipal park and reservoir in the United States. All are easy to catch. A bread ball will work for bait, as will a piece of canned corn. A night crawler works even better, and the ability to thread a wiggling worm onto a hook is what first separates those who can fish from those who cannot. For many, going to the pond with Dad or Mom to catch bluegills is a cherished memory.

By the time I began catching panfish, I had already fished commercially, braved 20-foot waves, and landed tuna in excess of 400 pounds. A born ocean fisherman, I never saw the point in trying to catch fish that, if they weighed a full pound, would be considered a trophy. It seemed like a waste of effort. Why spend hours staring at a bobber in hopes of catching fish smaller than the bait I was used to using?

Then I took a newspaper job in Fredericksburg, Virginia. Fredericksburg is far from the ocean, but ponds, reservoirs, and several great rivers surround the city. All the anglers I knew at the paper focused on freshwater fishing, especially bass. The smallmouth bass fishing in the upper Rappahannock River is exceptional, and catching a 10-pound large-mouth bass in some of the area reservoirs is only mildly noteworthy. You can only catch fish in the rivers at certain times of the year, so I increasingly found myself at local lakes and reservoirs, fishing off docks or out of rowboats.

From the start, I caught dozens of bluegills. Stupid 4-inch bluegills. Pesky, annoying bait-stealers. As soon as I tossed a worm into the reeds, these micropiranha would swarm on it, picking it clean. I'd always operated on the principle of big hook, big bait, big fish. But it wasn't working.

One day, after I came home annoyed and empty-handed yet again, my girlfriend at the time said, "Why don't we just eat the little ones?" "Because they're 4 inches long," I said, and left it at that.

Until the next time they began pestering me. I'd brought a little cooler with some ice, ostensibly for beer. But after the beer was gone, there was this nice cold container, which was just the right size to hold a few of these bait-stealers. So I switched to the smallest hook I had, a tiny brass baitholder hook. Baitholder hooks have little barbs on the shaft to hold the worm on. By this time, I'd seen that most of my fellow fishermen in Virginia did not use earthworms for bait. They used smaller red worms or even little maggoty things, one per hook. So I threaded a red worm onto my hook, let the line fly, and let it sink. Tap, tap, tap . . . boing! A bluegill had hooked itself and was trying to get free. I was surprised at how fierce the little bugger was. I was using light, 4-pound test line and a very light rod and reel I'd bought especially for this sort of "wimp fishing," as I was calling it at the time.

I had to admit to myself that it was kinda fun reeling a bluegill in with such light gear. I swung the fish over the rail of the dock and there it was, a little disc-shaped thing with a Betty Boop mouth flashing iridescent reds and yellows behind its gills. It was actually a pretty little fish. He smelled like the pond, a little green and swampy. I tossed him into the cooler and baited up again.

In short order, I had a dozen bluegills on ice, none more than 6 inches long. As I fished, however, I noticed something: Trailing behind the swarm of little fish would often be a much larger one, and this fish hung back while the midgets frenzied. Was this the mother? One fish was a monster, easily a pound. A 1-pound "monster." I had to laugh, but in the land of the blind, the one-eyed man is king. I felt like the Sioux chief Sitting Bull, who famously said that if there were no more bison, his people would hunt smaller animals to survive, down to mice in the fields. After catching tuna, sharks, bluefish, and striped bass all my life, these bluegills were my mice. I never did catch the big one that day.

The little bluegills seemed too small to fillet, so I scaled and gutted them, then rolled the fish in cornmeal and fried them in olive oil. A bit persnickety to eat, with all those little bones, but tasty. Tasty enough to keep fishing for them.

Not long after, however, I caught my first decent bluegill. It was so big relative to the bait-stealers that I weighed it on our kitchen scale when I got home. Eleven ounces. A giant. It reminded me of a porgy, an ocean fish I'd loved catching when I'd lived on Long Island. I decided then that I would spend some time fishing this reservoir to really learn it.

Learning a piece of water, whether it's a lake, pond, river, or stretch of shoreline, is what separates real anglers from those who just reel in fish. Catching fish is all about location and timing, but location is the toughest to master. An angler can fish all day in one spot and catch nothing, or move 10 yards to the left or right and catch fish for hours. Many new to the pursuit think that fish are evenly spaced below the surface, aligned in some sort of grid. All they need to do is drop their line down and wait. In a few places, that's true. But not many.

Fish like to be near structure. Sunken debris, logs, brush piles, even ships; when I lived in New York, I often fished for black sea bass and porgies over a sunken German U-boat off the Long Island coast. River fish orient to channels and current breaks, little places where they can hang out and rest away from the fast currents of the main river channel. Find the structure—either above or below the waterline—and you are a lot closer to finding the fish.

The lake I set out to master was Motts Run Reservoir. It is a smallish reservoir, and only rowboats with oars or an electric trolling motor were allowed. No gas. This made it a quiet, homey place to fish and kept the hard-core bass anglers away. My boat of choice was an aluminum rowboat with a cheap trolling motor attached to a car battery. Top speed: 5 miles per hour.

I started by looking for fish in coves. Coves are quiet places out of the main lake, meaning out of the path of wind-driven waves. Often they have fallen debris, excellent places for fish to hide. One such cove in Motts was textbook: About 10 yards wide at its widest, it was fed by a quicksilver sliver of a creek running down from the hillside above. The deepest channel in the middle of the cove was no deeper than 8 feet, and it shallowed rapidly toward either bank. The shoreline was steep, meaning few anglers without a boat could get to it. Overhanging bushes lined one side, and there was something of a mud and gravel "beach" on the other. An old dead tree behind this beach lay halfway in the water. Only at high noon did this cove lack shade, and fish like shade, especially those that frequent shallow water.

This idyllic spot, only 500 yards away from the boat ramp, became my larder. I almost never failed to catch fish there—usually better bluegills than at the fishing dock. The first time I fished there, I caught about 15 fish larger than 6 inches, which is largish for a sunfish. That proved to be too much, as the spot failed to produce as well for several months afterward. That taught me another key lesson: Don't overfish your spots. After that, I never took more than a half dozen bluegills from that cove.

It was an especially good lesson, however, because it forced me to continue my exploration of the reservoir. I found four or five similar coves, and learned that catfish lurked in the deep water behind the dam and that pickerel could be had at the opposite end, which was shallow, reedy, and cut through with beaver channels. I never did find a spot where I could consistently catch 11-ounce bluegills, but over the 4 years I fished Mott's, I did catch a half dozen fish heavier than a pound—big enough for the Virginia Department of Game and Inland Fisheries to give me a certificate for such a trophy.

CATCHING BLUEGILLS AND THEIR FRIENDS

A bluegill weighing a pound or so is probably between 4 and 6 years old. While most panfish don't get much bigger than a pound, real freak-nasty monsters of 2-plus pounds are caught every year. The record bluegill is a 4-pound goliath caught in Alabama in 1950. White bass are a little bigger, as are yellow perch. Crappies can outgrow the frying pan altogether and in some places can even top 5 pounds.

Fishing for panfish requires very little in the way of specialized gear. The light-action rod and reel combination available at any sporting goods store is inexpensive and more than enough to start catching fish. Rig the reel with light line, between 4- and 8-pound test. "Test" is a gauge of how heavy a fish the line is rated for, so you should easily be able to reel in a 4-pound fish with 4-pound test line without it snapping. Other good things to buy include:

- Small baitholder hooks and small lead-headed jigs with rubber curly tails in various colors. Crappies love these.
- A supply of split-shot weights in various sizes.
- Small sinkers, ranging from $\frac{1}{4}$ ounce to 1 ounce.

Barrel swivels, which connect your main line with the leader, the heavier line attached to the hook. Most hooks come prerigged on a leader line.

Bobbers. I prefer the narrow, cigar-shaped "competition fishing" bobbers over the typical round, red-and-white bobbers. Competition bobbers are more sensitive, allowing you to see whether a fish is just nudging your bait.

A selection of lures such as small plastic crickets and worms.

A stringer for your fish. A stringer is a nylon rope with a pointy end and a ring on the other end. The pointy end goes in the fish's mouth and out the gills, then through the ring. Secure the pointy end to land (the dock, the boat, a stick, etc.) and put the fish in the water. It will be able to breathe, but not escape.

A cooler for your beer and fish.

Bigger panfish tend to live in deeper water, often hanging out in between the surface and submerged hills or deep sunken logs. They tend to only come into shallow waters at dusk and dawn, looking for insects or small fish to eat. It's been my experience that larger bluegills prefer insects like crickets to worms or other baits, although I have caught my share on artificial lures such as small spinnerbaits and even chrome spoons. Crappies prefer

minnows or small jigs, as do yellow perch. White bass absolutely love night crawlers and, in the freshwater portions of tidal rivers, sandworms.

You can also try to catch large bluegills when they spawn, which is typically between late April and late June, depending on where you live. Look for water temperatures between 65° and 75°F, temperatures that trigger the fish to spawn. Spawning bluegills create nests that look like craters on the bottom of the pond or lake. Many times, good spots are so coveted that the "craters" touch and the pond bottom looks like a moonscape. The fish guard these spots and will strike anything intruding. This is the time of year you can literally sneak up on the colony, spot the larger bluegills, and fish exclusively for them. But again, remember the rule: Catch just a few, so you don't fish out the lake. Why not leave them alone? Because unlike many fish, the largest individuals in any bluegill population will be males, not breeding females. So you can take a few with a clear conscience.

A few other tips will help you catch panfish worth eating.

⊷ Use small hooks that are not shiny. I am convinced older bluegills shy away from brass hooks. If you are looking for a hook size number, I mostly use no. 8 baitholder hooks. White bass and yellow perch are not as picky.

⊷ Crappies can generally be caught with small jigs decorated with chartreuse rubber tails. Dance these lures around fallen trees and sunken brush where crappies like to hang out. Crappies also love to eat live minnows.

⊷ Don't forget winter fishing. At Mott's Reservoir, mid-winter was a decent time to catch bluegills. I've caught them on calm, sunny days when the water is somewhere around 45°F. I know lots of Minnesotans who catch crappies, perch, and bluegills all winter long through the ice, too. Yellow perch are especially good to fish through the ice, and the largest crappies I've ever caught were while ice fishing on Red Lake in Minnesota.

⊷ If you are looking for a place to fish for larger bluegills, look for lakes or reservoirs that have slot limits on largemouth bass. With a slot limit, you are encouraged to keep bass of a certain size, but must release both smaller and larger fish. Mott's Reservoir had a slot limit of 12 to 15 inches, meaning anglers could keep and eat bass of that size. A slot limit ensures there will be lots of bass in the lake, and those bass will control the bluegill population. Unchecked, bluegill populations can get so large the fish stunt.

🐟 Stunting happens. Some ponds and lakes have so many bluegills they crowd each other out, and none get larger than about 6 inches. Move to another pond if this is the case; you'll know if you fish it a few times and never see a large fish. If the pond happens to be yours, eat as many small ones as you can—you'll make room for others to grow large.

EATING PANFISH

Okay, so you've caught some fish. Now what? First off, toss your fish in a cooler with ice, or put them on a stringer. Once you are home, you need to decide whether to fillet your fish or just scale and gut them.

Honestly, the only panfish you'd ever want to fillet are those 10 inches or larger, dinner plate fish. You will need a fillet knife to properly fillet fish. They are available in any sporting goods store or in kitchen stores. To fillet a fish:

1. Lay the fish on its side with its back toward you. Anchor the fish by holding down its head. Slice down to the backbone with your knife from just behind the head of the fish to just behind the pectoral fin.

2. Still holding the fish by its head, slice down the length of the fish—using the backbone as a guide—starting from your first cut back to the tail. You will be cutting through ribs in the beginning of this cut, but once you get past the fish's vent, you should no longer feel bones. This frees the first fillet.

3. Flip the fish and repeat to cut the second fillet free.

4. To remove the skin, place a fillet skin side down with the tail closest to you. Use your fingers to anchor the fillet right at the tail end. You will need to exert some pressure to hold it steady. Now, using your knife, slice along the inner side of the skin toward the head end of the fillet. Press the blade down on your cutting surface to keep it close to the skin, not the meat.

5. Remove the rib bones by slicing along the edge of the ribs in the fillet down toward where the belly of the fish used to be.

6. Repeat the process with the other fillet.

As for the little fish, simply scale them with a fish scaler or a butter knife by scraping the scales off the fish from the tail end toward the head. Then cut their heads off with a stout chef's knife or cleaver, pull the guts out, and rinse well. If you angle your knife from right behind the head down toward the fish's vent, you can get most of the innards with that one chop. The result is little "fish biscuits," ideal for dredging in flour, egg, and bread crumbs and then frying. Frying is the ideal method for cooking most freshwater fish, as they tend to be very lean and rather bland-tasting, and need both salt and fat to bolster their flavor.

Bluegills are mild tasting and, if overdone, taste a little like skinless chicken breast. Done properly, bluegills are exceedingly delicate and moist, and with a little extra salt taste as good as a Dover sole. While frying is a wonderful way to eat small bluegills, save the large fillets for something more refined, such as steaming in parchment or in a Chinese steamer, or poaching gently in olive oil or fish broth.

Crappies and white bass are a little coarser but still firm and white. Yellow perch are the firmest of all panfish and are a delicacy in northern states; there is even a small commercial fishery for them. The skin of all panfish is delicious when crisped up in the pan.

RECIPES

OIL-POACHED BLUEGILL SALAD WITH SUMMER VEGGIES

What makes this recipe special is the way you cook the fish. You poach it in olive oil, which adds a little fat to otherwise lean fish. It creates a luxurious texture for what are often humble fish. Don't worry about the long cooking time or the amount of oil in this: You can strain and reuse the oil, and the stove is off for most of the cooking.

The quality of the ingredients is key. There isn't much being done to them here, so you will taste the difference between old corn and fresh, between a supermarket tomato and one from your garden. What happens if you want to make this dish in cold weather? Replace the tomatoes with roasted and chunked red and golden beets; the corn with cannellini, borlotti, or cranberry beans; the fresh chile with dried; and the cilantro with parsley. It will be delicious.

Serves 4

1 pound skinless fillets of bluegills, crappies, perch, porgies, walleyes, etc.

Salt

2–3 cups olive oil

Kernels from 2 ears of corn, or 1 cup frozen

1 chile pepper, finely chopped, anything from a jalapeño to a habanero

3 scallions, chopped

2–3 cloves garlic, finely chopped

2–3 tomatoes, seeded and chopped

3 tablespoons chopped parsley or cilantro

Freshly ground black pepper

Juice of 1 lemon

Rinse off your fish and pat dry. Sprinkle salt all over them and set aside at room temperature for 30 minutes.

In a heavy pot, add enough olive oil to submerge all the fish fillets. Heat over medium heat to 160°F. Turn off the heat. Slip the fish into the oil, then shake the pot to make sure the pieces do not stick to the bottom. Cover and set aside. The fish will cook slowly, as the oil retains heat well.

Let the oil cool for 45 minutes to 1 hour, or until you can place your hand on the outside of the pot and feel only slight warmth. Remove the fish carefully and set on a plate.

Pour a little of the poaching oil into a large skillet over medium-high heat. Add the corn, chile pepper, scallions, and garlic. Cook, stirring often, for 3 to 4 minutes.

Meanwhile, put the tomatoes and parsley in a large bowl. Flake the fish with your fingers and add it to the bowl. Add the corn mixture to the bowl, stir gently to combine, and add a little more of the olive oil, if you'd like. Grind some black pepper over it all, add the lemon juice, and serve.

DEEP-FRIED FISH BALLS, SOUTHEAST ASIAN-STYLE

No matter what kind of fish you use here, this recipe will knock your socks off. It's loaded with Southeast Asian flavors—lemongrass, garlic, cilantro, scallions, and just a touch of fish sauce. It's an ideal recipe for freshwater fish. I've made this recipe with catfish, largemouth bass, and bluegill, but any white fish will do.

You need fresh ingredients here to make the fish cakes pop; thankfully, good supermarkets are selling lemongrass nowadays. If you cannot find lemongrass, use lime peel. There is no substitute for fish sauce, and if you plan on making Southeast Asian food, you need to buy it. But if you want to make this recipe and have no intention of making other Asian dishes, you can sub in Worcestershire sauce. It will not be the same, but it's still good. Serve these fish balls as a party appetizer (the recipe can be doubled or tripled). You can make them ahead of time and let them cool on a wire rack. Then refry them at party time. This is a lot easier than dealing with the mess of making the balls while your guests are waiting.

Serves 4 as a main course, 6–8 as an appetizer

- 1–1½ pounds skinless fillets of white fish, such as largemouth bass, catfish, or bluegill
- 1 egg
- 2 tablespoons fish sauce or Worcestershire sauce
- 3 small hot chile peppers, finely chopped (you can use less if you want); wear plastic gloves when handling
- 1½ teaspoons finely chopped lemongrass or lime peel
- 4 cloves garlic, minced
- 3 scallions, chopped
- 2 tablespoons chopped cilantro
- 2 tablespoons rice flour (you can use regular flour, too) + about 1 cup for dusting

Peanut, vegetable, or grapeseed
  oil for frying
Lime wedges

Chop the fish into small pieces and put
in a food processor. Beat the egg and
add to the processor. Add the fish sauce,
chile peppers, lemongrass, garlic,
scallions, cilantro, and 2 tablespoons
flour to the food processor and buzz into
a paste. You want it pretty smooth but
not totally pureed. The reason you need
to chop all these ingredients before
putting them into the food processor is
because if you don't, some things will be
a pulp by the time others will be broken
down sufficiently.

Put about 1 cup of the flour in a bowl.

Fill a deep fryer according to its directions, or a heavy, high-sided pot about
halfway with oil. Heat the oil over medium-high heat to 350°F. (You can reuse this
oil a half dozen times if you strain it through cheesecloth after you've finished and
let the oil cool.)

Once the oil nears 350°F, start making your fish balls. Grab enough of the mixture to
make a fish ball about the size of a Ping-Pong ball and dust it in the bowl of rice flour.
Fry the fish cakes a few at a time so the oil temperature doesn't drop too much. Cook
for 5 to 8 minutes, or until golden brown.

Drain the fish balls on a wire rack set over paper towels.

Serve with lime wedges and cold beer.

PROVENÇAL FISH BISQUE

This is a curious, blended fish soup I've been making, in various forms, for many years. I like blended soups, which can seem creamy even without cream—although this one does have a little cream added at the end. They're just, well, more refined than a typical country soup. And sometimes I feel the need for a touch of elegance, even on a busy midweek night.

This soup only takes about 30 minutes to make. Yet, eaten with fresh bread and a glass of wine, you feel like you're sitting at an oceanside bistro in Provence. The flavor comes mostly from the stock (shellfish stock or a combination of fish stock and clam juice), the orange zest, and saffron. You cannot substitute something else for the saffron; its color and aroma are integral to the soup. A pinch of cayenne adds the faintest zing that brings everything together.

Use any mild white fish but bluegills are ideal. Other good choices would be cod, haddock, any flatfish (flounder, fluke, halibut, sole, turbot, etc.), walleye, crappie, or rock cod.

Once the soup is blended and you add the cream in, don't let the soup boil; it could break. And if you have leftovers, just heat them gently in a pot until warm enough to eat.

Serves 4–6

3 slices bacon, roughly chopped (or substitute 3 tablespoons olive oil or butter)

1 medium white or yellow onion, chopped

1 large celery rib, chopped

1 large carrot, chopped

Salt

1 pound white fish fillets, roughly chopped

2 plum tomatoes, chopped

2 cloves garlic, chopped

1 teaspoon orange peel

Pinch of ground red pepper

Large pinch of saffron

1 quart shellfish stock, or 16 ounces clam juice plus 16 ounces fish stock
   or water

¼ cup heavy cream

Dill or fennel fronds, for garnish

Cook the bacon on medium heat in a 6- to 8-quart pot until it is crispy. Remove the
bacon from the pot with a slotted spoon. Set aside on a paper towel to use for garnish
later.

Increase the heat to medium high and add the onion, celery, and carrot. Cook for 3 to
4 minutes, stirring often, until the onion is translucent. Do not brown. Sprinkle some
salt, to taste, over everything as it cooks.

Add the fish, tomatoes, and the garlic and cook for another 2 to 3 minutes, stirring
often.

Add the orange peel, red pepper, and saffron, then pour in the shellfish stock or
whatever stock you are using. In a pinch, you could even use chicken or vegetable
stock, but the flavor of the soup will be different. Simmer this gently—do not let it get
to a rolling boil—for 20 minutes, stirring occasionally.

Get another pot ready. Fill a blender a third of the way with the soup and blend it on
high (starting on low then increasing to high) for 1 minute, or until it is well puréed.
Work in batches to purée the rest of the soup. Pour the pureed soup into the clean pot.

Put the soup on medium-low heat and add the cream. Stir well and taste for salt,
adding if needed. Do not let this boil, or it might break. Serve garnished with fennel
or dill fronds, and alongside some crusty bread. A dry rosé or light red wine would go
well with this; I'd suggest a Beaujolais or a Pinot Noir.

10

CATCHING THE ORNERY CRAB

"Dude, I'm going crabbing up at Bodega. You wanna come?" My friend Jason knew of a great spot to catch Dungeness, red, and rock crabs off a breakwater in Northern California's Bodega Bay, and he wanted company. Little did he know that his casual offer was like waving crack in front of a junkie. Hi, my name is Hank, and I am a crab addict. . . .

I thought I'd kicked my addiction by first moving to the Midwest and then California, where I live 2 hours from shore. Guess not. I could barely sleep the night before the trip, my head filled with thoughts of these new and interesting crabs we'd catch. I've had a long-standing affair with the genus *Cancer*. As a boy I chased down little green crabs in New England and wondered why we couldn't eat them. One of my fondest memories as a teenager was going down the shore to Toms River, New Jersey, with my stepfather, Frank, and renting rowboats to hand-line crabs, using chicken legs as bait.

Years later, when I lived on Long Island as an impoverished newspaper reporter, I practically lived off the crabs I caught from the piers and jetties along the Great South Bay. They came in all stripes: pretty-but-shrewish calico crabs, docile rock and Jonah crabs, the occasional spider crab (which is an unappetizing vomit-brown when it's alive), and the prize, the blue crab.

Blue crabs are perhaps the meanest animal in nature, except for maybe the wolverine or a badger with its leg in a trap. Blue crabs are so mean that the watermen of the Chesapeake can stack them up in open bushel baskets: None will escape because as soon as one makes a break for it, another will grab his leg and hold him down. Talk about peer pressure.

Each crab had its purpose in those days. Some were for soups, some for crab cakes, some just for picking and eating. In college, I once ate close to 50 blue crabs at one sitting, in a hotel room in Delaware after a track-and-field meet. The maid refused to clean up the room the next day. Not sure I blame her.

Now I was getting a chance to toss a trap into the Pacific. We met early in the morning, armed with coffee and a slew of crabbing stories that made the 130-mile trek to California's north coast seem easy. We told stories of hundred-crab days and which unusual bait had worked—mine was a dead opossum I'd found on the side of the road that I wired to my trap. The crabs loved that nasty thing.

My traps back East were always boxes of stout wire mesh, about 1-foot square, made so all four sides of the cube dropped when the trap, which was weighted with lead, hit bottom. To use this trap, I attached nylon ropes to each side of the cube and joined them at the top, and then let this top line trail out for about 20 feet. You'd arc the trap through the air like a horseshoe or lasso into the water. You need to wrap the end of the top line around your wrist so it doesn't go into the drink. Some sort of stinky bait, typically fish heads, would be wired to the bottom. To spring the trap, you wait a while, then with a smooth motion lift the top line high and immediately start hauling it in; you know by the weight whether you have crabs inside. Once you get the trap on the rocks or dock, you let the sides drop and grab the crabs. It's a good idea to bring a pair of pliers and a set of heavy gloves to pry them off the sides of the trap. Crabs will hang on for dear life, gripping the trap with their claws.

Crab traps are different on the West Coast. Westerners use a circular hoop net made of nylon mesh. It looks like a bagel made of wire and mesh connected by a top line. This trap is easier to toss—you fling it like a giant Frisbee. Its main drawback is it can be tough to pry off all the crabs without shredding the nylon. Jason had several of these traps in the back of his truck, along with a giant propane burner and a kettle large enough to stew a sea lion.

"That's optimistic, don't you think?"

"Don't worry. We'll need it," he said.

We arrived at the end of a spit of land capped with a long breakwater. Armed with beer, crab traps, a bag of shad heads, and several 5-gallon buckets, we picked our way over the boulders to about midway out on the breakwater, where there were a couple nice flat rocks. It was June, and the weather was reasonably warm. Bodega Bay can fog up solid this time of year, so we could have been crabbing in the cold.

We tossed out our traps, cracked open a beer, and resumed our jawing. That's the beauty of crabbing: It is the best kind of lazy fishing. You bait the trap, toss it in the water, wait, drink beer, tell stories, read a book, do some other fishing, listen to the radio, catch a tan, whatever. So long as you have bait and a cooler or bucket, you're in business. Back on Long Island, I'd fill 50-gallon coolers full of crabs in an afternoon, enough to set me up with crabmeat for a couple of weeks. Meanwhile, I'd fish for flounder or mackerel or sea robins. You need a different cooler for them, though, as the crabs will tear apart a fish thrown in their midst.

After about 10 minutes Jason hauled up the first trap. It had three crabs inside. The only crab I'd ever heard of that lived in the West was the Dungeness crab. I'd eaten many, but all were store bought. These were not Dungeness in the trap. Jason said they were red crabs and rock crabs. Rock crabs I understood: They were like the Jonah crabs I'd caught back East. There is always some sort of sluggish, willful, "walking-around" crab that inhabits rocky nooks and crannies. Most of the meat in them is in the claws; the rest makes for superb crab-flavored soups. What were red crabs? Turns out they are merely Day-Glo crimson versions of rock crabs. And although reds are meaner than rocks, neither were anything like the bitchy calicos or the downright demonic blues back East. California crabs are just mellower.

For 3 hours, the crabbing went on pretty much like that first haul, and in no time we had three dozen good red and rock crabs as well as two legal Dungeness.

Dungies are the kings of the California crab world. They get huge, and their bodies are filled with sweet meat. They start running in November, and the season was very nearly done when we caught our pair; after July 1, you must toss them back until November rolls around again.

Laden with crabs, we carefully made our way back to the beach, where Jason's mega-burner was waiting. We got the kettle on the heat and cracked a few more beers. While we waited, we debated whether Zatarain's or Old Bay was a better crab boil. We clinked beers when we both voiced our preference for Zatarain's. Once the water came to a boil, we added the spice mix, tossed in a few crabs, and closed the lid.

We had so many crabs we needed to cook them in batches. So of course we ate a few while we waited. We broke open a pair of finger-searing-hot red crabs right in the parking lot. An old couple walking a little white terrier stared at us while we gorged ourselves, sitting on a curb with bottles of Pabst Blue Ribbon next to us. The crabmeat was sweet, flaky, and salty, with just a bit of zing from the Zatarain's. I added a smidge of the "mustard," which is the crab's liver, to the meat for an extra note of richness and fat. This was living.

THE NUTS AND BOLTS OF CATCHING CRABS

Catching crabs is pretty easy. You need bait, a cooler, some string, and patience. A trap of some sort helps a lot, but I've caught crabs hand-lining a chicken leg off a rowboat in a back bay or off a dock. You lower the chicken to the bottom and wait until you feel little tugs. Slowly bring the line up, and if you see a crab munching on the chicken, you carefully slip a net underneath him—he'll let go of the chicken as soon as he sees you or the boat.

Trap crabbing is basically a combination line and net. You toss the trap in and wait, then haul it in from time to time. Remove crabs from the trap and toss them in a cooler. Repeat as necessary.

Where to go? Piers are good places, as are jetties or breakwaters. You want to put the trap near places where crabs hide. They will run out and start eating your bait, and you can collect them. If you have a boat, look for underwater grass beds near rocks.

How deep? I've never tossed a trap in water deeper than 20 feet, but there's no reason not to. Conversely, I've sat there and watched crabs wander into my traps when they're set in only a foot or two of water.

When? Check with your state's fish and game department. Many states have seasons and bag limits on crabs, and many also require you to buy a fishing license. Dungeness crab season runs from November through June in California, but summer is the best time for blue crabs back East. I've found good crabbing in every part of the year.

As with all oceanic fishing, crabbing is best on a moving tide, either coming in or going out. Moving tides sweep possible food bits past crab hideouts, and they seem to be more active then. You can still catch a few in slack water, but you will generally catch more on an incoming tide.

What to use as bait? Really anything meaty and, preferably, stinky. Fish heads are a universal choice, as are chicken pieces, roadkill, and whole small fish like herrings or mackerel. I prefer the heads and bones of oily fish such as shad or mackerel.

WHAT YOU WILL CATCH

Crabbing is a crapshoot. You never know what will wander into your trap, although you can pretty much be assured you will never catch a Dungeness crab in the East or a blue crab in Oregon. What follows is a primer on the pros and cons of the common crabs. It'll be up to you to decide whether to keep them or toss 'em.

RED, ROCK, STONE, AND JONAH CRABS

Pacific red crab and its cousin the rock crab are the most common walking-around crabs on the West Coast south of Oregon. They share habitat with the prized Dungeness crab, which ranges down to about Santa Cruz. In the East, the Jonah crab is a close cousin of the Pacific rock crab, and in southern waters there is the vaunted stone crab, which is mostly harvested for one claw, then returned to the water; the missing claw regrows.

All live in and around rocky places—thus the name *rock crab*—and all are walking

crabs, meaning their last set of legs is pretty much like the rest. The last set of legs on a swimming crab, such as a blue crab, has fins. As with all crabs, you can tell the male from the female by the plate underneath the body: It is narrow in the male, wide in the female.

The main reason rock crabs live in the culinary shadows of blue and Dungeness crabs is because they are smaller and their meat is coarser. The body meat in rock and red crabs is also more difficult to extract than that of Dungeness crabs. And because they do not swim like blue crabs, they don't need the extra muscle power in their bodies that the blue crabs do. That muscle is the wonderful nugget called backfin lump meat, the tastiest part of any crab in North America.

The roe, bright orange eggs inside the female, is delicious and can be used in she-crab soup, although this soup is normally made with the roe of a blue crab. Some people also eat the yellow-green "mustard" inside the body; this is the liver. I eat a little of it, as it adds fat and richness, but remember this is a filtering organ, so any toxins the crab has ingested will be there. Best to eat it sparingly.

In all of these species, most of the meat is in the giant crusher claws. Florida stone crabs are legendary for the flavor of these claws, to the point where this is all we normally eat. When cooking, you can substitute the claws of red, rock, or Jonah crabs in any stone crab claw recipe you find. All of these crabs can grow to more than 10 inches across—especially Pacific red crabs—but 4 to 6 inches is more common. Watch for size limits where you catch them, and follow the law.

If you are looking to buy instead of catching your own, you will most often find walking crabs in Asian markets. New England markets will, however, often carry Jonah crabs, and Florida stone crab claws are so popular they can be bought online. All of these species tend to be inexpensive.

If you come across a mess of Jonah, red, or rock crabs, cook the claws like stone crabs—boiled or steamed in a seasoned broth and eaten with butter or mayo. Use the bodies of all but the largest crabs to make stock or sauces.

Cracking the legs and the cleaned bodies of any crabs will give you the fixings for an outstanding tomato-based spaghetti sauce. Like many seafood dishes, this sauce doesn't reheat well, so if you have lots of crabs, store the cooked bits in a bag and freeze until you want to use them.

DUNGENESS

Chances are, if you've eaten fresh crab anywhere in the West, it was a Dungeness crab. These are the most common crabs on the Pacific Coast and are among the tastiest, too. Dungeness meat compares well with eastern blue-claw crabs.

Dungeness partisans note that you get more meat per crab out of Dungeness—and not just because they are far larger, averaging nearly 2 pounds. You will typically get about 25 percent of the crab's weight in pure meat, which may not sound like a lot, but it is in the crab world. Blue crab yield is closer to 15 percent.

They are easy to catch in season, which runs from the winter and spring in California all the way through summer as you head up into Oregon, Washington, and Canada. They will be mixed in with the other rock crabs; Dungeness are also walking-around crabs that lack swimmer fins. All the tips about eating rock crabs apply to Dungeness, only dungies are sweeter and bigger.

There are strict limits on how many and what size Dungeness crabs you can keep, and these change often. So look up the regulations with your state's fish and game department before you go.

If you catch them, boil live Dungeness for 15 to 18 minutes in salty water. Pick out the meat and make broth from the shells. Don't recook any kind of crabmeat. Reheating is fine but only for a minute or two in soup, stir-fries, or sautés. No long cooking!

BLUE CRABS

Blue crabs are the dominant crab from the Gulf of Mexico up to about Long Island, and they are a cultural icon in the Chesapeake Bay area. Unlike the various walking-around crabs, blue crabs have a pair of swimming fins on their back pair of legs that allows them to do more than just scuttle.

Always grab blue crabs from behind—the only place those claws can't reach. Otherwise, they will nip you.

Blue crabs are relatively abundant, and in my opinion their meat is the sweetest of all North American crabs. The quarter-size lump of meat behind each swimming leg is one of the great delicacies of the seafood world. The roe from female blue crabs is a vital ingredient in she-crab soup.

BOILING AND PICKING CRABS

The first step in an old-fashioned crab boil is to gather your crabs. Figure on at least a half dozen blue crabs per person, eight red crabs or rock crabs (most of the meat is in the claws), 10 calico crabs, or one or two Dungeness crabs. These are general guidelines, so adjust to your eaters' preference.

While the briny sweetness of the crabs themselves will flavor your meal, I often add a spice mix to the boil. You can add anything you like, but I prefer one of two seasoning mixes: Old Bay crab boil or Zatarain's crab boil. Old Bay is the classic for Maryland or Virginia crab, while Zatarain's is a Cajun seasoning. And if you are on the ocean, there is nothing wrong with boiling your crabs in seawater, so long as it's not from polluted places.

Once your water is boiling away, drop your crabs in one at a time. Don't overcrowd the pot. Boil in batches if you need to.

The water will drop below a boil when you put the crabs in, so cover the pot and let it come back to a full boil. When it does, uncover and cook for 10 to 15 minutes; Dungeness take a few minutes longer. Once you see crabs floating on the surface, give it another 2 to 3 minutes.

When the crabs are ready, carefully extract them with tongs and set them aside to cool. You can start picking out the meat in a few minutes, or you can wait until they cool completely. You can also store and freeze whole crabs once they are cooked this way. Cooked crabs keep for up to a week in the fridge.

Picking and eating crabs is a down-home way to enjoy these tasty crustaceans, but crabs do not give up their treasures lightly. First, get a large work space ready. Lay down newspaper because you're going to get messy. I recommend a bowl for your cooked crabs, a bowl for good shells—use these for stocks and sauces—a bowl for the pure meat, and a trash can nearby. Once you have this all set, turn on some music, grab a beer or a lemonade, and get to pickin'.

There are many ways to go about picking crabs, but I start by removing all the legs and claws. Do this by grabbing the very base of each leg and pulling it away with a twist. Set them aside for later.

On the bottom of the crab is a plate. If it's a boy crab (a "jimmy" in East Coast terms), it'll have a narrow, pointy plate. If it's a girl crab (a "sook" in the East), it'll have a wide,

OTHER CRABS

Lots of other kinds of crabs can find their way into your pots. Here are a few you might come across that are worth keeping.

Spider crabs are the Atlantic cousin of the Alaskan snow crab and are very common along eastern shores. Spider crabs can grow nearly as large—in excess of 20 pounds, although 2 to 4 pounds is more common. Spider crabs have very thick shells, and most of the meat is in the legs, so you need a pretty big spider crab to make it worthwhile. I keep only large ones; look for a body about the size of a grapefruit. Spider crabs are slow and not terribly aggressive, and they are often covered in algae and barnacles, giving them the appearance of sluggish, ugly scavengers, which is in fact what they are.

Green crabs are also edible, but barely worth it. They are very common north of New Jersey and are, as you might expect, bright green. Green crabs have very little meat in them and are best used as bait for fish. Crack them open to make a crab broth, if you want to try eating them.

Similarly, the pretty calico crabs are often too small to be worth picking. Calico crabs have the back fins of a blue crab but a shell that is rounder, more like a walking crab. Watch their claws! Calicos are very abundant around sandy beaches and love little more than to pinch your toes. Any calico larger than about 4 inches across can be picked and eaten like a blue crab. Their meat is not quite as tasty as blue crab meat, but it's similar enough. Small ones make a great crab broth.

triangular plate. Slip your finger under the plate and peel it back. Grab the base of it and pull the whole thing away. Toss it, as it's not the best bit of shell for a crab stock.

Now it's time to open the body. Start where you removed the plate and wedge your thumbs on opposite sides of the body, then pull the top of the crab away from the bottom of the crab. There will be all sorts of icky-looking stuff in there. The bottom of the crab is where all the meat is, so start cleaning it by grabbing the face of the crab and pinching away the whole thing. It sounds grosser than it is.

The only truly inedible parts of a crab are the shell and lungs, feathery cones that line each side of the body cavity. They taste awful, so it is important to remove them all and discard them. After you remove the lungs, scrape out the gooey stuff in the center of the bottom part of the body, which, you will notice, is separated into two equal parts on the left and right of the crab. The greenish yellow stuff is the tomalley, or mustard; it's the liver.

If you have a female crab and you see bright orange stuff inside, keep it: It is roe, or eggs, also called *coral* in shellfish. Coral is delicious warmed and served on toast or in crab cakes, or added to crab soups.

A lot of good meat is located in cartilage-lined channels in the body of most crabs, especially blue crabs and Dungeness crabs. To get at it, grasp each side of the body and break the crab in half. Now comes the tricky part. You must fish out all the yummy meat from the maze of cartilaginous channels. Don't get discouraged, because after a few crabs you will learn how to navigate this maze and the picking will go much faster. Only bother to pick at this meat in Dungeness crabs, blue crabs, and any other crab whose top shell is wider than 6 inches. The bodies of smaller crabs are still tasty, but the work isn't worth what you

get. Instead, add the bodies of smaller crabs into stocks and sauces to get that sweet crab flavor. You will still need to remove the lungs and tomalley, however.

I always start picking the legs and claws by pulling the lower part of each claw off. This often pulls all the inner claw meat with it, but it'll be attached to a hard, cartilaginous, fin-shaped thing in the center. You just pinch the meat at the base of the claw and pull it away from the cartilage.

To get the leg meat in blue crabs, Dungeness crabs, or especially large crabs of other species, start with whatever meat happens to be attached to the end of the leg. The meat inside the legs can best be extracted by breaking the joints backward. Meat will usually remain attached to a thin piece of cartilage. Just slip the meat from this cartilage. In larger crabs, cut the shell open with kitchen shears or scissors to get at the meat within.

After you've done all this, you finish a crab by cracking the hard-shelled claws and knuckles. My mother likes the knuckle meat the best, and it is of exceptional flavor. Remember to use only the amount of pressure you need to crack the claw. Gently increase pressure until the claw is cracked, then pick away the shell and extract the meat. If you crush it too forcefully, you will mash the meat and bits of shell will get into it. If you'd rather, use the kitchen shears here, too. It works fine. All this sounds like a lot of work, and it is. But once you get the hang of it, you can pick a crab in just a few minutes.

RECIPES

CRAB RISOTTO

Seafood risottos are one of the great joys in life, especially when they are made with fresh stock and fresh ingredients. Unlike terrestrial meats and stocks, those made with the fruits of the sea are zephyrs—make them, enjoy them, and move on. They don't store well at all. The key here is good stock. You should make crab stock special for this recipe, but you could use a high-quality fish stock instead. If you don't have access to either, use good vegetable stock or even water. One note: If you use a salty broth or stock, taste the risotto as you go, and switch to water once the dish is salty enough for you.

Serves 4

> 5–7 cups crab stock, fish stock, or vegetable stock
>
> 2 tablespoons olive oil
>
> 4 cloves garlic, chopped
>
> 2 cups risotto rice (Vialone Nano, Arborio, Carnaroli)
>
> 1 heaping tablespoon tomato paste
>
> $\frac{1}{3}$ cup Marsala or white wine
>
> Salt
>
> 1 cup chopped parsley
>
> 1–2 cups crabmeat

Pour the stock into a pot and bring to a bare simmer.

Heat the olive oil in another pot over medium-high heat for a minute or two. Add the garlic, rice, and tomato paste and stir-fry them until the garlic just begins to brown.

Pour in the Marsala and stir vigorously. It will combine with the tomato paste to make a thick slurry, so start pouring in your crab stock, $\frac{1}{2}$ cup at a time. Stir well to combine. Sprinkle a little salt over everything now, unless your stock is already salty. Stirring constantly, let the liquid evaporate. When the pot is nearly dry, add another half cup of hot stock. Keep repeating this for 15 to 20 minutes, until the rice is al dente.

Once the rice is cooked, add a little more stock, the parsley, and the crab meat and stir to combine. Turn the heat to low and stir until the crab is heated through. Serve at once.

SPAGHETTI AND CRAB SAUCE

This is an adaptation of a recipe designed by my brother-in-law, Mark Cornaro. Mark makes his version with lobster, but I am on the West Coast, so I use crabmeat instead. You could use either. The sauce is tomato based, with lots of fennel and a hit of the anise-flavored Greek liqueur ouzo. The result is sweet, savory, and just a little spicy.

Serves 6

SAUCE BASE

3 tablespoons olive oil

3 shallots, chopped

½ cup chopped fennel bulb

2 cloves garlic, minced

1 pound crab or lobster shells

1 tablespoon finely chopped parsley

1 can (28–32 ounces) tomato sauce or crushed tomatoes

Salt

FINISHED SAUCE

2 tablespoons olive oil

¼ cup finely chopped fennel bulb

3 shallots, finely chopped

2 cloves garlic, minced

½ teaspoon ground red pepper

1 heaping tablespoon tomato paste

½ cup ouzo

Long pasta such as spaghetti, bucatini, or linguine

1 cup crab or lobster meat

1 tablespoon finely chopped parsley

TO MAKE THE SAUCE BASE: In a large pot, heat the oil over medium-high heat for 1 to 2 minutes, then add the shallots and fennel. Cook, stirring constantly, for 3 to 5 minutes, or until they start to brown.

Add the garlic and crab shells and stir to combine. Cook over medium-high heat for 5 minutes, stirring often with a wooden spoon. Crush the shells as they cook. They will soften.

Add the parsley and tomatoes, stir, and bring to a boil. Reduce the heat to a simmer, and cook for 45 minutes. Add water if the sauce gets too thick.

Set a large pot of salty water to boil for your pasta.

After the sauce base has cooked, turn off the heat and pick out all the pieces of shells you can find. Run the sauce through a food mill with the medium plate. If you do not have a food mill, pick out even more of the shells, then push the sauce through a colander or a medium-mesh sieve set over a bowl.

Taste the sauce. It might be gritty from bits of shell. If it is, run the sauce through a finer-mesh sieve. Add salt if needed. Set aside.

TO MAKE THE FINISHED SAUCE: In a clean pot, heat the oil and cook the fennel and shallots for 3 minutes, stirring often. You don't want them to brown.

Add the garlic, ground red pepper, tomato paste, and ouzo and stir well to combine. Turn the heat to high and cook vigorously for 1 to 2 minutes. Add the reserved sauce base.

Add the pasta to the pot of boiling water. Cook your sauce gently while the pasta cooks. Right before the pasta is done, add the crabmeat and parsley to the sauce.

Toss the sauce with the pasta and serve immediately. I like an Italian red with this dish, such as a Montepulciano or a Sangiovese.

SPRING CRAB SALAD

Springtime is when we emerge from deep, dark braised dishes and stews to enjoy the vibrant new growth of the year. This little crab salad is a clean, zesty way to savor the season. Success here hinges on the quality of your ingredients, especially the spring greens. Feel free to use other green things, such as chives, basil, cilantro, garlic chives, or ramps.

Serves 4–6

- 1 pound crabmeat (any kind will do)
- Peel and juice of 1 lemon
- 1 stalk green garlic, minced
- 1 spring onion, finely chopped
- 2 tablespoons finely chopped mint or chervil
- 2 tablespoons finely chopped parsley
- Salt and freshly ground black pepper
- ½ pound shelled fresh green fava beans (optional)
- ¼ cup high-quality olive oil or walnut oil

In a large bowl, mix together the crab, lemon peel, garlic, onion, mint, and 1 tablespoon of the parsley. Taste to see if you need salt. The crab may be salty enough.

Add the lemon juice, black pepper, and the fava beans, if using. Mix well.

Stirring gently all the while, slowly drizzle in the oil. Garnish with the remaining 1 tablespoon parsley. Serve with crusty bread and a fruity white wine, such as a Greek Rhoditis or an off-dry Riesling or Gewürztraminer.

11

HERRING AND SHAD: TIMING IS EVERYTHING

When I lived in Virginia, every spring, starting about April Fools' Day, I began my ritual. Wake up a little early and drive to the Rappahannock River. Look for other anglers; there usually weren't many so early in the season. If there were guys fishing, I'd see what they were doing. Were they casting? Were they catching? But usually no one was around, so I'd go to one of my posts along the bank, get out my spinning rod, and cast. And cast. And cast. Cast and repeat, cast and repeat—each toss into the turbid, springtime flood a little farther across the river, or a little to the left, or maybe with a slightly different rhythm of twitches to the line as I reeled it in.

Usually I did nothing but work on my casting skills, or catch my line on a stick or log floating downstream toward Chesapeake Bay. No matter. At Fredericksburg where I was fishing, the Rappahannock is still tidal, so maybe this wasn't the best tide. Maybe last night's frost affected the fish. Maybe it was something else. So I returned after work and repeated the same ritual. My girlfriend thought I was crazy.

But I kept on, because one day soon, there would be a fish on the end of my line. No one on the river could say with any accuracy when that might be, and it could be different for different anglers, some even crazier than me. But when that day did come, I'd be reeling in one of the thousand casts I'd flung into the river, and the line would shudder and stop. By then, I knew well what a snag on a log felt like, and this would be no dead stick. The shudder-and-stop meant They Have Arrived!

As soon as I felt this bump, I reeled in a little slack on the line and lifted my rod tip to about 60 degrees from the water; high, but not too high. This lifts the lure off the river bottom but keeps it steady for a second or two longer than it would be normally. The line started bouncing as the fish attached to it tried to escape. Sometimes that bouncing attracted his friends, and one of his more stupid colleagues would see another shiny brass hook bobbing in the river and attack it. Now I'd have two fish on the line. Rod held high to avoid snags, I reeled in, grinning like the Cheshire Cat. Finally.

When the fish arrived at the bank, I gently took them off the hooks and looked them over: Wriggling, flattened torpedoes, these fish looked out of place in the olive drab waters of the springtime Rappahannock. They were a flashing silver, laced with iridescence and topped with gunmetal blue backs. They had large eyes and wore the permanent frown caused by the worries of being so low on the food chain.

"Hello, Mister Herring," I said to the fish. "I've been waiting for you."

Mr. Herring and friends would be the first in a giant wave of Atlantic blueback herring that run up mid-Atlantic rivers to spawn every spring. They can come as early as March or as late as early May, but every year, the herring run comes. It has never failed. Herring were our harbingers of warmer weather.

The old wisdom says they arrive when the shadbush blossoms are fully formed but not yet open. Incidentally, the shadbush, also known as the Juneberry or serviceberry, sports delicious, blueberry-like fruit in late June. Fishermen rarely come back to the bushes that grow along the riverbank in June, as by then the herring are gone and they are off after other fish. We watch the bushes with a keen eye in springtime, however, because when those white blossoms open fully, the herring's successor enters the river: the shad.

But April belongs to the blueback. Once the run hit full stride, much of my social life dissolved, other than swapping stories with my friends on the riverbank. I'd spend an hour before work catching herring, then another few hours after work. On a weekend morning, I sometimes could catch a 5-gallon bucket full of them. It was almost always a bonanza, as few other fishermen targeted herring. Most preferred shad.

They are fools, in my opinion. Virginia anglers cannot legally keep the larger American white shad, *Alosa sapidissima*, and must settle for the smaller hickory shad, *Alosa mediocris*. (A hickory shad's lower jaw juts out beyond its upper jaw; an American shad's does not.) Hickories are larger than a half-pound herring but smaller than the grand white shad, which in some places can reach 10 pounds. And size matters. Herring and both shad species are extremely bony, but the smaller size of the herring means you can eat those bones without worry. Not so with the shad. And the ratio of bone to meat on a hickory shad is not as good as with a white shad. What's more, herring roe is just as tasty as the famous shad roe, only smaller. So I loaded up on bluebacks.

Once the herring run ended, I could cast until my arms fell off and not catch a one: They will swim back to the Chesapeake and ultimately the Atlantic. Timing is everything.

SHAD, KING of HERRINGS

The American, or white, shad is the world's largest herring. We'd see them from time to time in Virginia, but the fishery has long since been decimated. Shad in the East has become a largely symbolic pursuit: Catching more than a few shad, even in those rivers where you can still keep and eat them, is a rarity there.

Not so in the West's Columbia and Sacramento River systems, which sport the largest shad runs in the world. Our shad season in Northern California lasts a solid 8 weeks and is more of a hot weather fishery than is the East Coast run. June is the best time to chase them

in California. Like the herring, shad run to the rivers to spawn when the water hits a certain temperature. In the East, with wide rivers fed by rain and natural lakes, that happens in the spring. But in California, where the rivers are fed by melting snow, the frigid waters don't heat up enough until the air temperature is consistently in the 90s. I've fished for shad in the American River outside Sacramento in 110-degree heat.

Easterners brought the American shad, *Alosa sapidissima*, to California in the 1870s specifically to start a commercial fishery—*sapidissima* means "tastiest," after all. The fishery thrived for 80 years, but ended a half century ago when demand died off as consumers switched to less bony fish such as salmon. Few Westerners eat shad now.

Even so, a few thousand California anglers still meet the Sacramento shad every spring, at least in part because catching a shad is flat-out thrilling. The rush from hooking herring on the Rappahannock pales in comparison to laying into a big roe shad in swift current. The shad is one of North America's boniest fish, and those bones give them strength to fight like a fish twice their size. What's more, their soft mouths make them as difficult to land as they are easy to hook. Fished with light tackle, a big female, shouldering into the current of a fast-moving river, is as close to an immovable object as exists in freshwater fishing. If you try to horse in shad or other herring with brute strength, you typically lose the fish.

CATCHING THE RUN

Start your vigil by learning the general time frame for your local runs. For shad, it's February in the St. John's River in Florida, June in California and Oregon. A different herring, the alewife, comes into New England rivers starting in May. In the Great Lakes region, whitefish—not a herring but very similar from a cooking standpoint—begin spawning in late fall and can be caught all winter. Pacific herring can be caught all winter in the San Francisco Bay.

During that time, keep your gear in your vehicle, and keep your ears and eyes open. Watch for signs like the blooming shadbush. In Northern California, the best indicator is the cotton falling from cottonwood trees. When it blows like snow, it's time to go. Listen to the radio, and read the newspapers or online reports. Most places have a hunting and fishing report on radio (usually on the AM dial), and many newspapers have a hunting and fishing report at least once a week. Also look for online bulletin boards and forums:

The Fish Sniffer is one of the best of its kind for those who live in California. Weekly outdoors magazines like *Western Outdoor News* or *Game & Fish* also tell readers what's going on where they live.

It helps to have friends with the same obsession. When I lived on Long Island, I kept my gear in the car not for shad or herring, but for bluefish, which is essentially an ocean-going piranha that can grow to 25 pounds and take your finger clean off if you let it. Bluefish travel in packs like wolves and corral smaller fish, like herring, in shallow water near the beach. The water will boil with thrashing bluefish and fleeing baitfish. Anyone fishing near such a boil will have himself a hootenanny in a hurry. My friends and I would call each other if we ever found a bluefish boil, and we'd all drop what we were doing to get to the beach as fast as possible. By the time I lived in herring and shad country, all my angling friends had cell phones, so we could converge on the river even faster.

Generally speaking, the best times of day to catch herring and shad are at dawn and dusk. I've rarely caught them past 10 a.m. or before 3 p.m. Shad are especially sensitive to light, and many afternoons I've gone fishless until sundown.

HOW to CATCH HERRING AND SHAD

Tackle for these fish is pretty basic. You need a light rod and a spinning reel wound with nothing heavier than 8-pound test; anything more will be difficult to cast. Lots of people fly-fish for shad, but I'm not a fly fisherman, so I can't help you there. Where it is legal, I use a sabiki rig, a Japanese-style rig with five or six small hooks, each decorated with a neon red, green, or yellow pennant. Some states don't let you fish so many hooks. In those states, I use shad darts, which are small, brightly colored

lures with a little pennant on the back of them. Both rigs are readily available where shad and herring are caught.

Attach your lures to the line, leaving a loop at the bottom for a weight. Cast the lure as far as you can and reel it back, twitching the line a little as you go. Vary your distance, speed of return, angle, and color before you give up on a spot.

Buy lures in several colors and sizes. Sometimes chartreuse works like a charm, sometimes neon red. You don't want to be caught with the wrong color. Darts for shad should be heavier than for herring.

Look for deep channels or holes in the river or grassy, shallow areas in the San Francisco Bay. This is where the fish will be hanging out, more often than not. One tip is to fish across boat channels, which are dredged deep enough for larger boats. The fish will use the channels as highways.

Finally, know that you will lose many lures as they get snagged on sunken logs or rocks. It happens. Lose a rig, tie a rig. That's fishing.

EATING HERRING AND SHAD

Shad may be delicious, but cleaning them can be a chore. Before they've been cleaned, shad smell rank, like algae or decomposing grass. This smell goes away once the fish are filleted and washed. Shad and herring are unusually bloody fish, and they coat themselves with an eel-like thick layer of slime. Finally, while most fish have a single set of pin bones that extend from the backbone into the fillets, shad and herring have four sets of oddly shaped bones that almost reach the skin. An old Native American saying has it that a disgruntled porcupine begged the gods to change his lot in life, so they tossed him into the water and turned him inside out to become the shad. It is not far off.

That said, in all but the largest herring, the bones are so fine you barely notice them while eating. A big herring can sometimes taste a little "furry" from those bones, but you aren't likely to choke on one. Hickory shad and white shad are a different story.

Boning a shad requires a series of intricate, parallel cuts, leaving a skin-on fillet that has overlapping flaps of boneless meat. At eastern fish markets, you can buy professionally boned shad, but few fishmongers know how to do this anymore. The boning is worth it, though, as the boneless meat of shad and herring is sweet, silky, and rich.

There are alternatives. An old Virginia method of dealing with the bones is to dissolve them by baking the fish at 225°F for 6 or 7 hours. I've done it with hickory shad, and while it is true that you barely notice the bones, the already soft meat softens even further with this method, so I rarely do this. Another method is to pickle or smoke the shad. The acid in vinegar partially dissolves bones, salting the fish down performs a similar function, and both hot and cold smoking result in meat easily separated from its bony cage.

Both shad and herring are unusually high in the oils health experts extol, and both fish tolerate some overcooking because of their high oil content. That oil also makes shad and herring perfect for smoking, which is how most westerners prepare them. In the East, smoked shad is relatively rare. Instead, shad is usually broiled simply or planked. For the latter, the sides are nailed to a hickory or oak board, which is propped up before an open fire to roast the fish.

Both fish are wonderful salted down. Even properly cleaned and iced, a herring won't last more than 5 days or so in a fridge, and they are really best eaten within 2 days after they've come out of the water. Shad will last longer, up to a week. Neither fish freezes well; they turn mushy.

Salting is a traditional option for preserving the fish. After salting, some Italian families in California would then pickle the shad, rinsing off the salt and then sousing them with olive oil, vinegar, and spices. In Virginia, saltfish and corn cakes (think fish bacon with corn-based pancakes) is a breakfast that dates back to before 1700. It still can be had in some places around Fredericksburg.

To make saltfish, you lay down an inch-thick layer of kosher or pickling salt in a clean bucket. How many herring fillets you need depends on the size of the container; I'd start with a small gallon-size one. Fillet the herring, wash them well, and lay them skin side up in a radial pattern on the salt. Cover with another half inch of salt, add another layer of herring, and continue until your bucket is filled. Top with at least another inch of salt, preferably 2 inches. Put the bucket in the basement or another cool place. You don't need to refrigerate it. If you've caught your herring in the spring, leave them alone until autumn. The fish need at least 4 months to cure and, once cured, will last a year. Maybe more. Oh, and don't worry: You will not stink up your house by doing this. Done right, there should be no smell at all.

To use, unearth your herring and soak in milk or slightly vinegared water for a day or two. I once tried soaking the herring for 4 days and did not like the result. Too mushy. To eat, flour the soaked saltfish fillets and fry them in bacon fat. They will still taste fishy, however, and are definitely an acquired taste. Living in California, I miss them, although I suppose I could substitute sardines.

Of all the parts of shad and herring, the roe may be the greatest. Properly cooked, it is as light as a soufflé, airy with a taste of iodine and the sea. Each female has a pair of the orange, sausage-shaped roe sacs. To remove the sacs, carefully gut the fish by slicing with a fillet knife—blade facing away from the fish—through the vent toward the gills. You should see the orange roe sacs, which you can gently pull out. Traditionally, shad roe is brined overnight to firm it and remove any remaining blood. Then it is floured and fried slowly in bacon fat for about 10 minutes, until it is crisp outside and still slightly pink at the center. The roe is served with strips of bacon, a lemon wedge, and parsley. Recipes along these lines date back to the 18th century; Thomas Jefferson included shad roe in his spring menus at Monticello.

Like anything else, a roe has a life cycle. An underripe egg sac is thin and filled with a vaguely peach-colored mass of undifferentiated eggs. An overripe sac is bloated and watery; the eggs have become translucent and their flavor is bland. A perfect roe is full of opaque, brilliant orange orbs that look like the *tobiko* (flying fish roe) served in sushi restaurants. If you have excess roe, you can always salt it down, too, making yourself a rough version of the dried roe sacs called *bottarga* that are so loved by the Sardinians and Sicilians. When the roe sacs have dried solid, grind them over pasta like cheese.

Not everyone has access to fresh shad or herring, but there are fish that are similar. Alewives are another sort of herring that run up New England rivers in spring, and the Great Lakes have good schools of whitefish. Whitefish rival shad in flavor, and the canary-colored whitefish roe is an excellent North American alternative to flying fish roe, which is always imported; I prefer whitefish roe's flavor, actually. Herring do run in the San Francisco Bay, and this is a largely untapped fishery.

RECIPES

SHAD OR HERRING ROE WITH BACON

The eggs of shad and herring are valued more than the fish itself. Shad and herring roe tastes vaguely fishy but not overpoweringly so, and the texture is similar to a good meatball: soft, yet meaty. Shad roe cooked in bacon fat, served with lemon and a fresh spring herb, is the classic way to prepare this delicacy, which only comes around in late spring. The keys to this dish are very fresh roe, very good bacon, and a zingy herb to accompany it. Note: You need to start this dish the night before.

Serves 4

1 tablespoon salt

4–6 lobes of shad roe, or 6–10 lobes of herring roe (each female fish has 2 lobes)

8 pieces of smoky, thick-cut bacon

Flour for dusting

Fresh herbs such as chervil, fennel fronds, or parsley

1 lemon, quartered

In a medium bowl, mix the salt and 2 cups cold water until the salt dissolves. Submerge the roe in the salt water and let soak in the fridge overnight.

The next day, cook the bacon in a pan over medium-low heat until crispy. Set aside to drain.

Meanwhile, drain the roe and flour it. Set aside until the bacon is done.

When the bacon is finished, turn the heat to medium-high and cook the shad roe in the bacon fat for 1 minute. Turn the heat down to medium, then cook for another 2 to 3 minutes, or until golden. Turn and cook the other side for 2 to 3 minutes. Go with 2 minutes per side on herring roe, which is smaller; for shad roe, don't cook for longer than 3 minutes per side. Overcooked roe is chalky and nasty.

To serve, arrange the bacon on a plate, place the fresh herbs on the bacon, and then the roe on top. Serve with a lemon wedge.

"BONELESS" TEMPURA SHAD

I have solved the most vexing problem facing any shad angler: how to deal with the bones. The answer is honegiri tempura. What the hell is that? I saw an old episode of the TV show *Iron Chef* where they featured Kyoto chefs and the odd-looking, very bony "pike eel." To deal with the eel's bones, the chefs practice something called *honegiri*, or "pike-eel bone-cutting technique."

It goes something like this. Start with a side of the fish that has been cleaned and trimmed. Lay it horizontally in front of you and get the sharpest knife you own. You firmly yet gently slice across the fillet, through all the bones but not through the skin. Make your cuts every 5 millimeters or so.

What this technique does is slice the bones into many smaller pieces. By cutting the bones so small, it opens up far more surface area to the hot oil—and deep-frying softens bones to the point where you hardly notice them.

After doing the honegiri technique, cut the fillet into thick fingers, salt them, and fry them tempura style. One key to good tempura is not to mix the wet and dry ingredients until the moment you are ready to fry them. The wet ingredients also need to be very cold.

As for a sauce, I would suggest a traditional ponzu sauce, which is soy mixed with citrus, such as orange or lime juice.

Serves 4

⅛ teaspoon baking soda

½ teaspoon kosher salt

¼ cup cornstarch

¾ cup rice flour or all-purpose flour

Peanut or canola oil for frying

1 egg yolk

1 cup ice-cold sparkling water

Honegiri-cut sides from 2 shad, cut into 2–3-inch "fingers"

Mix the baking soda, salt, cornstarch, and flour in a bowl.

If you have a deep fryer, fill it with oil as per the instructions. If you don't have a deep fryer, pour oil 3 to 4 inches deep in a large, deep pot with a lid. (You'll need a lid to smother the oil in case it gets too hot and ignites—this should not happen, but better to have one handy just in case.)

When the oil reaches 360°F—and not before—whisk the egg yolk and sparkling water together, then pour it into the bowl of dry ingredients. You must move quickly from here on.

Rapidly dip a few pieces of shad into the thin batter—which should have the consistency of melted ice cream—shake them off a bit, and drop into the oil. Do this in small batches so the oil temperature does not drop too far. Do not crowd the pot.

Fry the shad for 2 to 3 minutes. Two tips: Move the pieces around in the oil with a chopstick, so they don't stick to the bottom of the pot or basket; and, to keep the shad warm while you do subsequent batches, put them on a pan lined with paper towels and place in an oven set on Warm.

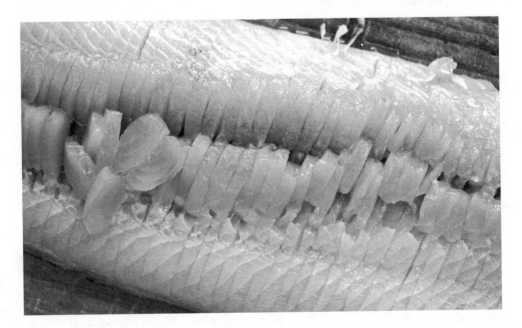

Smoked Shad, Herring, Sardines, or Mackerel

Smoked shad is like a refined version of smoked sardines or mackerel. Marinated in olive oil for a few weeks, homemade smoked shad—or mackerel, herring, or sardines—is far better than any store-bought product. This is my master recipe for any small, oily fish. This method also works well with whitefish.

Your fish should be brined, rested, and then smoked for several hours. I start with skin-on fillets, but you could use whole, gutted fish—which I recommend when smoking herring, sardines, or small whitefish.

You will need a smoker for this recipe, and keep in mind it will take a full day, although most of that time you can be doing other things.

Makes 10 smoked shad

4 cups water

¼ cup kosher salt

¼ cup honey, molasses, or brown sugar

4–5 bay leaves

1 onion, grated or finely chopped

2 cloves garlic, smashed

½ cup chopped parsley

3–4 crushed dried hot chile peppers (optional); wear plastic gloves when handling

2 tablespoons cracked black peppercorns

Juice of 2 lemons or 3 limes

10 shad, mackerel, or whitefish, or 20 sardines or herring

In a large stockpot, add the water and salt and boil to dissolve the salt. Add the honey, bay leaves, onion, garlic, parsley, chile peppers, peppercorns, and lemon juice. Boil for 1 minute. Turn off the heat, stir, and cover. Let stand until cool. Then add the fish to the brine and soak for 4 hours, or up to overnight. Don't go longer than that or the fish will be too salty.

The next step is to rest the fish. Take the fillets out of the brine, rinse, and pat dry. Lay on a rack in a breezy, cool place—lower than 70°F if at all possible—or run a fan on the fish. Turn the fillets from time to time, and let them dry for 2 to 3 hours.

Lay the fillets skin side down on a rack in the smoker and smoke slowly. I use almond wood, although hickory, oak, alder, or apple would also be good choices. Keep the smoker as cool as you can, no more than 140°F. This is tough in home setups, but you can help things along by loading your drip pan with ice and smoking on cool days. All is not lost if your smoker gets to 200°F or more. Just keep in mind you will want to take the fish out sooner. Under no circumstances should your smoker get past 250°F. Do whatever it takes to avoid this, as temperatures that high damage the structure of the fish and will cause the fat to weep out between the flakes of meat.

Don't open the smoker for at least an hour, as the smoking process typically takes 2 to 4 hours, depending on how hot it is. Check after an hour and then again every hour going forward. You want the fish to be firm throughout and a pretty golden color.

Remove the fish and let cool on a rack for several hours before storing it, preferably with a vacuum-sealer. Once cooked this way, smoked fish will freeze well for 4 to 6 months.

12

ROCK COD, PORGIES, AND OTHER BOTTOM DWELLERS

I have a thing about porgies. Porgies are to the rocks and sunken ships of the mid-Atlantic coast what bluegills and crappies are to the fallen logs and submerged brush piles of the nation's ponds and lakes. Small, fun to catch, plentiful, and easy to eat.

Most of my porgy fishing has been done on party boats, where you pay a fare and get on a fishing boat with 20 other dudes in the hopes that the captain knows where the fish are. But once in a while, when the tides were right and the wind wasn't too fierce, I'd venture out on my own.

The marina at Long Island's Port Jefferson rents rowboats with little outboard motors; most people use them to tour the harbor. I used the boats to fish—winter flounder in the back bays during the winter and early spring, and porgies outside the harbor in summer. It was tricky braving the inlet in a rowboat powered with an anemic 10-horsepower outboard. When the tide rushed through or the winds whipped too hard, the motor couldn't make headway against them. I learned to leave the harbor on the outgoing tide and return on the incoming tide. The tides didn't sync with the business hours of the marina every day, so I had to pick my trips carefully.

When I could catch the tides, however, I'd have myself a thrilling little adventure. Into a cooler went sandwiches, beef jerky, water, and a beer or two. Tackle and rods next, then a life preserver and the oars—going into the Long Island Sound without either could be fatal if a squall tore through unexpectedly. I'd motor out of the harbor past giant ferries, a forest of sailboats at the marina, the workingman's dock encrusted with rusty commercial trawlers, and sometimes even an old schooner or replica tall ship.

Years later, it's the salt spray I miss most. The rowboat would bounce on the waves, kicking up spray that would soak into every pore. In early May this could be bone chilling, but on a hot July morning it was exhilarating. As I got closer to the inlet, I'd feel the first flush of adrenaline: Be careful! Cut that big wave across the diagonal. Tack left. Mind that powerboat cruising past. Does that guy even see me?

Once out of the inlet and into the Sound, the water was usually much better. Another 15 minutes along the rocky coast and I'd be at my first porgy hole. Porgies, also known as scup, are the Atlantic cousin of the famous sea bream of the Mediterranean. Silvery gold, often with colored stripes, porgies have high foreheads, bodies flattened vertically like bluegills, and little mouths, also like bluegills. They travel in large schools, and each one will weigh anything from a half pound to 5 pounds.

Porgies live around sunken boulders and wrecked ships, often in close proximity to tautog, black sea bass, ocean perch, ling, little pollock, and, in late summer, triggerfish that have come up on the Gulf Stream. On Long Island's South Shore down to Virginia, this is a typical "wreck fish" mix. They are called wreck fish because these fish are often caught around sunken wrecks. South of Virginia, you begin to get another, larger porgy called a grunt or hardhead.

One day while fishing solo, I found a perfect porgy spot—a string of boulders and rocks that extended out from a spit of land. The waves had eroded the cliffside and carried away the soil, leaving only rock. I motored the rowboat to a spot up current from where I knew the rocks would be, and anchored.

I use a heavy spinning reel for porgies, weighted with a few ounces of lead and armed with two brass hooks baited with little strips of sea clam. I gently pitched the line, a few feet in front of me and let the current take it down and toward the rocks. Once I felt it hit bottom, I took up most of the slack and waited.

Being ocean fish, porgies aren't real shy. So a few minutes after the bait was down, I felt the rod jerk twice in rapid succession, then again, and again. Porgies grab the bait and shake their heads like a dog, then try to swim away with it. I set the hook and reeled. I felt weight. A nice one! Porgies jerk and shake all the way up, and, if they are especially clever, turn those flattened bodies broadside to the current in the hopes of breaking my line. Sometimes it worked, but not this time. Up came a nice little porgy, all glittery golden-silver. He was maybe a pound. I took off the hook and put him in the cooler, which I had half-filled with seawater after removing all my sandwiches. He swam around in the cooler looking confused. I shut the lid and rebaited the hook.

I managed to catch three more at that spot before it petered out. I could have stayed there and pecked at the spot for a while, but I decided to move on, to let the spot rest so I could come back to it again soon. But where to go? That's the beauty and challenge of fishing without a guide. You must use your own wits to sense where the submerged rocks or boats might be. I'd done some preliminary scouting the previous evening by scanning a chart, which helped. But it's only when you're out there that you realize that the likely-looking spot on the chart may not be rocky after all.

How can you tell where the rocks are, you ask? Fish long enough, and you can tell what your sinker is hitting by feel. Rock feels different from sand. Another giveaway is whether your line is getting hung up in rocks. This happens so much when you fish for tautog that you need to bring several dozen premade rigs when you fish for them. Tautog live so deep in crevices the joke is that the best time to set the hook on one is right before it hits the bait. There is one more surefire indicator that you are fishing sand, not rock: dogfish and skates. If you are catching either, you are over sand, not rock.

When I fished for porgies, there was no limit on them, although they needed to be at least 7 inches long. Now, in much of their range, there is a 10-fish limit and they must be at least 10½ inches long. Sad, really, as this means we were overfishing them then. I never caught more than 30 at a time, but would routinely catch in the teens and low twenties.

That day off Port Jefferson was one of those days. I hit a mother lode spot about 2 miles outside the harbor at the edge of a cove just a few hundred yards from the beach. Porgy after porgy came over the rail, and I even had two on at a time occasionally. I became more and more selective, which is one reason I kept the porgies swimming around in my cooler. Porgies are bony fish and really need to be larger than 10 inches to get a decent fillet off them; I typically ate them whole for this reason. So toward the end of the day, I began tossing back anything under about 10 inches until I had 20 good-size fish.

I headed home. Unfortunately, I had been having such a good time fishing I failed to notice the weather had worsened. A thunderstorm was heading up the Long Island Sound, and I was 2 miles away from the inlet. If the storm arrived before I could get inside the harbor, I'd need to beach the boat and wait for it to pass. Not good. I hauled up the anchor and began to make my way back to the harbor.

The skies had already darkened when the buoys marking the harbor came into sight. By this time, the wind was whipping about 20 miles per hour and the waves were pushing

6 feet—nothing earth-shattering for a normal boat, but scary for a rowboat with an under-powered motor. I was soaked with spray as every wave broke over the front of the boat. I eyed my life preserver. Thank God no other boats were near the inlet as I entered, because I needed to gun the motor over the waves and quickly slalom the other way to cut the next one at an angle. At some point, the rain began, but I didn't notice until later because I was so wet already.

Once inside the inlet the waves dropped considerably, but it was still slow going back to the marina. What normally took 30 minutes took more than an hour as I threaded my way through the choppy harbor waves, angling this way and that to cut the wind. When I tied up at the dock the boatmaster was standing there. "What the hell happened to you? Didn't you see the storm coming?" I said no, I was too busy catching porgies. "Porgies?" he said, shaking his head. "You risked your life for a garbage fish?" Satisfied that I was insane but that his boat was in one piece he hustled back to his office, out of the rain.

Back home, I dried off and sifted through my porgies. I had almost 10 that were big enough to fillet, and a couple monsters over 3 pounds. Beautiful fish. Standing in the rain in the backyard of the house where I was renting a room, I scaled the fish, gutted them, and filleted the big ones. I held one of the fillets up and looked at it: Porgy meat is rosy, firm, and a little iridescent. I felt a little warmer thinking about dredging a few fillets in cornmeal

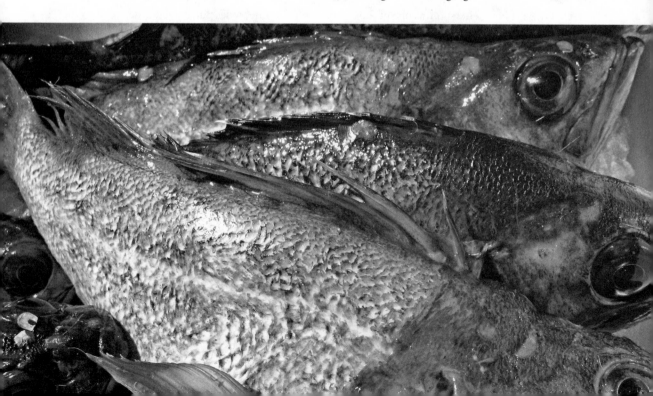

CATCHING THEM

The gear you need to catch wreck fish is generally pretty simple. For starters, any party boat will rent you gear for a small charge, so if you are not going to be a frequent angler, this is the best way to go.

I always bring my own gear, however, and over the long run it makes a difference and is cheaper. I had a rod for porgies, one for general boat fishing, and one for tautog, which are among the toughest wreck fish to catch. Your own gear feels better in your hands and is almost always more sensitive. This is important, as many wreck fish are slash-and-dash biters, meaning they will whip in and bite your bait and swim away, giving you a second at best to set the hook on them. Tautog are especially fast. You need to keep your wits about you when angling for these fish.

My favorite all-around setup is a short, 5-foot boat rod with a strong base tapering to a sensitive tip. You need the strong base to set on bigger fish. Believe me, hauling up a 5-pound sea bass from 200 feet of water is a lot harder than it sounds, and you want a rod that is up to the task. You also want a boat reel, not something geared for casting, with a good crank-to-reel ratio. What this means is that every time you turn the crank on the reel, it brings the fish up a certain number of feet. The faster you can reel in, the better, with a few exceptions.

As for terminal tackle, the hook, leader line, and sinker, wreck fishing is almost always bait fishing, so a simple baitholder hook (this is the one with the barbs on the back of the hook's shank) and some lead works just fine. You can get a little fancier by setting up what's called a dropper or a "high-low rig," which has two hooks coming off the main line about a foot or two apart. This lets you fish in two places at once. You can either tie this rig yourself or buy premade high-low rigs.

What sort of bait to use? When in doubt, buy sea clams. Everything eats sea clams, and it is one reason why wreck fish are so tasty: They are big shellfish and crustacean eaters. Squid is a good second choice. Dead anchovies will work but not as well. Green crabs are ideal for tautog and large black sea bass. Pacific lingcod are fond of eating whole sand dabs (a small flounder) or small mackerel, and many party boats will stop to catch live mackerel and sand dabs for just that purpose. The bonus is that both are delicious if you fail to catch a big lingcod.

The exception to the live bait rule is when you are fishing the Pacific for rock cod. They love an artificial lure called a Farallon Feather, which is a brightly colored pennant of feathers, wrapped in golden ribbon set around a hook. This is the lure of choice in Northern California, although bait works just fine.

and frying them in butter. A pint of Guinness would go well with these, as would some roasted potatoes. Maybe I'd toss in a carrot or two. Garbage fish? I think not.

Porgies and the other fish in this chapter are not all related biologically, but from a fishing and eating standpoint they are similar. They are known as wreck fish on the East Coast and rock fish on the West Coast.

I include a chapter on wreck fish largely because they were my staple when I was fishing primarily for food, and because it is an ideal fish to chase if you are a beginning ocean angler. In most trips, the value of the fish you bring home will be greater than the cost of getting on the party boat, and party boats are the most common way to catch these fish. It's pretty cheap, at about $30 to $80 per person per trip, usually close to shore, and you are very likely to catch fish.

My favorite thing about wreck fishing is the variety. You really never know what you'll catch. In the Northeast, from spring to winter you are likely going to catch porgies, black sea bass, ocean perch, and in winter, tautog and ling. Ling is a relative of the cod, not to be confused with the West Coast lingcod, which is actually related to the greenling. An eastern ling eats like a cod, while a western lingcod eats like a bass. West Coast bottom fishing is all about the rock cod, which are also known as rockfish. There are scores of species, covering all the colors of the rainbow. Rock cod are long-lived, firm, bass-like fish very close, culinarily speaking, to eastern black sea bass, snapper, and grouper.

These last are fish of warm waters. I have caught all sorts of snappers, groupers, and southern porgylike fish called grunts and hardheads in the Gulf Stream off North Carolina.

A little rarer but still in this category are triggerfish, Atlantic and Pacific sheepshead—two very different fish—kelp greenlings, tilefish, and wrasse.

The common denominator in most of these fish is that they are easy to catch, travel in large numbers so you are likely to catch several in a day, are relatively small—a 10-pound rock cod or black sea bass is huge—and have large heads and firm, mild, white meat. Grouper, which can grow to enormous size, are an exception to this rule.

WHAT YOU'LL CATCH

There are too many different species you will encounter in wreck fishing to go over all of them, but here are the main ones.

PORGIES

These are the bluegills of the ocean. Rarely over 5 pounds and usually only about a pound, these little fish are a staple of bottom fishing from New Jersey to southern Massachusetts, where they are called scup. Only large ones should be filleted. Porgies are best just scaled and gutted. Their meat is rosy when uncooked and white when cooked. It is very finely grained and mild tasting.

Once you get to North Carolina you find larger, coarser-fleshed porgies called grunts or hardheads. These are decent-eating fish, but not as tasty as the snappers they live with, so many anglers toss them back.

BLACK SEA BASS

This is the king of wreck fish in the East. It is basically a black, basslike fish that averages about 2 pounds, with a big head and nasty spines on its back. I've caught them heavier than 5 pounds, but this is increasingly rare. In New York and New Jersey, where you are most likely to catch them, the size limit is 12½ inches and the bag limit is 25 fish, which used to be a common catch but has become difficult.

From a cooking standpoint, there is little difference between a Pacific rock cod and an Atlantic black sea bass. A sea bass is a little less firm and slightly fattier.

TAUTOG OR BLACKFISH

My favorite eastern wreck fish, the 'tog is big and tough to catch. Fish for them in cold weather, once the best black sea bass and porgy fishing ends in October.

Tautog is the best chowder fish I know of, with the possible exception of tilefish. Super firm and snowy white, this crustacean-and-clam-eater is sweet and lean. They typically need to be at least 14 inches to keep, and 'tog of over 5 pounds are not uncommon. I once caught a 14-pounder and feasted on it for days. When I tired of chowder, I made the best deep-fried fish nuggets I'd ever eaten.

ROCKFISH OR ROCK COD

Pacific rockfish are the most common fish that live close to the shore along North America's West Coast. More than 70 varieties of this basslike fish swim around the shorelines down to depths of 300 feet or more. While there are taste differences in several varieties, all rockfish are firm, lean, and mild flavored.

The main difference is texture. China cod, a little black variety with a racy-looking yellow stripe along its back, is especially fine textured and often commands a higher price. Many also prefer the red ones, such as vermillion or copper rockfish, although I find them not so different than the common black, brown, and olive rockfish.

Rockfish run from hand-size up to 20 pounds or more. In California the limit is 10 fish per person per day, and I would advise you to keep everything you catch unless you are an excellent angler armed with a special device.

Here's why. Rock cod tend to live at lower depths, so when you reel them up, they often get the bends from the change in pressure. This makes their eyes bulge and can sometimes cause their swim bladder to expand and poke out of their mouths. This can't be fun for the fish. Just tossing fish that are suffering the bends back into the water isn't enough. They will be unable to swim back down, and will only become food for seagulls. This is a waste of the resource, especially since rock cod grow slowly and can live for decades. The only way to ensure that these fish are returned safely is to use something to forcibly send them back to the depths they came from. I use a device called a Shelton Fish Descender that you attach to your line. You reattach the fish you want to throw back to a curved hook on the device, let the line back down to the bottom and jerk the rod up sharply. This dislodges the fish at the proper depth; he'll be fine from there on.

If you don't have a fish descender, keep even the small rock cod you catch and count them toward your limit. They still taste excellent crispy-fried as whole fish. At least you did not waste them.

LINGCOD

These are large, predatory fish that live among the rock cod and eat them. Many times, I've had a small rock cod on the line and a 10-pound lingcod will grab it and hook himself. Lingcod are elongated, prehistoric-looking fish with mottled green or blue skin, bulging eyes, and lots and lots of razor-sharp teeth. Don't be scared—they are stupendous eating: firm, white, and close grained. There is even a rare color phase of the lingcod that causes the uncooked meat to be a translucent ice blue. It's very cool. Lingcod are generally caught with bait or large chrome, diamond-shaped jigs.

SNAPPER AND GROUPER

These are the premier wreck fishes of the South Atlantic. You can catch them in the Gulf Stream wrecks of North Carolina all the way down to the Florida Keys and into the Gulf. Like Pacific rock cod, there are lots of species besides the world-famous red snapper. All are tasty. Grouper is even tastier than snapper, but angling has been severely restricted due to overfishing. If you catch a legal-size one, savor it: Grouper has a certain dense meatiness to it that no other wreck fish possesses. It is concentrated umami, something I've encountered elsewhere only in Pacific white sea bass or cobia from southern waters.

CLEANING AND COOKING

Wreck fish all seem to have huge heads for their bodies, as well as high, round rib cages. This means your yield on a fillet is not nearly as good as on a tuna or salmon. Add to this their relatively small size and you have a recipe for skinny little fillets with a lot of waste.

That's why I fillet only large fish and eat the smaller ones whole. All should be scaled, because their skin crisps up well and is delicious. Exceptions to this rule are the tough-skinned blackfish, large groupers, and tilefish, and especially triggerfish, which have skins so sturdy they are literally used as leather to make shoes.

All wreck fish are fairly lean, which means the leftover heads and bones will make excellent fish stock; in general, all lean fish make good stock. Be sure to rinse them well to remove traces of blood, and cut out the gills before making a stock. Gills will make the broth bitter and cloudy.

In the market, you will usually find rockfish sold as skinless fillets—usually misleadingly called Pacific snapper, although rockfish are nowhere near as fine flavored as real red snapper, which only lives in the Atlantic. If you have a skinless fillet, use it in any normal fillet recipe. Dredged in flour and sautéed, rockfish is excellent. It's also good batter-fried or made into tempura. Snapper and black sea bass are normally sold skin-on.

Rock cod, porgies, and black sea bass are often sold whole, or scaled and gutted. You'll find whole fish mostly in Asian markets, but they're being sold this way increasingly in high-end Western markets as well. If you buy a whole rock cod or black sea bass, I'd advise one of three treatments: grill it, crispy-fry it in oil, or steam it Asian style. Each suits this fish perfectly. You get a smoky hit of flavor with grilling, while crispy-frying takes advantage of the fish's firmness. Steaming highlights its delicate flavor.

Crispy-frying and steaming have been perfected by the West's Asian American community, so look to Asian sources for your inspiration. In the Mediterranean, fish are often grilled simply and served with lemon and salt, and this technique works well with all wreck fish.

Porgies are best done in this Mediterranean style. The fish is a good stand-in for the gilt-head bream, one of that region's most sought-after fish. I prefer porgies grilled whole over charcoal or fruit wood, but I also like them dredged in chickpea flour and crispy-fried. The chickpea flour adds a nice earthy note.

All of these fish are good raw in homemade sushi, but make sure to freeze them for a few days (after gutting and scaling) to kill any possible parasites. You will find rockfish and black sea bass sold as "suzuki" in sushi bars. These fish are also excellent "cooked" by citrus in seviche or chopped into a *tartare*.

Being lean, they all freeze well, too. I've eaten rockfish that had been vacuum-sealed for a year and was still edible, although I would not recommend storing them longer than 6 months.

RECIPES

Sicilian Grilled Fish with Oregano Oil

This is a simple recipe from Sicily for a well-marinated grilled fish. Use whole fish like porgies, rock cod, or black sea bass that have been scaled and gutted. If you are inland, do this with largemouth or smallmouth bass, freshwater drum, trout, or walleyes.

You must use fresh oregano here. It is easy to find in supermarkets, or you can grow it yourself. If you want to serve the fish with the marinade, make a second batch. I don't like reusing marinades unless they've been cooked first (it's a germ thing), and cooking this one would destroy the flavors.

Start with a scaled and gutted fish that has had the gills cut out. Slash the fish to the bone perpendicular to the spine, on both sides, every 3 inches or so. This helps it cook evenly. If you don't do this, the thick part of the fish will still be raw when the tail end is overcooked.

Don't forget the cheeks of the fish, which are my favorite part. They will be orbs of yummy meat right under each eye. And the tails, if not burnt black, are crunchy and nutty tasting. You can also pick at the meat between the ribs, as well as in the belly. Eating a whole fish makes for a primal, deeply satisfying meal. It may not be dainty, but it sure is good.

Serves 2 (can be doubled)

1 teaspoon salt

1 teaspoon freshly ground black pepper

⅓ cup olive oil

3 cloves garlic, chopped

5–6 tablespoons chopped fresh oregano

1–2 whole fish, 12–15-inch long, scaled, gutted and slashed vertically
   every 3 inches

Vegetable oil

Lemon wedges

Put the salt, pepper, olive oil, garlic, and oregano in a blender and puree. Pour the marinade in a resealable plastic bag and put the fish inside. Massage the marinade over the fish so all the pieces are well covered. Seal the bag and put it in the fridge for at least 2 hours, or up to 10 hours.

Preheat the grill to a medium heat. A good test of how hot it should be is to hold your hand about 6 inches over the grate: If you can just barely hold your hand there without it burning, the heat is perfect. If you can't, the grill is too hot. If you can keep your hand there for several seconds, it's too cool. Clean the grates well. Using tongs, grab a crumpled piece of paper towel, dip it into some vegetable oil, and wipe down the grill grates.

Take the fish out of the marinade and shake off any excess. Lay the fish down on the grill with the tail facing farthest away from the heat. It will cook much faster than the head end, even with the slashes you made. It is very important that you do not grill fish over high heat. They will burn to a crisp on the outside before the center is cooked through. Steady medium heat is what you want.

Grill them for 4 to 7 minutes, depending on how thick the pieces are. You want a good char, with a little blackening, but keep an eye on the fish for flare-ups. If you're getting lots of flare-ups, turn the heat down. Don't move the fish just yet. While the fish is cooking, baste once with the marinade.

Gently lift the fish up with tongs or a spatula and flip. Grill for another 2 to 4 minutes. Baste one more time.

Serve with lemon wedges and some freshly cracked black pepper.

SICHUAN SWEET AND SOUR CRISPY FISH

One of the great Chinese restaurant dishes is a whole fish crispy-fried and then served with sweet-and-sour sauce. It is a dramatic presentation, and the combination of sweet-sour-hot-savory can't be beat. I developed a home version of the recipe, and it is as good as any restaurant version. Use small whole fish that have been scaled and gutted. It is traditional to leave the head on, but you can remove it if you like. I prefer to use Pacific rock cod, black sea bass, perch, porgies, or any type of bass— largemouth, white, smallmouth, spotted—for this recipe.

Serves 2–4 (depending on the size of the fish)

FISH AND MARINADE

2 whole rockfish or other pan-size fish, scaled and gutted

3 scallions, chopped

1-inch piece ginger, peeled and finely chopped

1 tablespoon Chinese cooking wine or Japanese mirin

1 tablespoon soy sauce

1 teaspoon freshly ground black pepper

SAUCE

5 tablespoons tomato sauce or ketchup (I use pureed tomatoes)

5 tablespoons water

3 tablespoons sugar

1 tablespoon Chinese cooking wine (or Japanese mirin)

1 tablespoon soy sauce

1½ teaspoons cornstarch

VEGETABLES

3-inch piece ginger, peeled

½ medium onion

3 cloves garlic

4 cups peanut or vegetable oil

2 cups flour

½ finely chopped habanero chile pepper, or 1–2 Thai chile peppers,
   or 1 serrano chile pepper (wear plastic gloves when handling)

GARNISH

1 tablespoon finely chopped cilantro

1 tablespoon finely chopped scallions or chives

TO MAKE THE FISH AND MARINADE: Cut off the fins of each fish with
kitchen shears or scissors, and cut out the gills of the fish, if they are still attached.
Make three slices parallel to the ribs along each side of the fish, evenly spaced up and
down its length. If you have a long fish, make four slices. Rinse the fish under cold
water and pat dry.

Mix the scallions, ginger, wine, soy sauce, and black pepper together and pour the
mixture into a glass or plastic container or a resealable plastic bag. Place the fish in
the container and make sure the marinade surrounds the fish. Let this sit in the
fridge for 30 minutes to 2 hours.

TO MAKE THE SAUCE: In a medium bowl, mix the tomato sauce, water, sugar,
wine, soy sauce, and cornstarch. Stir vigorously to combine. Set aside.

TO MAKE THE VEGETABLES: Julienne the ginger. (The 3-inch size is just a
guideline, so the piece of ginger can be a bit larger or smaller.) Cut the ginger into a
rectangle, then slice it into thin rectangles about ⅛-inch thick. Slice these rectangles
into very thin strips, as thin as you can make them.

Slice the onion into very thin half moons. Slice the garlic as thin as you can along the long side of the clove, to make long pieces.

To prepare the dish, pour the oil into a wok and turn the heat to medium. If you do not have a wok, use the largest, deepest skillet you have. A wok really matters here, as its shape prevents the tail fin from burning to a crisp. Take the fish out of the fridge.

Check the oil temperature. You want it to be about 300° to 325°F. If you do not have a thermometer (you should buy one!), the oil is ready when a little flour sprinkled into the oil sizzles immediately. You are probably going to have room to cook only one fish at a time. If so, turn the oven on to Warm.

Remove the fish from the marinade and dredge in flour. Shake off the excess, and when the oil is hot enough, slip the fish one at a time into the oil. Fry the fish for at least 5 minutes per side. You want it to be golden brown. With 300°F oil, fry a 1-pound fish for 8 minutes on the first side, 5 minutes on the other side. Larger fish will need more time.

When the first fish is done, remove it to a plate and put the plate in the warm oven. Fry the second fish the same way as the first.

Once the fish are cooked, ladle out all but about ¼ cup of the oil from the wok. Toss in the chile peppers and the prepared ginger, onion, and garlic. Cook over high heat, stirring frequently, for 2 to 3 minutes. Add the reserved sauce and stir well to combine. Bring this to a rapid boil, stirring constantly. Cook for 2 to 3 minutes.

To serve, pour some sauce on a plate, place the fish on top of it, and garnish with the cilantro and scallions. This dish goes best with simple steamed white rice.

13

THE MISFITS OF AMERICA'S OCEANS, PONDS, AND RIVERS

Up to now, I've dealt mostly with fish prized to some extent or another by most people who cast a line, set a trap, or drag a rake through the sand. These fish are all fine creatures. I love all fish—even salmon, which has become the boneless, skinless chicken breast of the aquatic world. But I love my misfits most. Eels, odd bony fishes that lurk in rivers, hideous spiny sea robins, tiny fishlings that school near boat docks. These are my children. Part of it is my love of the underdog, a common American trait. Part of it is because most of my angling brethren haven't a clue about these creatures, and understanding how to properly cook them has been knowledge I have protected closely. Until now.

This chapter is about the oddities you might find on the end of your line or sitting unwanted in the corner of larger fish markets. All are more than edible, and most offer some special delight if you know what to look for or how to prepare them. A few are commonly eaten among certain ethnic groups here in America, and it is from generous fellow anglers—Chinese, Portuguese, African American—that I learned most of what I know about these fish.

I sometimes use the term "white people's fish" to mean large boneless, skinless fillets of easy-to-love fishes like tuna, bass, salmon, or flounder. I get bored with these fish and often find myself cruising ethnic markets in search of saltier treats. I'll take a bowl of whitebait, a grilled eel, or skate wings in a delicate broth over a pretty square of unrecognizable fillet any day. And don't even get me started on tilapia, the *Soylent Green* of fish. . . .

What follows are the stories of how I discovered my favorite misfits and what to do when you encounter them.

THE OYSTER TOAD

It is fitting that the weirdest of my misfit clan was the first shown to me by a fellow angler. I will never forget the morning. I was in high school, and I had driven down to Point Pleasant, New Jersey, to fish for fluke off the party boat *Norma K III*. I set up in the waist of the boat next to an old black dude. He wore a well-loved army jacket, and his beard stubble was gray. Next to his tackle box was a lunch box like the ones you see construction workers carry in cartoons. He said "hey," and I said "hey" back. We both set our poles up on the rail.

Within a few minutes, he set up a simple bottom fishing rig, just a sinker and a bait hook, threaded a big piece of sea clam on it, and flicked it into the water. We hadn't even left dock yet.

"What are you doing?" I asked.

"Fishing for oyster toads," he said.

"What the hell is an oyster toad?" He said if I was lucky, he'd show me in a few minutes. Sure enough, his rod jerked, and he reeled in what looked like something from a horror movie. All head, spiny, mud brown with some yellow on the body, bulging eyes, and the biggest, nastiest set of jaws I'd ever seen. "That's an oyster toad," he said.

The fish grunted and writhed back and forth on the deck. My new friend grabbed a pair of needle-nose pliers and twisted the hook free. "Watch these jaws. They'll take your finger off."

"Well, what do you do with it now that you have it?" I asked. He looked at me sideways, as if I'd asked what to do with the flounder we were all about to catch. "Eat 'em, of course. Look, I'll show you." The old man produced a fillet knife from his belt and stuck the oyster toad in the back of the head, killing it. He then used the point to work around the cheeks of the ugly little fish, producing an orb of snow-white flesh nearly the size of a Ping-Pong ball. "Old oyster toad here eats oysters. He cracks the shells with these muscles. I catch all I can, and my wife fries 'em up for me."

"Holy shit! Look at the size of that cheek meat!" I'd eaten cod cheeks before, but to get one that size, the codfish would need to be more than 2 feet long. This oyster toad was maybe 8 inches long.

"Tails are pretty good, too," he said, and cast his line back in the water. He offered me some sea clams, too, and I fished alongside him for the 45 minutes or so before we headed out to catch fluke. Sadly, I can no longer remember his name, but I did see him from time to time after that first meeting, and we always sat next to each other and caught oyster toads before heading out for other fish.

Looking back, I probably should not have eaten so many oyster toads off the dock in Point Pleasant. Oyster toadfish, also known as oyster crackers, can live in horribly polluted water, so avoid fishing for them in crowded marinas. Oyster toads rarely grow larger than a foot, and most I caught were between 6 and 10 inches. They are disgusting-looking fish. No scales and coated in slime, they are very similar to their larger cousins, the monkfish. Fillet their little tails and remove the skin, which is nasty.

The best parts are those giant cheek muscles. Don't expect to feed a crowd on oyster toads, but they are a good little dinner for two or an appetizer. I've never caught more than five at one time, and although there was no limit on them when I fished New York and New Jersey, now they must be 10 inches long and you can only keep three. To remove the cheek, work the point of your fillet knife all around the meat, angling it the way you

cut the top off a pumpkin. Carefully slice off the little patch of skin attached to the cheek.

I have never done anything with oyster toads but fry them. Fry them in a good beer batter or as a tempura.

REDHORSES, DRUMS, AND GIANT MINNOWS

I am not a natural freshwater angler. I grew up so close to the Atlantic I never saw the point in freshwater fishing. I also grew up with no one telling me this fish was good to eat and that one was not. I was free to make my own decisions. So when I finally began freshwater fishing as an adult, I was a clean slate.

The Rappahannock was the closest river to me at the time. Most anglers don't bother to fish it until the herring begin their run in late March, but I wanted to know what was in the river in winter, when the waters run high from rain and snow and were at their coldest. So I'd fish a few spots with worms or lures day after day. And day after day I caught nothing. Maybe there wasn't anything here, I thought. Maybe the other anglers were right.

Then one day I caught a fish. It was a nice-looking fish, too, about a foot long, silver, with big scales and reddish fins. Looked like it should be tasty, so I kept it. I paged through my guidebooks and figured it was a dace. The fish, while pretty, had a suckerlike mouth. I suspected it was a kind of carp, which meant it would have an extra set of bones. I was right. I dusted the fish fillets with flour and fried them simply. The meat was white, firm, and clean tasting, although I did need to pick through the extra bones.

Next day at work, I asked my friend Rusty, who was an old hand at fishing the Rappahannock, what the heck it was. I described the fish, and he said it was probably a sucker or a redhorse. "Most people don't eat those," he said. It tasted just fine by me, so I returned to the same spot once a week through the rest of the winter and caught a dozen more of these fish. After more checking through my guidebooks, I determined they were indeed redhorse, which are related to carp. Which species of redhorse it was I still have no idea. The fish disappeared once the water warmed up. Not once did I catch one after May or before October.

Later, when I moved to Minnesota, I lived just a short drive from the St. Croix River. I found redhorse there. Carp, too. Again I encountered the fish snobs. "Trash fish. You going to actually eat those? They're poisonous, aren't they?" No, they're not. In fact, redhorse and their cousins the suckers can only live in clean water, and biologists consider them indicators of whether a body of water is healthy or not. Carp can live in anything, but suckers die in polluted water. The two fish may look alike, but they're not.

Another day on the St. Croix River, I was fishing with a friend when I caught what looked like the croakers and spot I caught by the cooler-load in the Chesapeake Bay. Croakers and spot are smallish silvery fish ranging from 6 inches to 2 feet long with hard, bony heads and downward-turned mouths. They will actually croak when you catch them, making a sound like "er er er er er."

"Hey, Chris, what the hell is a croaker doing in the St. Croix?"

"Oh, that's just a freshwater drum." We were fishing for walleye, so he was not enthused. I kept it anyway, and Chris humored me. I've learned that if a fish looks similar to one I'd eaten before, there's a good chance it'll taste similar, too. This holds true for freshwater drum: Drum, croakers, and spot are all firm, with white meat that's loaded with delicious oil that, unfortunately, can go rancid fast. Freshwater drum are also known as sheepshead, not to be confused with a striped variety of porgy living off New York and New Jersey, or with another fish that lives in kelp beds off the coast of California—both of which are also called sheepshead. Sigh.

Unlike the suckers, carp, and redhorses, these freshwater drum were common, easy to catch—simple night crawlers are all you need—and did not have that extra set of bones that so bedevils most American anglers. They are best caught in the warmer months, meaning you need not don your parka to catch them. For a freshwater fish, drum are high in healthy omega-3 fatty acids.

Freshwater drum average 2 pounds and can reportedly grow beyond 50 pounds, although any fish larger than 10 pounds is probably a big breeding female and ought to be let go if it hasn't swallowed the hook. Freshwater drum live in schools and prefer open water and slower, more open channels. Like their Atlantic cousins the croakers and spot, they cruise around eating shellfish and crustaceans along grassy underwater plains. It is rare to catch just one. Their only drawback is they don't freeze very well; they turn mushy. You can freeze freshwater drum for a month or so, but that's about it.

My home is now near the Sacramento River. Soon after I moved here, I learned about a mysterious fish called the Sacramento pikeminnow, the largest minnow in the world, lurking in the depths and capable of swallowing toddlers and stray pets. Okay, maybe that is an exaggeration, but I had heard that these "minnows" could top 3 feet long. That's one big minnow.

I have never targeted pikeminnows specifically, largely because they are long-lived, voracious predators living in a compromised river system. What this means is that pikeminnows accumulate biological mercury at higher levels than any other freshwater fish in California. Now, I am neither a child nor a pregnant woman, so I am not overly concerned about eating pikeminnow. But I would not recommend that the very young or the pregnant or nursing eat too many of them. That said, eating one now and again will not hurt you.

Pikeminnow is like a combination of the redhorse and the freshwater drum: It has a redhorse's extra set of bones and is oily like the drum. Seeing the sheen on my cutting board, I immediately decided to smoke the pikeminnow the same way I smoke shad, mackerel, or herring. So if you ever catch one—they live only in large western rivers—follow my recipe for smoked shad in Chapter 11.

EELS AND FRIENDS

Eels are not snakes, just odd-looking fish. Still, I've seen grown men freak out after hauling up a conger eel, which is actually a fish called a cusk or ocean pout. They couldn't grab their knives fast enough to cut the line. It's odd, actually. Most people hate these fish because of what they look like, not because of how they taste. Both cusk and eels have very firm, very white meat. Eel is among my favorite fish.

To be sure, lots of people eat eels. The British have their jellied eel, which I happen to find appalling, the Italians smoke them for their Christmas Eve Feast of the Seven Fishes, and nearly anyone who has ever eaten sushi has eaten the Japanese barbecued eel *unagi*. Spaniards love baby eels so much that a dish of *anguillas* can cost a small fortune. The Dutch are also big eel eaters, and there has always been a little cottage commercial eel fishery in the eastern United States.

I ate a lot of smoked eels when I lived on Long Island—it's a great bar snack—but the first one I found on the end of my line was in Virginia. It fought like a catfish or a white bass, but as I reeled it in closer to the riverbank, there it was: a 2-foot-long, olive drab–colored eel. I then made a fatal mistake: I netted it. If you should ever catch an eel, by all means keep it, but under no circumstances should you try to net it, unless you have a stiff wire net on hand. Eels wriggle, as everyone knows, and they are slimy. That combination turns a netted eel into a squirming ball covered in snot. Your only recourse is to cut the net free and drop bits of it, along with the eel, into your bucket. So next time you catch one, lift it onto the boat or onshore with one smooth swing of the rod. If it falls off and back into the water, you were apparently not meant to catch that eel.

Know, too, that eels won't die in your bucket. They can live for very long periods out of the water, so you will most definitely have a live eel to deal with when you come home from the river. The best way to kill them is to dump salt on them—lots and lots of salt—and then pour in just enough water to cover them. The salinity kills the eel and strips it of its protective slime layer, which is a big bonus.

So you have a relatively slime-free dead eel. Now what? One last bit of gruesomeness. The best way to skin an eel, which has no scales, is to nail its head to a piece of wood, then slice the skin in a circle around the back of its head. Using a pair of pliers, grab the edge of the skin firmly and wrench it back toward the tail. It should come off all in one piece or, at worst, two pieces. Do you need to do all this? No, but I am not a fan of eel skin, as it never seems to crisp up very well and has a gelatinous underside where it meets the meat. Some people just chunk the eel and cook it that way. I prefer my eel skinned.

You then gut the eel and either fillet it off the backbone or chunk it. I chunk little ones and fillet big ones.

How do you cook an eel? Any way you'd like, really. Eels are fatty, white, very firm, and mild flavored. If I could get them more often, I'd eat eel every week. They are great batter-fried (but what isn't?) and even better barbecued or grilled. Their firmness holds up really well in fish soups, too. Maybe put them in bouillabaisse.

Eel does not freeze too well, however; the fat can go rancid even in a freezer. I would recommend vacuum-sealing them and keeping frozen eel no more than a month or two.

The cusk or ocean pout is a solitary, eel-like fish that lives among cod, pollock, and haddock. They are ugly and blotchy, and typically run about 5 pounds, and their fillets are long, skinny, and white. Very few people ate them when I fished off Long Island and New Jersey, but I started keeping cusk when the cod fishing began to drop off in the late 1980s. They're just like the more common ling, which is a cousin, although cusk are larger, leaner, and less sweet. Apparently lots of us have eaten cusk without knowing it, as it is one of the codlike fishes that go into fish sticks and other processed fish foods. They have been fished so hard, however, that scientists are worried about their population status. So should you keep a cusk if you catch it? Sure, but if you catch two, you might want to let the other one back into the water.

A cusk is a good candidate for poaching, especially oil poaching. It dries out easily, so baking or broiling is out. It is pretty firm, so you can put it in soups, and of course it is good fried. Cusk freezes well for up to 6 months.

FLYING GARGOYLES

"Another goddamn sea robin!" If I had a quarter for every time I've heard that expletive, I'd have enough to buy a boat. Such a sweet name, *sea robin*. You'd think this fish would be pretty and birdlike. Well, sea robins are red. And they do have "wings," really large, wide pectoral fins. And they do actually "sing," although instead of a lovely tune it's more like "er, er, er, er, er." In fact, they sound a lot like croakers or drum.

Sea robins won't win any aquatic beauty contests anytime soon. Big head, bulging eyes. Lots of spines. They look like gargoyles. And those pectoral fins—they even have spiny "legs" in front of those fins they use to walk along the bottom. You could actually use the fins as a fan on a hot day.

Sea robins swim in the same water as fluke, also known as summer flounder, and they range from Florida to Maine. They like sandy bottoms and use those big wings to probe the bottom, looking for shellfish. They adore the combination of cut squid and minnow that most fluke anglers use. And, as sea robins are far more numerous than fluke, catching them while fluking is a matter of course.

I was taught as a little boy to throw them back. No one we knew ate them. But I always saw the Asians keep them—and even ask other anglers for theirs. At first, I thought these people were crazy, that they must have had some weird Asian tastebuds impervious to this ugly fish. But as I reached college age, I decided to keep one and fillet it like any other fish. I sautéed it simply in butter and ate it with salt. Then I realized I had been the crazy one all these years.

As fluke populations fell, with minimum size limits reaching an astoundingly large 21 inches (it was 12 inches when I was a boy), more and more anglers began keeping sea robins, which can grow to 5 pounds. Normal robins are only about 1 to 2 pounds, however. Now you can search for "sea robin recipes" online and find lots of examples. So maybe this fish is no longer an oddity.

Regardless, sea robin is firm, white, lean, and a little sweet, reminiscent of scallops. A similar fish is a required ingredient in the famous French soup bouillabaisse and, like most fish, sea robin is good breaded and fried. I've never heard of anyone eating it raw, but I have found no evidence that it is regularly parasitized the way drums and many fish are, so you could give it a go as *crudo* or sushi.

The downside to sea robins is their yield, which is low. These fish have huge heads and wide rib cages, so you will get twice as much meat on a 2-pound flounder as you will on a 2-pound sea robin. That said, sea robin carcasses are good for making fish stock, so they'll get some use. Remember to cut out the gills of any fish you use for stock, as the gills will make the stock cloudy and bitter.

Sea robins will last a good week in the fridge, kept over ice, and the meat freezes well for up to 6 months, especially when vacuum-sealed. All of this also applies to a Pacific cousin of the sea robin, the cabezon. Oddly, Pacific anglers don't seem to be put off by the cabezon's hideous appearance, and it is considered a fine food fish from British Columbia to San Diego.

BLOWFISH

When I was just starting out as a reporter, I struggled to make enough money to pay for rent, gasoline, beer, and the other necessities of life. Groceries often got the short end of the stick in this equation, but unlike my ramen noodle–eating friends, I was a fisherman and a good one at that.

One spring evening after work, I was in Cavanaugh's, my neighborhood bar, when the talk turned to fishing. I'd been on a hot streak lately, having caught fish every day for nearly a month. The mackerel season had just ended, and winter flounder, snapper bluefish, and crabs were all on tap. I'd even caught a few striped bass and weakfish. I was eating like a king, with fried fish, grilled fish, fish in tomato sauce, fish cakes, and so on every day. "I bet I can go the whole summer without getting skunked," I told my friends.

The bet was on. If I failed, I owed my friends beer for a week, and as they were epic drinkers, this was no small wager. I did not fish every day—that's not what the bet was; the bet was that when I did fish, I would always come home with something. Privately, I wondered whether I could eat nothing but seafood until Labor Day. This would save a lot of money. Money for more beer at Cavanaugh's. Fishing went well for more than a month, until I hit the inevitable rough patch. Nothing was biting, and the crabs were nowhere to be found. I was getting desperate when I noticed that there were swarms of minnows and shiners milling about behind me, on the marina side of the dock I fished from. After several failed attempts, I scooped up a few shiners and used them to bait the smallest hooks I had in my tackle box.

Within minutes, I almost leapt for joy—a tug on my line! I reeled it in, and on the end was a blowfish, looking as surprised at being caught as I probably looked having landed it. Weren't they poisonous? I'd heard the Japanese ate them as sushi and died from it on occasion. But then I also remembered Asian anglers catching and keeping puffer fish right next to me at this very dock some months ago. I also dimly thought I'd seen puffers sold in the local fish market.

"Sorry, man," I said to this blowfish. "A bet's a bet."

Into the bucket he went, and before nightfall, so did five of his closest friends. Or enemies. Not sure what, exactly, their relationship was to each other. I only know that blowfish travel in schools.

On my way home, I swung by the fish market and asked the fishmonger what to do with these blowfish. He was a good guy and told me that you only eat the skinless tails of puffers, and you want to avoid the fish's liver, which is the most poisonous part. The fishmonger also said that the Japanese puffer was a different fish, way more poisonous than these. He called them "chicken of the sea" and told me to batter-fry them.

I did, and man, were they good! There is only one bone to deal with, so you have a tail with meat on it and a central bone. A dressed puffer is nature's fish stick. It really does taste like chicken. I once ate 15 of them in one sitting, which was a little too much: I got enough toxin to make my mouth a little numb but suffered no other effects. Keep them as an appetizer, not a main course.

Other than batter-frying, a great way to serve puffer fish is to slow barbecue them, teriyaki style. Their dense texture makes them a dead ringer for chicken teriyaki—and who doesn't like chicken teriyaki?

Keep in mind this is the puffer fish that lives in the North Atlantic. There are lots of different species of blowfish, and most are really toxic. But if you live from North Carolina on up to Maine and catch a puffer, go for it.

The toxin concentrates in the liver, skin, and organs of the fish, so you want as little contact with them as possible. To clean a blowfish:

1. Put the fish belly down on a board, and take your knife and cut down behind the head. Do not cut all the way through, but sever the backbone. Leave the belly skin attached.

2. Flip the blowfish over and anchor its back on the board by holding it down firmly. Alternately, grip the backbone with a pair of pliers. Grab the head, which will still be attached to that belly skin, and yank it back toward the tail. This should remove the head, organs, and skin all in one motion. It leaves the tail, one fin, and the meat.

3. Rinse the meat well and cook away! Blowfish go bad quickly, so eat within a day or two of catching them.

SKATES AND SHARKS

Sometimes I feel the need to be in a support group for shark eaters, given the abuse I've taken for it over the years. Of all the dirty looks I get for eating weird fish, the ones I get for keeping sharks are the worst.

I catch Cain not from other anglers, but from ill-informed conservationists. I hear the chorus of "How can you eat sharks when they're all endangered?" whenever I mention sharks as food. Well, no shark commonly eaten for food is endangered, although several are under heavy fishing pressure. But still, if you happen to catch one of these by hook and line, go ahead and keep and eat it. It's commercial fishing that is responsible for damaging the populations of sharks, skates, and rays, not recreational angling. The demand for shark fin soup is especially abhorrent. Asian fishermen in this trade slice off the shark's fins and toss the still-living shark back into the ocean, allowing it to spin helplessly into the depths where it is killed by pressure or eaten by other fish. Shark fin soup made from a leopard shark you happened to catch in the San Francisco Bay is no problem, but I view it as a moral crime to buy commercially harvested shark fins. I won't buy shark or skate—I don't want to support a commercial fishery on them—but I will eat them if I catch them. A contradiction? Maybe.

Why all this fuss about sharks, skates, and rays? They are all prone to population crashes because they grow and reproduce slowly. The same can be said for rock cod and many other deepwater fish, by the way. This slow rate of growth also means their meat is dense and, properly prepared, flavorful.

Catching sharks happens as a matter of course. I rarely target sharks or skates, but you'll catch them periodically while fishing for flounder, halibut, or cod. No special tackle or gear or bait is needed; they'll bite on anything. If you really want to catch sharks, though, use a steel leader that connects the hook and bait from the main fishing line. Otherwise, the shark will bite through the line more often than not.

When I do specifically fish for sharks, it can be thrilling. I've run into huge schools of dogfish (a small shark) in the North Atlantic, caught leopard sharks within sight of the Transamerica Building in San Francisco, and hooked mako sharks as large as a man off the coast of New Jersey. Mako was considered a poor man's swordfish when I was growing up, but I like it better.

Most sharks are edible, but the most common ones caught and eaten in North America are the various species of dogfish—they live on both coasts—as well as leopard sharks in California, soupfin sharks all across the West Coast, and thresher and mako sharks, which can be found in both the Atlantic and the southern Pacific Oceans. Makos and threshers tend to live far offshore, however, so few anglers encounter them accidentally.

Skates are wide and flat, with a long tail trailing behind them. In general, skates have thicker, fleshy tails, and rays have narrow, whiplike tails. All skates are edible. Rays can be eaten, but the meat of most species is full of ammonia (sharks, skates, and rays excrete their urine through their skin), so I avoid eating them.

Once landed, process skates and sharks immediately. Kill them with a knife between their eyes or a thump with a club, then slice off their "wings" as close to the body as you can. Rinse these with seawater and put them on ice. With sharks, bleed them immediately by slicing until you hit the backbone just in front of the tail and by slicing the gills. Let them bleed out and then gut them right on the boat if you can. The guts are great chum to attract other fish. The reason for this special handling is because of that ammonia. Improperly processed shark can stink of urea, which is most definitely not good eats.

To fillet a shark, start by slicing off the top fins. If you are into shark fin soup, save them. Watch out for East Coast spiny dogfish, which you will recognize by a stout spine in front of its dorsal fin. Don't get spiked, or it'll hurt like the devil and will probably get infected. Use your fillet knife to slice off the top strip of the shark. Do the same on the bottom (no spines there).

Now fillet the shark as you would any other fish. Remember that they make boots out of shark skin, so it'll be tough. You can slice off the skin like you would on a normal fish, or you can peel it off with pliers the way you do an eel's skin, and then fillet off the meat. I fillet off the meat and then remove the skin like I do with a normal fish. I find this easier than the peeling method. Once the skin is off and you have two rather long, skinless fillets, soak them in milk or salted water overnight before eating. This rids the meat of any stray ammonia. Really fresh shark might not need this step. Use your nose as your guide.

As with many things in this chapter, dogfish and leopard shark are at their best fried, preferably in beer batter. In fact, dogfish is the primary fish for fish and chips in some parts of Britain.

Skate requires slightly different handling. Small skates need only be skinned and soaked like sharks before eating, but keep in mind there is a tough line of cartilage separating the top and bottom of the wing. In small skates and rays, you just eat around it. In larger skates, those with wings an inch thick at the base or wider, you will want to fillet off the meat from the cartilage. Do this with your fillet knife. Just run it along the "bone" gently, filleting the meat off the cartilage. The top fillet will be thicker than the bottom fillet.

Skate wings are delicate in flavor and unique in that the muscle runs in lines, which looks like wide-wale corduroy. This also makes handling the fillets tricky. It is traditional to age skate wings for up to 48 hours before serving, as this firms them up. Skate is one of the few fish that benefit from aging.

The classic way to prepare skate wings is dusted in flour and sautéed in brown butter, then served with capers and lemon juice. This dish is a linchpin of French haute cuisine, and as I rarely catch more than a few skates a year, I see no real reason to stray from it with any other recipe. Skate also can be eaten raw like seviche, and at least one restaurant in the San Francisco area strips the strands of the skate wing apart and serves them as if they were thick pasta, which I think is pretty cool.

RECIPES

SPANISH SHARK WITH TOMATOES AND PINE NUTS

This is a knockout recipe. Calvin Schwabe, in his classic book *Unmentionable Cuisine*, writes about a dish called *Tiburón con pasas y piñones*. He provided no real recipe, just ingredients. So I made it up from there. The dish Schwabe describes has both pine nuts and raisins in it. I don't much like raisins, so I left them out. You could put in 2 tablespoons if you'd like.

Shark is a firm, white fish. I used leopard shark, which I caught in San Francisco Bay, but you could also use dogfish or any small shark. This recipe would work just fine with sturgeon, tilefish, white sea bass, tautog, halibut—really any very firm, white fish you can slice into chunks.

Have everything prepared before you start this dish, as it comes together fast. Serve with saffron rice, potatoes, or just crusty bread.

Serves 2 (can be doubled)

12 ounces skinless shark fillets (or other firm white fish)

Salt

¼ cup pine nuts

3 tablespoons olive oil

Flour

2–3 cloves garlic, slivered

3–4 Roma or other paste tomatoes, seeded and finely chopped

Freshly ground black pepper

2 tablespoons white wine or water

2 teaspoons Spanish smoked paprika

¼ cup chopped parsley

Cut the shark or other fish fillets into cubes about 1 inch across. Salt well and set aside.

Put a large skillet over medium heat and add the pine nuts. Toast them well. Do not walk away from the stove, because pine nuts can burn in a hurry. Toss the pan frequently to toast the nuts on all sides and to check if any are burning. Once even a few nuts have turned dark brown, turn off the heat and pour the nuts into a bowl. Set aside.

Wipe the pan with a paper towel and add the oil. Turn the heat to medium-high.

Dust the shark in the flour and cook in the oil. I cook two of the four sides well, for 2 to 3 minutes per side, and then just "kiss" the other sides to lightly brown them. Set the cooked shark on a paper towel to drain.

Add the garlic and pine nuts to the pan and cook, stirring frequently. Add a little more olive oil if the fish soaked up too much. The second you see the garlic brown, in 1 to 2 minutes, add the chopped tomatoes and toss to combine. Grind some pepper over everything.

Add the wine or water and scrape up any stuck-on bits from the bottom of the pan with a wooden spoon.

Sprinkle a little salt over the tomatoes, then add the fish back to the pan. Sprinkle with the paprika and parsley and toss to combine. Cook for only another minute or so, just to coat everything evenly. It is very important not to cook the tomatoes so much they break down. Just a couple of minutes are all they need.

Serve at once. I'd recommend a nice white wine, maybe a Torrontes or an Albariño.

BLOWFISH TERIYAKI

Modern teriyakis are often too sweet, and while you need the sugar to help caramelize the sauce, too much is cloying. Mirin is readily available in most supermarkets. This is a very simple recipe that takes very little time to prepare, and you can use the sauce on other fish. I'd recommend yellowtail, tuna, swordfish, mackerel, striped bass, bluefish, catfish, or cobia.

Serves 4

> Salt
>
> 1½ pounds blowfish tails (or other fish)
>
> 4 tablespoons sake
>
> 4 tablespoons mirin (a Japanese sweet wine)
>
> 4 tablespoons soy sauce
>
> 1 heaping teaspoon sugar
>
> 2 tablespoons vegetable oil (peanut is best)

Salt the fish tails well and set aside at room temperature for 15 to 25 minutes.

In a small pot, bring the sake, mirin, and soy sauce to a boil. Stir in the sugar. Boil until reduced by half. Turn off the heat and set aside.

Get a grill hot. Wood fire works best, followed by charcoal, a gas grill, or broiler.

Coat the fish with the vegetable oil, then paint the teriyaki sauce on the tails. Grill them over medium heat for 5 minutes, turning them after 3 minutes. Blowfish is very dense and needs to be cooked gently to heat the center without overcooking the outer edges. Spoon some more sauce on the tails and cook for another 3 minutes, turning often.

Remove from the grill. Before serving, bathe the tails in the pot with the remaining teriyaki glaze. Turn the heat to medium and gently shake the pan so it doesn't stick. Cook for 1 minute.

Serve immediately with steamed rice and a salad.

PART III

HUNTING FOR FOOD AND FULFILLMENT

14

WHY HUNT?

For most people, foraging for wild plants poses no moral problem. Some, mostly vegetarians, have a tough time with fishing, but there are 30 million anglers in the United States. Hunting, however, is another story. Let's face it: If you are not a hunter, and you did not grow up around hunters, the pursuit can seem alien. The hunting world is largely male, rural, agrarian, white, and conservative. If that's not you, gaining access to this world can seem impossibly daunting. First off, you will need to become comfortable with guns—no small thing for many. You will need to take a hunter safety course, which in some states can take more than a day. For the most part, unlike fishing, you can't just walk into a sporting goods store and buy a hunting license. Once you do have the license, then you need to purchase the right tags and stamps, which can seem bewildering (the extras all help raise money for habitat restoration, so they're for a good cause). There is equipment to buy, notably a gun or bow. Finally, you need to find a place to hunt, either public or private, or you need to work with an outfitter and a guide.

What follows are chapters intended to introduce you to the world of the hunt, including a primer on hunting a particular set of game animals, proper care of the meat, and how to break the animals down into usable portions, as well as recipes both simple and complex. This is the payoff. This is why you go through all the prep work to be a safe and competent hunter. To me, there is nothing more satisfying than possessing the skills to venture into the field and find, kill, and clean a game animal—and then to come home and portion it out yourself and put a meal made with that animal on the table for your family. It's a powerful, addictive feeling, knowing you've done it all yourself. No butchers, no supermarkets, no one telling you what you can and cannot do. While it is true you can substitute commercially available game meats or even domestic meats for the wild game recipes in these chapters, it is my hope that this section of the book will spark into action those of you who've always thought about hunting but had no idea where to begin.

I won't sugarcoat it: Hunting is a helluva lot more work than buying a 1-day fishing license and stepping aboard a party boat on a whim. But the rewards are worth it. After several years as novice hunters, Holly and I have become proficient enough that—with the exception of pork fat for sausages, and whole lambs and goats for parties—we have not bought more than a few stray pounds of meat for our home in years. We eat pheasants and wild boar and venison. I find I'm losing my taste for beef these days. It seems so fatty, so coarse. Wild meat is leaner, denser, and more flavorful than almost any domestic meat. This means you need less to feel full.

Hunting your own meat changes your eating habits in other ways. Where before you might have just eaten steaks or chicken breasts or pork loin, with hunted game you learn how to cook the rest of the animal, including the offal. I've become skilled at cooking the various bits in this "fifth quarter" of the animal, largely because I've not wanted to waste a venison heart, a rabbit kidney, or a goose gizzard. As you get better at cooking the less glamorous cuts, you develop an appreciation for things like braised shanks or heart cutlets or the little flank steaks you can get off a deer. Anyone can sear a tenderloin. You become a serious cook when you can pull off elk shank osso buco or braised wild turkey legs.

But hunting is more than a pursuit of free-range meat. Hunting has given us a sense of self-sufficiency, a sense of honesty, and a clear-eyed understanding of exactly where our meat comes from. No factory farms, no hormones, antibiotics, and, arguably, no cruelty. Every animal we kill had been living the life God intended until it met us that one fateful day. We practice our marksmanship all year long to do our best to make sure that, when the day comes, the animal dies quickly and cleanly. I always put myself in the animal's position: Would I want to go out like that? It's why those less-than-perfect shots, which are an unfortunate part of this pursuit, can gnaw at me for months afterward.

Hunting has been the primary pursuit of humans for more than a million years. Consumption of meat is widely seen as the engine behind our brain development (the brain burns a lot of fuel, calories best obtained from protein and fat), and when we made the jump from scavenger to hunter somewhere in our protohuman past, scientists generally agree that it was the pursuit of large animals that drove us. Large animals provide more reward for similar expenditure of energy. Chasing a rabbit and chasing a deer are pretty similar, but you get a lot more meat from a deer. The pursued have evolved with us, and the eternal chase, man against deer, continues to drive us. So the next time a hunter seems overly wrapped up in a story about the deer that he shot this year, cut him a little slack. Or at least understand why he's doing it.

Hunting also fills a gap in an electronic, urban lifestyle. When I am out pursuing ducks or pheasants or deer, nature surrounds me and I become lost within her. I am a set of eyes and a quiet footstep, a straining pair of ears seeking, say, the source of that whistle or quack—which I know through experience to be the sounds a hen and drake pintail make when they are looking to land somewhere. Will it be in my decoy spread? When you hunt, much of the rest of the world falls away, if only for a few hours. I've learned more about how and why nature does what she does in a morning spent hunting in the marsh or forest than most could in a year. I am still and silent, watching and listening, giving all my senses to my surroundings. Hikers, for example, tend to be chatty and relatively noisy. Several times, while I've been in the woods hunting, I have heard hikers coming and seen them walk right past me unawares. If I can hide in plain sight and be forewarned of their approach, what must wild animals think about them?

Over the years, I've had tiny kinglets alight on my shoulder. I've shared the shelter of a dead tree with a ghostly white owl. I've unknowingly stalked a wild pig alongside a mountain lion stalking blacktail deer, and stared rapt watching two tarantulas wrestle for dominance. It is beautiful out there, and I wouldn't trade those experiences for anything.

It might surprise some of you to learn that I did not start hunting until I was 32 years old. I shot target rifles a little as a teenager but never hunted. I'd fished and foraged since I could walk, but our family owned no guns, and I knew only one person my age who hunted. I grew up in suburban New Jersey, where guns were for video games or movies or criminals, and deer were pests, eaters of azaleas and backyard flower beds.

Decades later, when Holly and I moved to Minnesota, I became fast friends with Chris Niskanen, the hunting and fishing writer for the newspaper we worked for, the *St. Paul Pioneer Press*. I was lamenting the limited fishing in early winter (before ice-up brought a long ice fishing season), when Chris asked if I wanted to join him on a pheasant hunt in South Dakota. I'd eaten pheasant and thought the idea of catching my own wild chickens would be pretty cool. I knew nothing about shooting a shotgun or how to actually shoot pheasants, but I tagged along. We drove out to Aberdeen with Chris's black Labrador Finn and stayed in a modest little motel that was fine with hunting dogs as added guests.

It was cold. We were hunting the last week of the season, between Christmas and New

Year's, and there was snow on the ground. Chris said it'd be a hard hunt, and it was. I couldn't shoot worth a damn, and I caught a marsh reed in the corner of my eye that made it tear up uncontrollably—and it was so cold the tears froze to my face. But Chris is an excellent hunter, and he shot his limit of three birds on both days of the hunt. I was deeply impressed, both with his skill and the bottom-line fact that we would come home with six ditch chickens to eat.

Chris gave me three of them to take home. He told me to skin them and break the carcass down like a chicken. I said no. I was determined to pluck them because to me, the skin on a chicken is the best part. "Pluck them gently then," he said. "The skin rips." We were living in an apartment in downtown St. Paul at the time, and the only place that seemed suitable for this sort of dirty work was the parking garage beneath the building. So I grabbed a couple of plastic bags and a knife and went downstairs. Chris wasn't kidding about the skin. It tore up everywhere, and I soon broke down and followed his advice.

There were other surprises. The pheasants had been eating when he'd shot them, and out of their crops spilled what seemed like a full cup of milo, corn, and other seeds. It was alarming. Then I slipped the knife behind the breast to gut the birds. I reached in and felt a cold, squishy mass, yanked it out . . . and almost gagged. I'd broken the intestinal tract, and the guts reeked. So this was death, I thought. This was where my meat comes from.

I honestly wasn't sure I could go on. The smell and the mess and the blood were so different from fishing, which seemed almost antiseptic by comparison. But I decided that if we killed these birds, it was my duty to eat them. So I washed the pheasants well and let them age a bit in the fridge. A few days later, I cooked them in a tomato sauce, and we ate them with some potatoes and bread.

The taste was very much like chicken, but like no chicken I'd ever eaten. It felt firmer, denser, more substantial, more vital. I wanted more. My head began whirling with cooking possibilities. As a larval hunter, I wanted to learn the skills my friend possessed. I wanted that easy competence and calm knowledge that if you read the wind and the terrain and the weather correctly, you would probably come home with food for the table. That hunt began what has become a way of life for me.

I offer my experience as a road map for anyone like me: a clueless enthusiast who wants to eat wild game but has no idea how to proceed.

The first thing you'll notice is I had a mentor. A mentor is wildly helpful, as he or she can steer you clear of obvious errors. I did not always have Chris, as we moved soon afterward, and I learned a lot through trial and error for some time afterward. But Chris helped me through the license process, and showed me the ropes of a gun range and the basics about where and how to chase rabbits and squirrels and pheasants.

If you know any hunters, ask them to help you. Chances are they will be more than happy. Most hunters love nothing better than to introduce others to our pursuit. We want more people to understand what it is we do, and I've met only a few hunters unwilling to let a newbie into the "club." If you don't know any hunters, seek out groups like Ducks Unlimited, the Rocky Mountain Elk Foundation, Pheasants Forever, or the Delta Waterfowl Association. These groups are made up of hunter-conservationists who raise and spend millions protecting, maintaining, and restoring habitat for the animal they're associated with. All are eager to help new hunters and will probably have a chapter near you. There are more regional groups, such as the California Waterfowl Association, which, if you live in the Golden State, are even better at helping you get started. You can also call your state's fish and game department (they all have different names, depending on your state) and ask them to point you to your state's hunter safety program, which will teach you a lot. Books are another great source of basic information. I read scores of hunting how-to books when I got started, and I include a list of some of my favorite at the end of this book.

You can use the following as a rough guide to getting started.

Before you do anything else, go out on a hunt as a nonshooter if it is at all possible. Hunting is an involved pursuit, and you want to be out there, seeing the good, the bad, and the ugly before you spend time and money gearing up. Try to be a guest on several different kinds of hunts to see where you might want to begin. Some people love the walking and the open fields of pheasant or partridge hunting. Some love the rush of stalking deer or seeing a turkey inch ever closer to you. Others love that magic sight of incoming ducks with cupped wings and feet down, ready for a landing. I love it all, and so might you, but it's best to start hunting one animal and move to another as you gain experience.

When you decide to take the plunge, you will first need to get licensed. Most states require that you take a hunter education course; in other states, it is optional. My advice is to take the course if offered. It is the best primer on safety, hunting etiquette, ethics, equipment you will need, basic shooting, tracking, and handling of game. The courses range from a few hours to a few days, and you take a test at the end. If you are paying attention, you should pass with no problem. The cost is usually less than $50 and sometimes far less. In California, the cost is typically less than $20.

Once you are certified, you can buy your license. Most states have a basic license that lets you hunt a limited number of animal species, and then you will need to buy stamps and tags on top of that. A typical set of stamps and tags includes an upland game stamp, allowing you to hunt pheasants, quail, grouse, and such; state and federal waterfowl hunting stamps, which let you hunt those animals; deer tags, each of which allows you to kill one deer and which must be attached to that deer once it's down. Pig, elk, moose, antelope, etc., operate on the same tag system as deer. Costs vary widely. In general, however, it is far cheaper to hunt in your own state than in another.

Now you're licensed and certified. Consider what sort of hunting you want to start with. I started small, with rabbits and squirrels. Your first big choice is equipment: rifle or shotgun, or even bow? If you hunt birds, you will need to use a shotgun. Big game you can hunt with a rifle, shotgun, or bow. Small game such as rabbits and squirrels can be hunted with either a small rifle, like a .22 caliber, or with a shotgun. (Some people hunt small game with a bow, but it is difficult for a beginner.) Guns can range in cost from a few hundred dollars to a few thousand.

I shoot a pretty standard rifle, a Remington 700, chambered in .270 caliber. Sound like Greek to you? Remington is the manufacturer, 700 is the model, and the width of the bullet that the rifle shoots is .27 of an inch. This is an ideal deer gun for a westerner, as it shoots fast and flat—perfect for shooting in wide-open spaces—and the gun will not kick you like a mule. It cost me a few hundred dollars, but I spent nearly $1,000 on the scope. Quality optics are handcrafted and cost big bucks. That said, you can get a decent scope for a few hundred dollars.

My shotgun, and I only shoot one, is a pretty 20-gauge over-under from Franchi called the Veloce. I've named her Tinkerbell. It's an Italian gun with two barrels, one over the other, whose width is "20 gauge," which is smaller than the standard 12 gauge. Shotguns range from cannons like a 10 gauge down to the dainty 28 gauge, and, just to confuse you, there is an even smaller .410, which is the only shotgun geared to the "caliber" of rifles: Its barrel is .41 of an inch in diameter. Most hunters shoot a 12 gauge, which can kill any bird you hit, and can even kill deer and wild pigs if you load it with buckshot or slugs, which are solid blobs of lead like a handgun or rifle bullet. I shoot 20 gauge because it kicks less, and as I have become a good shot, I can kill anything with it. The difference between the different-size shotguns is the number of pellets you shoot, not the speed or distance you can shoot. My 20 gauge shoots as far and as fast as a 12 gauge, only with fewer pellets. I need to be a better shot to kill as cleanly at a distance as someone shooting a 12 gauge.

As for rifles, my .270 will kill cleanly anything from a jackrabbit to an elk—which is pretty much anything in North America short of a bull moose or a grizzly bear. Unless you plan on hunting those animals with some frequency, you don't need the really high-powered magnum guns. They'll just kick you harder, and you really, really want to be comfortable shooting your rifle. Other good calibers are the venerable 30-06, a .243 (which kicks even less than the .270), the ancient 30-30 (often lever-action rifles like you see in western movies), and a 7mm. When you go to the gun store, talk to the staff and tell them what you want to hunt and where (the West, eastern forests, the desert). Pick up a few rifles to see how they feel. If you are a big person, maybe you want a magnum, which are the muscle cars of the rifle world. If you are a woman of average height and build, you might want to try out junior models. There is no one answer.

My bottom-line advice is, if at all possible, to shoot other people's guns before you buy. You can often rent guns at a shooting range to give them a try, and this is an excellent

option. Buying a gun is an investment, and if you take care of it, the gun will outlast you. I know several people who shoot their father's or grandfather's gun. Another route is to buy a used gun from a reputable gun dealer. Ask around to find out who those might be. Do not buy a gun online unless you have tried it out beforehand and unless that dealer is well regarded. A gun is a very personal thing, and you want to feel it before you buy.

Once armed, get thee to the gun range. A gun is a tool you must understand before you have any business being in the field trying to kill something with it. When you buy the gun, ask about nearby gun ranges or go online: The National Shooting Sports Foundation maintains a national online registry of gun ranges. Call your nearby ranges and tell them you are a new shooter, and ask if they have anyone available to give you a lesson or two. Many ranges have pros around. This is especially important with shotgun shooting, which can be more frustrating than rifle shooting for a beginner.

If you have the money, I also recommend you get your shotgun fitted, like a custom shirt. Unlike a rifle, where you hit a target by lining up the front and back sight of the gun, the "back sight" of a shotgun is your eye. So if your eye does not line up perfectly with the front sight, you will miss. A lot. Getting a shotgun fitted to you makes this split-second alignment work without thought. Some people can shoot well with an off-the-rack shotgun, but those are lucky folks. Left-handers and women take special heed: Most off-the-rack shotguns are made for right-handers, and a sizable percentage of women are what is called cross dominant, which means the eye opposite their dominant hand is the dominant eye. So a right-handed woman might need to shoot left-handed because her strongest eye is on the left.

I cannot stress enough the importance of practice, even though it can be expensive. A typical trip to my local rifle range costs me $15 to walk onto the range, and, since I shoot nonlead bullets, which are spendy, each cartridge I shoot costs me more than $2. But it's worth it. When you hunt, you may only have a second or two when the game is close enough for a shot. If you are not comfortable with your gun, you can easily get flustered and botch what might be your only chance of the day. When you are at the range, visualize yourself hunting. Imagine the rifle target is a deer, and a shotgun clay is a duck or dove or pheasant. Put yourself in your imaginary hunt and then, when the real time comes, you will be better prepared. Expect to miss often when you start out. We all do.

Each animal pursuit requires different equipment. Blaze orange gear (also known as "hunter orange," a Day-Glo color we can see but many animals cannot) is almost always required for pheasant, quail, or deer hunting. Buy a sturdy upland game vest with blaze orange on it and a large game pocket in the back: You can use it for deer hunting if need be, but it's mostly for upland birds or rabbits. Deer hunting has a whole industry behind it, but in reality you only need drab, tough clothing, a blaze orange vest or hat, a good pair of binoculars (buy the best you can afford), a sharp hunting knife, and a comfortable pair of hiking boots. Deer don't see color, so breaking up your outline is more important than any particular camouflage. I've successfully hunted deer, pigs, and antelope in a T-shirt and jeans. Waterfowl hunting is a whole different matter. Unlike deer, ducks and geese do see color, and you do need to be camouflaged as much as is humanly possible. Clothes are only one part of the equation. You will need to hide in the reeds and cattails, too. A warm pair of chest waders is a must, and these run more than $100. Warm jackets are vital, too. You spend long hours in crappy weather awaiting ducks, and you will need to layer better than in deer or upland hunting, where you are often walking. A good hat and maybe some chemical hand warmers are good to have.

Then there is the question of duck calls and decoys. To be a good duck hunter, you need both, but learning a duck call takes some practice, and it is better for a beginner to not call at all than call badly. As for decoys, buy at least a dozen. You'll want more, but a dozen is a good start. Don't have room for lots of decoys? Apartment dwellers should look into inflatable decoys, which are pretty lifelike and store in small boxes. You can also schlep dozens of them in a compact car, something you cannot do with standard decoys.

I highly recommend that you begin your hunting career with either an experienced friend or a paid guide. A friend is best, of course, but even so, you should hunt with guides often at first. They will know things your friend probably doesn't. Tell the outfitter you are a new hunter and want to learn on your hunt, and then follow this one iron rule: Do whatever your guide tells you, then ask why later. You will have a better hunt, you will earn the respect of your guide, and you will learn something you can use when you go out on your own. Always tip your guide at least 10 percent; they're like waiters and mostly work for tips. Twenty percent is better.

All of this is intended as a rough guide to get you started as a hunter. You will want to do your own reading and talk to more experienced hunters, shooting instructors, and hunting guides as much as you can. Hunting can have a steep learning curve at first, but fear not: We're here to help.

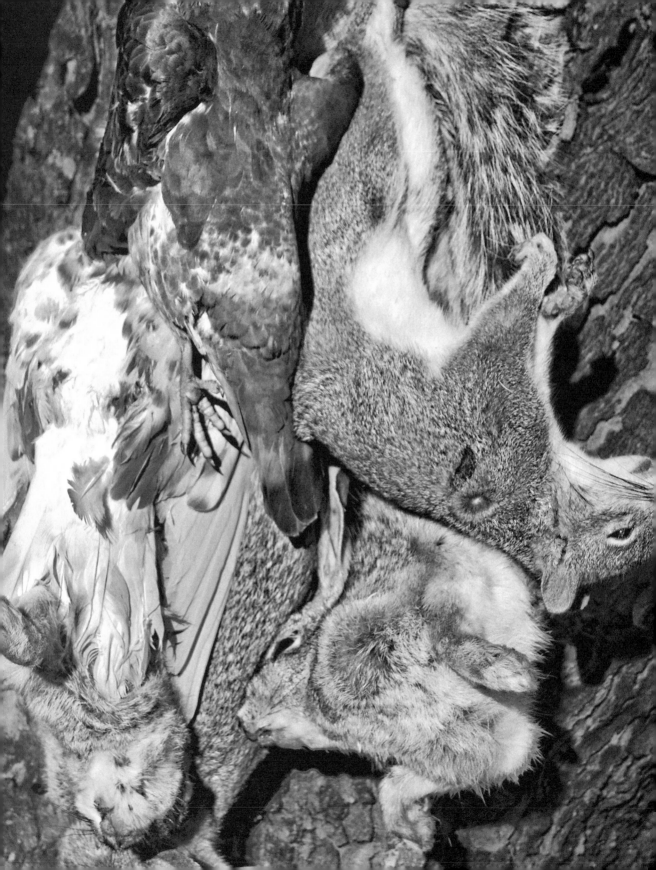

15

RABBITS, HARES, AND SQUIRRELS

It was so cold the corners of my eyes began to freeze as I crept as quietly as I could through a snowy Minnesota woodlot, looking, listening, searching. Somehow I caught a glimpse of a twitch in a skeletal walnut tree about a hundred yards away. I held still and swiveled my eyes toward the twitch. It was a gray squirrel. I crept over to the side of a nearby sapling and raised my rifle. I steadied it over my right arm, which gripped the tree. For a long moment, the crosshairs weaved like a drunk driver around the image of this squirrel, which was waking up to the morning's light. I inhaled deeply, and as I exhaled, the crosshairs settled on the animal's head. Crack! The squirrel fell with a soft thud into the snow.

I ran as fast as I could toward the walnut and found the limp squirrel near the tree trunk. I was at once elated and horrified at what I'd done. This squirrel was the first mammal I'd ever shot, and when I reached into the snow and picked it up, I was unnerved by its startling warmth. Fish are cold, but this squirrel was still warm and soft as I slipped him into my game vest. I officially had blood on my hands. I was now, finally, a hunter.

The great Spanish hunter-philosopher José Ortega y Gasset said, "One does not hunt in order to kill; on the contrary, one kills in order to have hunted." Various thinkers have debated the meaning of this since he wrote that in the 1920s, but to me it meant that I'd stepped out of the audience and into nature's drama, which can be terrible and awe inspiring and crushingly beautiful all at once. Killing and then eating an animal you have hunted is the final act in this play. Shooting with a camera as a nature photographer doesn't cut it: To me, that just means you had a front-row seat in the audience.

But the eating is as vital to the whole act as is the killing. Ortega y Gasset could have continued by saying that while one kills in order to have hunted, one eats in order to have the right to hunt again. Wanton killing is a sin against nature.

I was most definitely going to eat this squirrel. I shot another one that morning, enough for dinner for Holly and me. I'd read that squirrels can be tough. They can live for several years in the wild, unlike cottontail rabbits, which rarely live longer than a year. Braising is the safest way to go. So I skinned and gutted the squirrels, jointed them out, and made the first wild game meal I'd ever cooked with animals I'd shot myself: braised squirrel in walnut sauce.

Squirrel hunting is essentially a primer for deer hunting and was once the way every child started his hunting career. If you can stalk quietly through the forest and sneak close enough to a squirrel to hit it with a shotgun or a .22 rifle, you have the skill to graduate to larger game, such as deer.

Rabbits have always been the other "gateway animal" for a young hunter, as has Rabbit's cousin Jack, who is really a hare. In the northern regions, snowshoe hares fit this bill, too. Rabbits are the krill of the forest: numerous, fecund, and prey to just about everything. It is their curse to be born delicious.

The first rabbit I shot was not far from that walnut tree where I felled the squirrel. It was a rabbit I'd flushed from a snowy brush pile. I had a feeling there would be a rabbit in a pile of brush in the woods, so I kicked it. Zoom! The rabbit burst out of the opposite side of the brush, at the only angle where I could not get a clear shot. Damn. But rabbits, once flushed, will often return to their brush piles eventually. A wily hunter hides nearby and waits for the bunny to return. Which is exactly what I did—I'd read about this trick in a book—in temperatures that were well below zero. I remember being so cold, and the forest being so quiet, that when I heard the crunch-crunch of a rabbit's stealthy approach in the snow, it sounded like a cow. I dared not move my head, but when I swiveled my eyes I could just barely see movement. The rabbit was almost behind me, hunched down and sneaking back to his hidey-hole. I whirled, brought the shotgun up, and in the instant before I squeezed the trigger, we stared at each other. I swear he had a look of "oh, shit . . . " before I shot. Like the squirrel, he was spectacular in a classic cacciatore.

Hares are another matter. Many Americans know our most common hare as the jackrabbit, and there are several species of Mr. Jack all over the country. Jackrabbits are good table fare and are very dark; rabbit is a white meat. Jacks do tend to be tough, though, and are best braised. Cold regions have the most delicious hare, the snowshoe. Smaller than a jackrabbit but larger than a cottontail, snowshoes offer the accessibility of rabbit (they too are a white meat) but are large enough to feed two to three people. Catch a young one and you can even fry it like chicken.

Why hunt rabbits, hares, and squirrels? The easiest answer is that they are ubiquitous and delicious, and that even includes the much-maligned jackrabbits. Every state in America has a species of rabbit, hare, or squirrel, and in many states there is no closed season on jacks. You can hunt them all year long, although summer hunting can be dicey because the animals are stressed and susceptible to parasites.

A better answer to the question is because hunting rabbits and squirrels will make you a better hunter. It is not every day you can head out and shoot a deer or elk or wild boar. Even avid hunters typically shoot only a few big game animals each year. Learning to stalk squirrels will make you a better big game hunter, and learning the quick reflexes needed to hit a rabbit fleeing for a briar patch will make you a better bird hunter. You need patience to hunt squirrels and a Zen-like intense relaxation to consistently kill rabbits with a shotgun.

SEASONS

All states have a rabbit season that is more than a month long, and some are as long as 6 months; California's goes from July to the end of January. Many states have no closed season on jackrabbits. Snowshoe hares, which are more sought after than jackrabbits, typically follow the rabbit season. Squirrels usually have a long season, too, and a few states even have a special early spring squirrel season.

TYPES OF RABBITS, HARES, AND SQUIRRELS

RABBITS

Some sort of cottontail rabbit lives everywhere in North America. This is your standard little brown rabbit with short ears and a white tail. A few subspecies are larger than others, and the big Minnesota bunnies were nearly twice the weight of the wiry desert cottontails I now hunt in California. American rabbits do not dig extensive warrens the way European rabbits do. Instead, they live in shallow scrapes, often under briar bushes. Look for cottontails around rural homesteads, old junk piles on farms, the edges of meadows, and along riversides.

European rabbits have been introduced into a few eastern states, such as New Jersey, New York, and Connecticut, and around the eastern Great Lakes. These rabbits are much bigger, weighing up to 7 pounds—far heavier than the average 2-pound cottontail—and they dig deep warrens. Some states have no closed season on these invaders; as they are surpassingly tasty and large, shoot as many as you will eat.

HARES

We have three main hares in America: the white-tailed jackrabbit, the black-tailed jackrabbit, and the snowshoe hare. Jacks tend to be wiry, live in the open plains or deserts, sport gigantic ears, and have dark, full-flavored meat. Snowshoes live in forests, can be plumper, have ears like rabbits, and have lighter meat like a true rabbit. Hares are not rabbits, although they are cousins. Jackrabbits can be very large. The largest I've seen weighed more than 10 pounds, and some will grow to 14 pounds. In the far north, there is an Arctic hare that routinely weighs more than 10 pounds, but it is limited to the polar regions. You will rarely find them around trees, although they will wander into fruit orchards to eat.

SQUIRRELS

As for squirrels, there are really only two kinds you need to know, gray and rusty-colored. The gray ones are actually two species: an eastern gray, which can in fact be a little brownish red or even black; and a western gray, which is larger and will always be a beautiful blue-gray. Easterns can be found everywhere, as they were introduced into the West decades ago. Westerns live in the coastal states, rarely straying into the Great Basins of Nevada or eastern Washington or Oregon. Easterns weigh a pound or two, and westerns are typically close to or a little more than 2 pounds.

The other squirrel worth hunting is the rusty-colored fox squirrel, which can surpass 2 pounds. I've even heard about someone shooting a three-pounder, which is an awfully big tree rat. Fox squirrels are concentrated in the center of the country, as they were denizens of the Great Forest that once stretched from the Atlantic to the Great Plains. They like cottonwood trees and big gnarly oaks as dens, although I've seen them in lots of different kinds of trees. Fox squirrels tend to be reddish and, compared with the incredibly wary (at least outside city parks) eastern gray, seem a bit slow on the uptake. This is why people love to hunt them.

HUNTING TIPS

Seasons for all these animals vary widely depending on the state. Many states have no closed season on jackrabbits, so they can be hunted all year long. Most rabbit, hare, and squirrel seasons open in September and close in January. A few states have a spring squirrel season.

Unless the weather is brutally cold, the absolute best times to hunt these animals are the half hour before dawn and the half hour after dusk—the first and last moments you can legally hunt them. Many rabbits and hares are seminocturnal, and catching them out grazing early is a great way to put bunnies in the bag. When the weather is really cold, rabbits and especially squirrels will sleep in until the sun warms the area a bit. In subzero weather, I've had my best hunting at about 10 a.m.

Hunting around the full moon can be iffy. Rabbits and hares will often congregate in great numbers by the light of the full moon, frolicking, mating, and gorging themselves in an odd-looking midnight party. I saw one of these parties once as a boy, and was mesmerized. There had to be 200 rabbits in a meadow grazing, scampering around, and boxing—yes, the males get on their hind legs and flail away at each other in dominance fights. It's pretty wild. And just like any partygoers, the bunnies sleep in the following morning.

If you live in snowshoe hare country, some of the best times to hunt them are when the snow comes early or late. Snowshoes turn from brown to white at a predetermined point in

early winter, and if the snow doesn't match their coat, these hares become fuzzy bull's-eyes. Spotting a white hare in brown countryside, or a brown hare in snow, is pretty easy. If you come across a bonanza, take some pity on the poor things: I might shoot a limit one day, and maybe come back one more time, but after that the hares need to be left alone for later in the season or even next year.

Always be ready. Rabbit hunting is an exercise in active relaxation. You never know when a rabbit or hare will show itself, and then you might only have a second to make the shot. Peering intently at everything will wear you out in an hour, so you need to let yourself go and absorb everything as you slowly move through an area. Listen. You can often hear rabbits before you can see them. I've heard rabbits chewing before I could spot them.

Move more slowly. Once you get to an area with squirrels or rabbits, slow down. Use your ears and eyes more than your feet. Move only with purpose, and watch where you plant your foot. Try not to step on dried leaves, especially if you are trying to get close to a squirrel. Fortunately, squirrels themselves can be noisy, so you can move when they drop a nut from a tree or rustle through the leaves. Use the wind. A strong breeze can mask the sound of you stalking closer.

Above all, watch. Don't look for the body of the rabbit or the hare, look for its eye or an ear. I've spotted hares staring at me that were standing stock-still. I never saw the hare; his coat melted into the surrounding scrub, but his eyes looked like polished pebbles.

Aim for the head, especially with a shotgun. A full blast with a shotgun in the body can destroy the meat on a rabbit or squirrel. A head shot is both more humane and wastes less meat. Remember, the most and best meat in any of these animals is in their back legs.

Look for brush piles, briars, and scrap heaps. Rabbits and hares love to hide in them. Small piles you can approach quietly and then kick—ready to shoot if a bunny bursts from the other side. Large piles are best done as a team: One person kicks the brush while the other stands off to the side, ready to shoot. Be careful about your shooting lanes, though, so you don't swing your shotgun near your friend.

Rabbits love junk. The best cottontail rabbit hunts I've ever had were in and around abandoned buildings, junked cars, log piles, and other human detritus. I was boar hunting once and walked into a hidden valley littered with the hulks of ancient farm equipment. I knew immediately there might be rabbits. I was not disappointed. There were bunnies everywhere that had made these hulks their home. I didn't come home with a boar that day, but I did have a rabbit for dinner.

Both rabbits and hares, when flushed, will generally circle back to where you originally flushed them. I've killed a few rabbits by being patient enough to find a spot nearby to wait for their return. Each time I waited nearly an hour. Hares, however, have such large territories that they might not return until after dark. So don't bother waiting for a jack or snowshoe to come back. You lost. Move on.

For squirrels, find nut trees, including oaks. Find the nut, find the squirrel. Approach each oak or hickory or walnut tree as if it has squirrels already in it, and, if they're not around, look at the base of the tree for chewed nuts. If you find a lot, this is a place to ambush. Find a comfortable tree nearby and sit at its base with a clear view of the nut tree. Wait. The squirrels will come eventually. This is a time-honored technique that can actually be better than moving through the forest. But you need to know it is a tree the squirrels are using. And that takes time and patience.

EQUIPMENT

This is another beauty of hunting rabbits, hares, and squirrels: You need little more than good boots, a shotgun, and something to hold your quarry in. Most states require that you wear blaze orange for safety, and the same sturdy orange vest you buy for upland bird hunting will do just fine for rabbits and hares.

Squirrels are another matter. Squirrels react to color, so you want to wear the minimum amount of blaze orange that the law requires, and camo up everything else. I don't go overboard the way many turkey hunters do, with face mask, head-to-toe camouflage suit, and a camo shotgun; that's not necessary with squirrels. But I wear at least one thing that is camouflage, and something else that blends in with the forest.

Boots for walking are a must for pretty much any hunting. If you live in a cold climate, wear well-insulated boots, especially for squirrels, as you will be moving very slowly or not at all, sometimes for hours. If you still get cold feet, you can buy chemical foot warmers that will keep your feet warm for a long time.

Brush pants are a good choice. These are canvas pants with a water-resistant, thick front, like built-in chaps. These pants will get you through a lot of upland bird hunting, too, and are great on wet mornings or when you need to bushwhack through briars to either flush rabbits or retrieve them.

As for a gun, my 20-gauge shotgun is a perfect fit for rabbits and hares, and it's great for squirrels, too. Any shotgun is fine, although the larger 12 gauge will throw an awful lot of pellets at a 1-pound squirrel. Remember, aim for the head. As for ammunition, anything will kill a rabbit, even the standard No. 7½ target shot. Jackrabbits are made of sterner stuff and are better shot with No. 5 or No. 6 shot; ditto with squirrels. I would not shoot these animals with anything larger than No. 4 shot.

Your other option is a .22 caliber rifle. A .22 is an excellent choice in winter when the leaves are off the trees and when you are hunting for jackrabbits, which live in open, scrubby terrain. A shotgun is not accurate much beyond 40 yards, and in the open you might not get much closer on a jackrabbit. A .22 is accurate to 100 yards. If you are hunting in open country, you could use the fast-flying, hard-hitting "varmint" rifles, such as a .17 Hornet or even a .22-250, which is a standard .22 bullet sitting on top of a lot more powder; it's accurate to 400 yards and beyond. No matter what you use, make sure you are not shooting around houses. Rifle bullets can travel a long ways, so be sure you know what's behind the rabbit or squirrel you are shooting at.

Finally, you'll need a good hunting knife. It's always good to have on hand in the field regardless, but if you're successful, you'll need your knife to dress the animals you've taken.

HANDLING YOUR GAME

The pocket of your hunting vest is a fine place to store your game until you get back to your car or truck, unless it is hot out. Putting a warm animal into an enclosed pouch when temperatures are much above 60°F is a recipe for rapid spoilage. In those cases, I bring the game strap I normally use for duck hunting. It's a leather shoulder strap with various smaller straps hanging from it, each with a loop at the end from which to hang the animals. Keeping them in open air will keep the meat safe.

Bring a cooler with ice if you are hunting in hot weather. Lay an old towel or piece of burlap over the ice, and then put the rabbits or squirrels on it. You don't want to get them wet. Right now, water is the enemy.

If it is cool out, and it usually is in hunting season, you can just keep the animals in a cool place until you get home, unless that's several hours away. In this case, bring the cooler.

There is a caveat here: Squirrels have a tough hide and are harder to skin once they cool. So I will often skin them in the field but leave them ungutted. I then put them in an open plastic bag. To skin a squirrel, cut through the tail from the bottom up without actually cutting the tail off. Holding the squirrel with one hand, step on the tail. With the squirrel's back facing your shin, grab both hind legs, straighten yourself, and you will pull the skin right off. It'll hang up around the feet and head. Cut these off and discard. Some people eat squirrel brains, but not me. You'll be left with the squirrel's "pants." Grab the skin along the belly and pull back toward the hind legs, holding onto the squirrel around the rib cage with the forelegs as a brace. Again, cut off the feet and you're good to go.

If you live in the West, before you gut rabbits you should put on rubber gloves. Why? There is a disease called tularemia that some perfectly edible rabbits and a few hares carry that can be transmitted to humans through contact with the viscera. It gives you flulike symptoms that can degenerate into more serious, chronic problems. Tularemia often shows itself in a rabbit's liver: Look for striations or weird whitish markings in the organ, and if you see them, throw the liver out and mark this rabbit for braising. Proper cooking kills the disease. I've eaten a dozen rabbits with weird-looking livers with no ill effects, but I was sure to braise them well.

I don't hang rabbits. Hanging, for the uninitiated, is when you hang your game in a cool, airy place for it to age; it's a little like aging beef. Rabbits are mostly young and are almost always pretty tender already. Hares can benefit from hanging, though. An old hare, which you can identify by its tattered ears, blunt claws, and worn-down, yellow teeth, can hang as long as a week, in my estimation. Gut your animals first, though, and stuff the cavity loosely with clean paper towels. Watch to see if the paper towels get soaked with blood. If they do, replace them. Again, right now moisture is your enemy. It can breed germs. If you are going to hang, this is how you gut: On the underside of the hare or squirrel, feel the paunch up to the rib cage to where the sternum would be if it were you. Slice across the sternum to open the fur and skin. Then take the knife—blade facing up toward you and away from the guts—and run it down to the anus. The guts will want to fall out. Reach in and grab them, and gently pull them out. Watch the bunghole, and if you see any feces, push them out the anus and away from the carcass. Cut out the entrails with a knife. Save the heart, liver, and kidneys for later. Toss the rest. Wipe the inside with a paper towel. Loosely stuff with clean paper towels, and you're ready to hang. Some people do not gut their hares before hanging, and while they haven't died from the practice, gutting a hare that's been dead for 5 days will be a very smelly, nasty business. Guts rot fast.

I always hang hares from the neck, but some people hang them by the feet. Your choice.

Make sure the hare neither freezes nor warms beyond 55°F. I hang my game in an old refrigerator fitted with a temperature regulator that lets me dial in precisely 55°F. Never hang a hare that has been gut-shot. (For more on hanging game, see Chapter 18.)

Skinning a rabbit or hare is easy. Do this after hanging, if you are doing so. Snip off the tail and the feet at the first joint with kitchen shears. Grab the fur at the center of its back and lift it up. Slice the skin and fur open perpendicular to the length of the animal. Now grab either end of the opening you just created and pull hard in opposite directions. The skin will pull right off. You will need to cut off the head. Again, poultry shears work well for this. Squirrels can be skinned in the same way, but as their hide is stronger, it'll take some muscle.

Once you have a skinned, gutted animal, you can now joint it out.

I break down rabbits, hares, and squirrels in much the same way. I begin with the forelegs, which are not actually attached to the rest of the body by bones. You will need a good cutting board, a cleaver, kitchen shears or stout knife, and a short, sharp boning knife. Turn the animal on its back and spread the foreleg away from the body with your fingers: You will see a gap you can slice through. Try to cut as close to the body as possible, and get the knife underneath the shoulder blade. The foreleg and shoulder will come right off.

Now move to the hind legs. Again with the animal on its back, take the hind legs and

bend them backward to break the joint; the hind legs are attached to the body by a ball-and-socket joint. You will hear a pop when the joint goes. Now take your boning knife and gently slice as close to the bone as you can around the socket. Slide the blade along the bone to free the leg from the body. It is a lot like taking the thigh off a chicken, if you've ever done that.

After both legs are free, slice off the belly flaps of meat. Add these to a braise or stew, and you'll have a nice little boneless morsel for someone. Snip off the ribs with shears.

Now you are left with the saddle, or

loins. Here's where the differences come in. With a squirrel, you get two pieces; a rabbit, three or four; and a hare, well, we'll get to that. First, you'll need to remove as much silverskin as possible. This is the luminous sinew that covers the loin. Use your sharpest small knife to slip under the sinew and above the muscle. I take the silverskin off in sheets; there are two layers. Don't worry if you cut into a little muscle. It happens. Just take your time and be patient with it. If you don't do this step, the sinew will contract hard when you cook the loin and squeeze the meat out from either side of the cut. No bueno.

To portion the loin, take your boning knife and gently cut down to the vertebrae in the portion sizes you want. Now use your cleaver, stout knife, or shears to break the spine. The reason you don't just hack without a guide cut is because you can get weird cuts if you are not really comfortable with a cleaver; if you are, by all means chop away. The way I make this cut is to get my cleaver blade on the spine and rap it hard with the heel of my palm. You can also use kitchen shears.

Remember, the very end of the spine, where the hind legs were, is not usable as a saddle piece. It's mostly bone. Just chop that last inch or two off, and save it for stock.

With hares, you can either portion the saddle like a rabbit, only with more portions, or you can actually bone it out. A really large hare will give you two little tenderloins that are fun to use in an amuse-bouche, a playful, one-bite appetizer. You'll also get two long boneless loin pieces with the diameter of a nickel or even a quarter.

To bone a saddle, start with the tenderloin, which is on the underside of the spine. Slide your boning knife along either side of the spine to free one side of the tender, then gently swipe the knife over the ribs to separate the tenderloin completely. Be gentle, as this is a small but very delicious piece of meat.

Do the same with the loin on the top of the spine. Start with the edge along the spine, then free the loin by slipping the knife in short strokes over what's left of the ribs. It takes practice, but you are left with a pretty piece of meat. Incidentally, hare loin should be served medium or medium-rare because it will always be tender. Loins of rabbits and squirrels are best served medium to medium-well.

You are now left with a carcass. This will go into the stockpot. Any portions that have been shot up—which happens—also go into the pot after you have cut out the really bloody areas. Sometimes you've poorly shot the animal, and it must all go into the pot. Oh, well. It happens, and at least you will have a wonderful broth to make polenta or risotto with later.

RECIPES

BRAISED SQUIRREL AURORA

I almost always cook squirrels with some sort of nut sauce. Call me macabre. An adaptation of a Spanish rabbit recipe I found in *Delicioso! The Regional Cooking of Spain* by Penelope Casas, this dish is a luxurious, thick stew that cries out for crusty bread. The almonds and olives are also perfect with squirrel, which tastes like a combination of rabbit and chicken thigh meat.

Be sure to brine the squirrel—this makes it moister. Figure on one eastern gray squirrel per person, two fox squirrels or western grays for three people, or one cottontail for two people. Or, if you are not a hunter, one domestic rabbit for two to three people. And yes, you can use chicken thighs and legs, too.

Serves 4

¼ cup kosher salt

4 cups water

3 bay leaves

1 tablespoon cracked black pepper

1 teaspoon dried thyme

2–3 squirrels or 2 cottontails, jointed

¼ cup almonds

5 cloves garlic

20–30 green olives

3–4 tablespoons olive oil

Flour

1 large onion

1 cup white wine

½ cup chicken, rabbit, or other light broth

1 small hot chile pepper, finely chopped (wear plastic gloves when handling)

1 pound fingerling potatoes (optional)

Parsley

Mix the salt, water, bay leaves, black pepper, and thyme in a large pot. Bring to a boil, then turn off the heat, cover, and let cool to room temperature. When cool, add the squirrel or rabbit pieces and refrigerate for 6 to 8 hours—no longer, or the meat will get unbearably salty.

Toast the almonds in a dry pan over medium-high heat if they are not already roasted. Pound them with the garlic and a pinch of salt in a mortar; you could also buzz them in a food processor or chop them fine by hand.

Pit and slice the olives in half or chop roughly.

Preheat the oven to 300°F.

Pour the oil in a Dutch oven or brazier—something ovenproof with a lid—and heat it over medium-high heat. Remove the squirrel or rabbit from the brine and pat it dry. Roll it in the flour. Lower the heat to medium and brown the meat on all sides. Take your time and cook the squirrel in batches so you do not crowd the pan. It should take 5 to 6 minutes to properly brown each piece. Remove the meat from the pot as it browns and set it aside.

While the meat is browning, slice the onion in half. Grate one half through a coarse grater and roughly chop the other half or slice it in half moons.

When all the meat is browned, remove it to a large bowl and set aside. Add the wine and broth to the pot and scrape off any brown bits stuck to the bottom. Bring this to a rolling boil. Here is a tricky part: You want to cook it down on the stovetop to the point where, when you put the meat back into the pot, the liquid comes up only about halfway. You do not want to submerge your squirrels completely. How long you'll need to boil it depends on the size of your pot.

When the liquid is boiling, add the almond-garlic mixture, chile pepper, and grated onion. Mix well and let boil for a minute. Add the squirrel back to the pot. Make sure it is not totally submerged. Halfway is ideal.

Cover the pot and put it in the oven. Cook for 45 minutes.

Remove from the oven and add the sliced onion, olives, and potatoes. Mix everything together. If the stew looks too dry, add a little more broth, but remember this is a dry stew, not a soup. I eat this with a fork and a piece of bread, not a soup spoon. Add just enough broth to keep everything from drying out. Cover the pot again and return to the oven for 45 to 60 minutes.

Check the meat and potatoes. The squirrel should be about falling off the bone, and the potatoes should be cooked through. When ready, remove from the oven and let it cool, covered, for 10 minutes on the stovetop.

To serve, spoon out portions and garnish with parsley. I'd drink a robust, complex white wine with this, such as a white Côtes du Rhône or an older Chardonnay. An Italian Grillo might be nice, too, as would a white wine from Friuli.

Sardinian Hare Stew

I love the flavors of Sardinia: saffron, capers, lusty sauces, stews, and game meats. This stew has it all. The recipe has its origins with a rabbit recipe I found in Giuliano Bugialli's *Foods of Sicily & Sardinia and the Smaller Islands*. It is traditionally done with rabbit or chicken, but I had some jackrabbits—really, hares—I wanted to cook, so here it is. The dominant flavors here are the full-flavored hare, vinegar, saffron, and capers. Use the best saffron you can afford here; it matters. It is a heady mix that needs a powerful wine; I prefer an Italian Aglianico with this, but any heavy red will do.

There is nothing especially difficult about this stew, but it needs lots of time. I cooked my hares for more than 2 hours, and yours might take 3. Domestic rabbits and chickens will be tender in half that time. Eat this hearty stew with crusty bread, *fregula* pasta, or my favorite, a soft polenta with butter and cheese.

Serves 4–6

Salt

4 hind legs from large hares or rabbits, or 6 chicken or pheasant legs/thighs

4 tablespoons olive oil

8 tablespoons capers

1 cup very warm water

Large pinch saffron

1 onion, chopped

5 cloves garlic, chopped

¾ cup chopped parsley

¼ cup high-quality red wine vinegar

Salt the hare or rabbit pieces well and set aside at room temperature for 30 minutes.

Heat the oil over medium-high heat in a large pot or Dutch oven.

Pat the hare pieces dry and add to the pot. Brown well. You might need to turn the heat down to medium if they are sizzling too violently. You want a calm, steady sizzle. Cook in batches, placing the browned pieces in a bowl, and take your time. Browning all the legs could take 30 minutes.

Meanwhile, chop half the capers.

Get your tap water running as hot as it will go and measure 1 cup. Crush the saffron in your palm and sprinkle it into the water. Get every bit of saffron into the water, and let this soak while the hare is browning.

Once all the meat is browned, set it aside in a bowl. Add the onion to the pot and sauté until browned. Add the garlic and cook for 1 to 2 minutes.

Add ½ cup of the parsley, the vinegar, and the saffron water to the pot. Nestle the hare pieces in tightly. If the liquid does not come at least halfway up the sides of the hare pieces, add some more water. Do not add wine or stock—the point is to have pure flavors here.

Cover tightly and simmer gently over low heat for at least 90 minutes. Chicken and domestic rabbits should be done by then, but hares need longer. Check the hare after 2½ hours. You want the meat to almost be falling from the bones.

Pull the meat out and strip it from the bone. Return it to the pot with the remaining ¼ cup parsley and mix well. Turn off the heat and cover for 5 minutes.

Serve over polenta or Sardinian *fregula* pasta, or with crusty bread. Don't forget the wine. You will want a big, heavy red here.

Buttermilk Fried Rabbit or Squirrel

If you are blessed with a cottontail rabbit, a young squirrel, or a young snowshoe hare (look for white teeth and ears that tear easily), you can do what anyone who buys a domestic bunny can do: Fry it like a chicken. This recipe is based on one for fried chicken that I picked up from my friend Elise Bauer, who runs the blog *Simply Recipes*. I kicked up her spice mix by adding more garlic, ground red pepper, and paprika, which gives it a red color.

As a general rule, one domestic rabbit will serve 2 to 3, as will a jackrabbit. A snowshoe hare will serve 2, a cottontail about 1½, and a squirrel just 1.

Serves 1–3 (can be doubled)

- 1 domestic rabbit or snowshoe hare, or 2–3 cottontail rabbits or squirrels, cut into serving pieces
- 2 cups buttermilk
- 2 tablespoons Italian seasoning, or ½ cup mixed chopped fresh herbs like oregano, thyme, and parsley
- 1 tablespoon paprika
- 1 tablespoon garlic powder
- 2 teaspoons ground red pepper
- 2–3 cups vegetable oil
- 1 teaspoon salt
- 2 cups flour

Mix the buttermilk with the Italian seasoning, paprika, garlic powder, and ground red pepper. Coat the rabbit with the mixture and put it in a covered container in the fridge overnight or at least 8 hours.

When you are ready to fry, pour the oil into a large pan—a big cast-iron skillet is ideal—and heat over medium-high heat. The general idea is you want the oil to come halfway up the side of the rabbit.

Meanwhile, take the rabbit out of the buttermilk mixture and drain in a colander. Don't shake off the buttermilk or anything, just leave it there.

Let the oil heat until it is about 325°F. This is the point where a sprinkle of flour will immediately sizzle. Do not let the oil smoke or it will taste acrid.

When the oil is hot, put the salt and flour into a plastic bag and shake to combine. Put a few pieces of rabbit into the bag and shake to get it coated in flour. You will probably need to fry in batches, so just leave the rabbit pieces in the colander until you are ready to flour them up and fry them. Don't let the floured pieces sit.

Fry gently for 12 to 15 minutes. You want a steady sizzle, but nothing raging, and you definitely don't want the rabbit to just sit in oil. You might need to adjust the heat a bit.

Turn the rabbit pieces and fry for another 10 to 12 minutes. The belly flap pieces and the forelegs will come out first, followed by the loin, and the hind legs will come out last.

When the rabbit pieces are good and fried, let them rest on a rack set over paper towels to drain away any excess oil. Serve hot or at room temperature.

16

VENISON: DEER, ELK, ANTELOPE, AND MOOSE

"Shoot that deer!"

Why was my friend Tim shouting? "What deer?"

"THAT ONE! The one right over there!"

Tim was pointing wildly at a doe mule deer that had frozen at our approach. We were in a pickup, Tim driving, me in the passenger seat. We'd driven to an abandoned homestead in northeastern Montana in search of mule deer. We liked this spot because it had a feral apple orchard on it, and deer love to eat apples.

I grabbed my rifle from the backseat and slipped as smoothly and as quietly from the truck as I could. In one motion, I worked the bolt action on my gun to chamber a round and sank to the ground, cross-legged. I knew I could hold steady from this spot. The deer just stared at me. My heart was beating so hard the crosshairs were jumping between the deer's back and belly. I took one deep breath, steadied the rifle, squeezed the trigger . . . and the world exploded.

The events of the next few seconds are a blur, but Tim later told me I took aim and shot in about 10 seconds. All I remember after that was hearing Tim, who'd leapt out of the truck as soon as I pulled the trigger, shouting at me to run around the other side of an old barn. The doe had been standing to one side of the barn, and it had bolted away when I'd shot.

"Ohmygod, ohmygod, ohmygod," I thought, running around the barn. I tried to chamber another round on the run but dropped the cartridge. I fumbled for another, stuffed it into the rifle, looked up, and saw a deer standing 5 feet away. What?! Then three things happened, all at once. I realized it was not my deer—"my deer" . . . how can we come to possess another living thing in such a short time? It was not my deer because this one had tiny antlers on it. I also heard Tim screaming, "Don't shoot the deer!" And the little buck bounced off. Where was my doe?

Then I realized Tim was 10 yards away from me, at the back of the barn. We'd both come around the barn at the same time and saw the young buck, who had apparently been traveling with the doe. What Tim saw that I did not was the doe at his feet. She had not gone more than a few feet, and lay there dying.

"You mind if I shoot her?" Tim asked. "I hate to see them suffer." I said okay, and Tim shot the doe in the head, killing her instantly. In retrospect, we wouldn't have needed that second shot, because mine had gone through both lungs. But to my mind, a quicker death is worth an extra bullet.

And there she lay. My first deer. She was not very big, maybe a hundred pounds or so. Her fur felt more like hair. It was coarse. There was dirt in her hooves. Tim stood back a few steps to give me room. Maybe he noticed my hands were trembling. We'd hunted for 3 days, and in an instant the hunt was over. We'd marched miles and miles through canyons and across hillsides, through farm fields and cattle ranches. And yet here we were, just a few feet from the truck.

Tim helped me with the skinning and gutting, which was strangely not as terrifying as I'd expected. I'd gutted rabbits and squirrels and very large fish before, and this was not so different. We broke down the deer in the little kitchen of the hotel where we were staying— the place looked like a scene from a mafia movie afterward. Blood is indeed thicker than water, I learned, and harder to clean up. But as we worked, the deer became venison. And I finally began to think of all the wonderful dishes I could make.

I've shot many deer since then. Some were easy, one was very hard. I remember them all, with every bit as much detail as that first doe in Montana. There is something special about big game hunting. It seems more primal than hunting small game. I know I am affected more by the death of a deer than the death of a rabbit. Maybe that's not fair to the rabbit, but it's how I feel nonetheless.

SEASONS

Somewhere in America, you can hunt deer from July to the end of January. In California, deer hunting begins in July, and many states close down their seasons on the final day of

January. There are also game preserves that essentially ranch deer and exotic species such as African antelope, and these often have seasons that extend before and after the regular deer season. Some places offer challenging hunts, some are little more than shooting galleries. Do your research before you decide to hunt a high-fence ranch.

Most states separate deer seasons by weapon: Archery season is always first, followed by regular gun season. I say "gun season" because rifle hunting in many eastern states is illegal: You must hunt with a shotgun loaded with slugs or buckshot. A slug is a single lump of lead or copper, and buckshot is a collection of a few large balls encased in the shotgun shell. Buckshot, incidentally, is not legal in all states, as it is especially good at killing people. In the East, most deer hunting is in close quarters and in places where you're likely to be within rifle range of another hunter. A rifle bullet can travel for a mile or more, while a shotgun slug will travel only a few hundred yards at best.

Many states also have special muzzleloader rifle seasons. A muzzleloader is a single-shot rifle loaded from the muzzle, not breech of the rifle near your trigger. Some people hunt deer with replicas of traditional rifles, like the Kentucky long rifle used in the 18th century, and it's a rare person who can shoot these guns accurately beyond 100 yards. That's why many more hunters take advantage of the special muzzleloader season by using high-tech, modern guns that can accurately shoot 200 yards or more. It's still a single shot, so you'd better be sure of your aim, but it ain't Daniel Boone's rifle, that's for sure.

TYPES OF VENISON

Venison is really a cooking term for the red meat of a wild critter with four cloven hooves and, if it came from a male, antlers or horns. The word *venison* covers the meat of all kinds of deer, elk, antelope, moose, and caribou.

The white-tailed deer is by far the most sought-after big game animal in North America. This is the deer that dominates the landscape everywhere east of the Great Plains. Whitetails are scarcer west of the Rockies, although there are a few isolated populations in eastern Washington. Many books have been written about whitetail deer habits and biology, but for our purposes it's most important to know that this is the deer that lives near people. Whitetail bucks range from the skinny desert deer of Texas and Arizona to the monsters of the Canadian plains, which can approach 400 pounds. A big doe rarely tops 200 pounds, which is the size of a typical buck.

Whitetail hunting is excellent in farm country, especially where grain is grown extensively. They absolutely love abandoned orchards and, in natural forests, will gravitate in the fall to oak trees heavy with acorns. And yes, you can find them in your backyard eating your azaleas. Look for them in river bottoms, too.

Whitetails share habitat with the West's primary species, the mule deer. Muleys don't much like people, although if you live in a rural area you will have them in your yard. They tend to be bigger than whitetails, and big bucks over 300 pounds are not that unusual; reports of 500-pound muley bucks surface from time to time. I've shot a 200-pound doe, and it felt like dragging a horse back to the truck.

Mule deer have very different antlers from whitetails, and they have a white rump, a dustier-looking coat, and much bigger ears. The ears really make them stand out—they do have a mule's ears. I once stalked a bedded muley doe that I could have sworn was a jackrabbit. All I could see was the ears. When she got up and bounced away, I almost had a heart attack. Once the deer runs, there is no mistaking which kind it is: Muleys do something called stotting, which is essentially bouncing on all four feet very fast. Boing! Boing! Boing! Whitetails never do this.

But blacktail deer do. This is the main deer of the Pacific Coast. And while it is thought to be a subspecies of the mule deer, it looks and acts more like a whitetail, although it has the same big ears as the muley. Blacktails tend to be small. A mature buck I shot in the Coastal Range of Monterey County only weighed about 140 pounds on the hoof. And their antlers are rarely as spectacular as those of trophy mule deer or whitetails. Most blacktail are creatures of the forest, and they hang around edges in close cover. Another set live in the arid coastal regions of California. These tend to be smaller and leaner. Blacktails and mule deer hybridize in the Sierra Nevada, so it's tough to tell which species you're hunting. They all taste good, though.

The West is also home to the pronghorn antelope, which is not, biologically speaking, an antelope. Pronghorns are the fastest land animals in North America and love nothing better than to run around in wide open plains grazing and generally having a good time. Antelope can be very hard to hunt. Their eyesight is incredible—the equivalent of you looking through powerful binoculars—and if they see you, they'll run. Getting a clean shot can be tough. Unfortunately for the antelope, they also happen to be curious animals. I've seen people attract curious bucks by hiding behind a sagebrush and waving a big white handkerchief. I've also seen archery hunters walk up within range of antelope by hiding behind a cardboard cutout of a cow. Pronghorn are plentiful in Wyoming, Montana, Colorado, and New Mexico, and if you can cool their meat down rapidly (an antelope's body temperature is so high it will spoil the meat if you don't skin it quickly), pronghorn is one of the finest wild game meats on the continent.

Elk are making a massive comeback, too. A generation ago, elk were isolated in a few states, but now they can be hunted in every western state, and there are limited hunts in the Appalachian regions of Kentucky and Tennessee. Elk hunting has not been this good since before the Civil War, and considering that even a cow elk averages 500 pounds, one will feed a family for a year. Bull elk are one of the most impressive deer species in the world and can top 1,000 pounds. Be prepared to hike for an elk, however, as they spend a lot of time on mountainsides in open pine forest at high elevations. If you want to bag an elk, you need to be fit—especially for the trip home, where you'll be packing out several hundred pounds of meat.

Farther north lives North America's largest cervid, the moose. A bull moose is even larger than an elk, and bulls weighing nearly a ton have been recorded. An average bull is more than 1,200 pounds, with cows averaging 700 pounds. Moose hunting is one of the more difficult pursuits on the continent. Moose are solitary and ornery, and they frequent swampy areas. I can't tell you how many stories I've heard of hunters shooting moose and seeing them die in the middle of a shallow lake. They then had to drag the moose to shore before they could even begin to pack it out. If you want a moose, which will feed two families for a year, you need to be as fit as an elk hunter and not be afraid to get wet.

The best moose hunting is in Canada, although Maine, Idaho, Alaska, and parts of Montana, Wyoming, and Utah all have huntable populations. Minnesota offers a handful of moose hunts a year, open only to state residents.

HUNTING TIPS

I am a competent deer hunter and have shot at least one deer, antelope, or elk every year since I began hunting nearly a decade ago. But that doesn't make me an expert, so I am happy to share with you some advice from my friend Phillip Loughlin, who is an expert. Loughlin runs the *Hog Blog* and is a part-time hunting guide; his tips are also in Chapter 17. What follows is a compilation of tips from both Phillip and me.

The prime directives in deer hunting are practice, patience, and perseverance. To become a good deer hunter, you need to hunt deer. A lot. This can be tough considering time constraints and the fact that in many cases you will only squeeze the trigger once each year. But you don't have to go out with a gun to practice.

Before the season starts, get out to where you expect to hunt and walk around at dawn or dusk, when deer do most of their moving. Use your binoculars. Move slowly. Listen. I've heard deer long before I've been able to see them because I was tucked with my back to a tree, sitting motionless, breathing lightly. I melted into the countryside. And as an aside, I was wearing blue jeans and a flannel shirt. No camo. Camouflage is not as important as knowing where the wind is coming from. Remember that deer don't see color, but they can outsmell you big time. And try as you might, people stink. Scent-blocking clothing is not foolproof.

If you do your scouting, you will learn where the deer like to go. You will know where the water is, and everything needs water. You'll see what they are eating, which is important because deer can eat all sorts of things and you want to know what strikes their fancy here and now. You also will be able to spot the deer trails and see where they go. Remember, move slowly, listen, and stop often to look around. I've done this a few times, looked up, and saw a doe staring right at me, just a few yards from my face. I waved and she bounced away.

If you are a stand hunter, meaning you plan to set up a tree stand, platform, or just sit on a stack of hay bales, the same applies. You'll need to know which tree, where to erect the platform, or which hay bales to set up on.

Phillip points out that once you get closer to the season, about the last 2 or 3 weeks before Opening Day, lay off. Let the place rest. Even your quiet excursions are intrusions on the deer's playground, and you want everything calm for the opener. You can't control what other hunters do, but you can hope that your little spot will be ready when you do bring the gun or bow.

Another Phillip maxim is that once you are set up in your spot, stop wondering what's over the next ridge. In the West, there is a lot of open land, and we're all subject to the lure of the allegedly greener grass just over that hill. If you want to walk, then by all means walk. But you'll be better served to do your preseason scouting, identify key areas, learn them, and then hunt those specific areas hard rather than trying to hunt new turf. Hunt where you know the deer are, not where you hope they might be.

Remember you can glass a lot more ground with binoculars than you can walk, and binoculars don't spook game like big feet and human stink. In the West, it's better to spend more time with the binoculars and less time wandering around.

Patience pays off. When you're pretty sure you've done everything right, you probably have. Just calm down, enjoy the sunrise or sunset, and don't second-guess yourself. Wild animals do not follow a script, but there are three things they consistently need: food, water, and shelter. If you've found one (or more) of these key areas, and the signs show that the animals are definitely here, then stick to it. Sit tight. They'll come. And if they don't show up today, come back tomorrow. That's where perseverance comes in.

After dawn, most deer will find a spot to bed down for the day. This makes them harder to find, as a deer's back blends well with the countryside. But deer seldom bed down in one place for an entire day. Find an observation point above a place you've seen bedded deer—usually you've bumped them by mistake—make yourself comfortable, and watch with your binoculars. You'll see animals as they move in their beds, switch beds, or get up for that midmorning/midday/midafternoon water/snack/stretch. Incidentally, this applies to pig hunting, too.

Get as close as you can. Then try to get closer. There's no such thing as too close for a good, clean shot. Well, maybe 10 feet might be a little close, but you catch my drift. The idea of hunting is not to see how challenging you can make the shot, but to make it as simple as possible. This is a living thing you're trying to kill here. It feels pain and suffers. You want to take every opportunity to minimize that pain. I've shot an elk at 375 yards, and I am proud of that. But I would much rather have shot it at 75 yards.

Here's one from Phillip I never would have thought of. If you're looking for fresh deer signs that indicate an active area, look for the things that last the shortest time: hair and moisture. Hair can be found on fence crossings, on tree trunks, and where they bed down. It disappears fast, even on a fairly calm day. If you find hair, the animals are probably close by. Likewise, moisture tends to dissipate almost as soon as it appears. Look for water droplets on grass or leaves, wet tracks exiting water crossings, or moisture in the bottom of a track in marshy ground. Scat can be dependable for a few hours, after which it's really tough to determine how old it is with any certainty (depending on weather). Wet, mushy shit means a deer was here recently. Dry tracks, however, can last for weeks, and again, depending on the weather, they really lose their value within hours.

Does usually mean bucks. If you've found an area where you're consistently seeing does and youngsters, and if you've got the time, then stay in that general area. The bucks will eventually show up, although it may be later in the season as the rut gets closer. Unless there are lots of other hunters in your area—like in certain public hunting areas—the bucks will generally be relatively close to the does. If pressure is high, though, the bucks will spend the early season in higher, less accessible ground. An old buck did not get that way by being stupid.

Unless you spook deer off a feeding spot or water source, they'll come back to it within a day or so, and sometimes even later the same day.

In the West, blacktails and mule deer have a fatal flaw. When spooked, they will almost invariably run off a short distance (20 to 50 yards) and then stop to look back. If you get busted, don't panic and don't take a bad shot. Wait for the deer to do his trick, and then be ready to shoot. You'll only get about a second, so be ready. White-tailed deer might do this, or they might run like rabbits clean out of sight. But like rabbits, whitetails will often run in something of a circle.

Another Phillip nugget: If you are tracking a deer, avoid following directly in his trail. Deer will often stop or backtrack to see if someone is following them. Instead, move uphill and somewhat parallel to the tracks, and keep an eye out on the trail ahead. If the tracks start to meander, slow way down and start watching carefully. The animal is either feeding or looking for a place to bed down.

When it comes to actually shooting a deer, aim for the "boiler room," which is a spot the size of a dinner plate right behind the animal's front leg. This is the conjunction of the heart and lungs, and is the easiest place to kill the deer quickly. Put a shot in the boiler room and the deer dies. Period. You might need to track it, but it should drop within 200 yards and probably a lot less.

Finally, I advise you to start your deer hunting with does, if that is legal in your state; it's not easy to score a doe tag in California. Does tend to taste better than bucks (testosterone and all that) and you will not contract "buck fever." I never thought buck fever would happen to me until I hunted antelope and saw a striking buck with horns that were spaced unusually far apart. I couldn't get a shot off the first time I saw that buck because I was mesmerized by its horns. Only when I got a second chance at him was I able to will myself to ignore the head of the animal and focus on that boiler room. If you find yourself looking at a truly great buck through your scope or peep sight, you will know what I mean. I think it is genetic in all humans, and yes, even women get the fever. Just remember: Focus on the boiler room.

EQUIPMENT

Deer hunting can be as complex or as simple as you want it to be. At a minimum, you will need a weapon—rifle, shotgun, or bow—good walking boots, a sharp knife, and, if you are in the West, binoculars. That said, there is a whole industry geared toward selling you products intended to help you hunt deer, mostly whitetails. Most people hunt deer close to home, in woodlots, the edges of farm fields, from tree stands on your property, hidden among hay bales, etc. If this is the case, you can probably drive a truck or an ATV to where you are hunting and pick up the deer you shot.

In these cases, the equipment I recommend above is necessary, as is something that is blaze orange. Most states require that hunters wear blaze orange when deer hunting. Deer can't see color, but fellow hunters can, and that's the point.

But, if you are going to be walking any distance while hunting, which is what I do when I hunt in Montana and Wyoming, buy a comfortable backpack and make sure it has the following:

- A quality compass.
- Several lengths of stout rope for hauling a deer or pulling it up over a tree limb to skin, hang, or gut.
- A little knife sharpener.
- Some way to purify water. If you are lost and find a stream, you will want to ensure that the water you drink is safe. Use iodine or buy a camper's water purification kit.
- All-weather matches.
- Latex or rubber gloves for gutting, if you so desire. I don't always use them, but it is a good precaution in case you see anything odd-looking in the viscera. Deer are not normally parasitized, but it can happen. Parasites rarely affect meat, but you would not want to eat a liver that looked speckled, misshapen, or flecked with white spots or lines.
- A game bag, which is a large cheesecloth bag you can get a whole deer into. Good for hauling to keep flies off the meat.

- Binoculars, the absolute best you can afford. This is recommended in the East, mandatory in the West.

- A rain slicker that doesn't make noise. Many hunting gear companies sell these. In the arid West, skip this unless you are very high in the mountains.

- A rag for your hands.

- Two water bottles. You need more water than you think out there.

- Many energy bars, like Clif Bars, granola, PowerBars, etc. Fig Newtons are good, too. You need concentrated energy. I dry figs and carry them.

- A camper's first aid kit that includes a snake bite kit. This is especially true for the West.

- A spare knife.

- Extra ammunition.

- A flashlight with a few extra batteries.

- A thin warming blanket made from Tyvek or some other microfiber.

- A cell phone, fully charged. It might not work where you are, but it's good to have in case you can get to a spot with cell service.

As you can see from this list, when you hike in search of deer, elk, moose, and the like, there is a very real chance you might get lost and have the sun go down on you. If that happens, just sit down and stop moving. Collect yourself and try to remember where you came from, and if you are not sure, you might have to spend a night in the field. The things in this pack will make your life easier until the sun rises again. Obviously a cell phone is your first line to the outside world in an emergency, but they don't always work in remote places. Best to be prepared.

Close-to-home hunters might want to buy these things, too. Doing so allows you to range farther while you are hunting in, say, the Adirondacks of New York or the Smokies of Tennessee.

A final piece of equipment that is useful out West is a set of shooting sticks or a bipod on your rifle. It is not uncommon to take a shot longer than 200 yards. You won't always have something nearby to steady your rifle or be able to shoot lying down, which is the most stable position to shoot from. Shooting sticks help a lot.

HOW TO SKIN AND GUT A DEER

You have a deer on the ground. Now what? Whole books have been written on how to field dress and butcher a deer, and a truly detailed tutorial is beyond the scope of this book. But the following should get you started.

Take your sharp knife and cut around the deer's anus, as if you were cutting it a new, larger one. I know, I know. Ew. Do it. You need to because you don't want deer shit on your meat. Once you cut around, pull on the cut part to pull the intestine out a bit. Tie the intestines off with string or a twist tie.

Now get the deer on its back. It's helpful to have a partner hold the deer up and secure while you cut. Run your hand down the centerline of the deer's belly and feel for the end of the rib cage, where your solar plexus would be. When you get there, pinch up a little skin and slice perpendicular to the length of the deer until you get through the hide.

Run your knife—blade pointed up away from the guts—from this first incision all the way back to the anus. You'll have to cut off a buck's 'nads en route; slice around them and discard. It helps to insert two fingers under the belly skin, one on either side of the blade, as a guide while you are making this cut. Hold the knife with your good hand, and use the fingers of the other as the guide. Do your best to not pierce the stomach. This should not be a problem if your blade is facing up and you are cutting with just the tip. You should begin to see the innards as you cut.

Once you have that cut made, roll the deer on its side and the offal will come part of the way out. This is why it is called offal, by the way: It is what "falls off" the animal once you gut it. But the innards will not come completely free. Now you get messy. Reach in and forward toward the ribs and find the gullet, which is the pipe from the front of the deer to its stomach. Cut this and you can pull the whole shebang free, but do it carefully. You may need to use the knife in a few places to free the intestines from the body cavity.

Now in this wobbly mess are the liver and probably the kidneys. You want these. The liver is a big burgundy blob. Cut it free from its attachments. The kidneys on a deer look like human kidneys. You can't miss 'em. They might be covered in fat and could still be attached to the rib cage. Leave them if that's the case; you can cut them free later.

You will notice that the rear end of the innards is still attached. Go back to the anus, and cut out everything still attaching that tied-off bung to the pelvis of the deer. You'll mostly be cutting glands and things, so it might get a little whiffy. But try to not cut the intestine itself. Once this is free, pull all the guts away from the deer.

Next you'll need to deal with the heart and lungs. Be prepared for blood, because if you did your job and shot the deer in the boiler room, the animal will have bled out in this area. There are several ways to take care of this. You can use a stout knife or bone saw and saw apart the centerline of the breastbone, then spread the ribs, grab the heart and lungs, and pull them away. You will need to sever the windpipe before it'll come free, however. This method works with does, small bucks, and antelope, but not on larger critters like moose or elk. For them, you'll need to climb on in and pull things out as best you can. If it is not freezing out, take your long sleeves off. Save the heart in a plastic bag, as it is delicious, but lose the lungs unless you plan on making haggis in the near future. Leave the remaining guts in the grass for the other animals. Coyotes and buzzards love them.

Roll the deer over to let any remaining blood drain. If there are two of you, each person grabs two legs and lifts the deer up to let everything drain. Paper towels are good for this, too, if you've packed them.

Now you're ready to drag the deer to the truck. Do this with the deer on its back, so you don't get dirt in the body cavity. Grab the antlers if it's a buck or the forelegs if it's a doe. Before you start, find some sticks and use them to prop open the chest cavity. This helps the meat cool faster.

Don't skin the deer until you are back at the truck, unless you are quartering it out. Most people skin elk and moose in the field and cut off large pieces—often whole legs—and carry them in backpacks back to the camp or truck. A 1,000-pound elk is too large to drag, so you'll need to do this if you shoot one.

To start skinning, take your knife and cut around the legs right above the hooves. Slip the point of your knife under the skin on the inside of the hind leg and, with the blade facing outward from the leg, slice upward. If the deer is still warm, this should be easy. Go all the way up to the belly and toward that first belly cut you made. Now pull and slice the skin off. You can pull a lot of the skin off when the deer is warm, using the knife only to free the skin in the places where there are strong attachments.

Work methodically, and try your best to not get hair on the meat. It sticks and can possibly contaminate it, but it isn't the end of the world if you get a little hair on the carcass.

Just do your best. You can also have your friend start at the foreleg and work up toward the neck while you are working on the rear of the animal.

When you are quartering out a large animal, skin one side first, then cut off the legs, tenderloins, and backstraps from one side. Only then do you turn over the animal to skin the other side. You don't want to get your meat dirty.

BREAKING DOWN A DEER

Again, whole books have been written on this topic. I'd suggest either buying one—my favorite is the classic *Basic Butchering of Livestock & Game*, by John Mettler Jr.—or taking your deer to a local butcher. If you don't plan on breaking down the deer by yourself, call around to butchers ahead of time to see if they will do it for you. Many will, especially in rural areas and even in suburbia. If you are traveling to hunt, many butchers will, for a fee, break down your deer and ship your meat to your house. It's expensive, but until you learn to butcher, it's a solid option.

RECIPES

SWEDISH MOOSE MEATBALLS

This is a recipe adapted from my grandmother, who was a Massachusetts Swede. They call these meatballs *Svenska Kottbullar*, and they are traditionally served with a lingonberry sauce. In Scandinavia, the meatballs are sometimes made with reindeer, so it's not a stretch to switch to moose. You could use any red meat.

In keeping with the Northwoods theme, I switch out lingonberries with highbush cranberries. Moose and highbush cranberries share the same habitat, and there is a golden rule in cooking: What goes together in life can go together on the plate. You can by all means use lingonberries, but you can buy highbush cranberry jelly online or make it yourself.

Serve these little meatballs in the sauce over mashed potatoes. A salad or sauteed greens would round things out. This is a large recipe, so you can either halve it or freeze extra meatballs after you brown them.

Serves 8–12

2–3 pounds meat (moose, beef, venison, lamb, elk, etc.)

1 pound pork or beef fat (preferably pork)

⅔ cup milk

4 slices stale bread, crusts removed

1 yellow onion, grated

2 teaspoons kosher salt

2 teaspoons ground allspice

1 teaspoon caraway seeds

1 teaspoon freshly ground black pepper

2 eggs

1 cup flour

Butter or oil

1 quart beef or wild game stock

½ cup highbush cranberry or lingonberry jelly

½ cup sour cream

Put the moose and pork fat in the freezer for an hour, until they are partially frozen. Cut both the meat and fat into ½-inch chunks. Grind through your fine die in a meat grinder. If you do not have a meat grinder, use a food processor. Don't crowd the processor. Chop in pulses until you get something that looks like ground meat—it will not be as good as with a grinder, but it is easier than hand-mincing everything. Place the mixture in a large bowl and put it in the fridge.

Pour the milk into a medium pot and set it on low heat. Break the bread into pieces and add to the milk. The bread will begin to absorb the milk. When it does, turn off the heat and mash everything into a paste. Let this cool to room temperature.

Take the meat bowl out of the fridge and add the onion, salt, allspice, caraway, and pepper. Crack the eggs into the bowl, then pour the bread-milk mixture in. With clean hands, gently mix everything together. Do not knead it like bread, and do not squeeze things together. Just gently work the mixture. Think cake, not bread.

When it is mostly combined—you need not get everything perfect—grab a tablespoon and scoop up some of the mixture. Roll it into a little ball with your palms, not your fingers. Pour the flour into a medium bowl and gently roll the meatballs in the flour. You may need to reshape the meatballs before putting them on a baking sheet lined with wax paper or parchment.

When the meatballs are all made, get a large pan ready. I use a big, old cast-iron skillet. Fill it with a little less than ¼-inch of oil. I use canola oil with a little butter tossed in for flavor. Bring it up to temperature over medium-high heat. When a bit of flour splashed in the oil immediately sizzles away, lower the heat to medium and add the meatballs. Do not crowd them.

You want the oil to come up halfway on the meatballs. Add a little oil if need be. Fry on medium heat for 3 to 5 minutes. You are looking for golden brown. Turn only once. The other side will need 2 to 4 minutes.

Set the cooked meatballs on a paper towel or wire rack to drain. They can be used right away or cooled and then refrigerated for a week, or frozen for several months.

Once the meatballs are cooked, drain all but about 3 to 4 tablespoons of the butter/oil from the pan. Over medium heat, add an equal amount of the flour left over from dusting the meatballs. Stir to make a roux and cook slowly until it turns a nice golden brown. Think coffee with cream.

Add the stock gradually and turn the heat up to medium-high. Stir well to combine and add more stock or some water if need be. You want this thicker than water, thinner than Thanksgiving gravy. Taste for salt and add if needed.

Put the meatballs in the pan, cover, and cook for 10 minutes over medium-low heat. Add the jelly to the pan. Let it melt and then mix it in gently. Coat all the meatballs with the sauce. Cover and cook another 10 minutes over very low heat. Add the sour cream and just warm through for maybe 3 to 4 minutes.

Serve over mashed potatoes or spaetzle, or with German egg noodles.

VENISON MEDALLIONS WITH MOREL SAUCE

Morel mushrooms paired with venison, antelope, bison, or even the common steak is a marriage far more successful than most pairings between mushrooms and meat—which often compete with one another. This dish is simple, deep, and delicious.

But don't skimp on the morels or the quality of any ingredient: You and your guests will notice. Can't find them in your grocery store? You can buy morels online, or you can substitute shiitakes from the supermarket.

Serves 4

A handful of dried morels, about ¼ cup, soaked in water for
    several hours, or about 20 fresh morels, chopped

1 cup venison or beef stock

4 venison medallions, cut ¾–1-inch thick, or the tenderloins
    from a large deer

Salt

4 tablespoons unsalted butter

1 shallot, finely chopped

2 tablespoons grapeseed oil, or another oil with a high smoke point

1 tablespoon flour

½ cup port wine (something you would drink)

Freshly ground black pepper

If you are using dried morels, remove the morels from the soaking water once they've rehydrated and pour the liquid into a small saucepan. Reduce the soaking water over high heat until you are left with about ¼ cup of liquid. Turn off the heat, pour into a small bowl, and set aside.

Pour the stock into the same saucepan and reduce it to ½ cup over high heat. If you are using dried morels, add this reduced stock to the mushroom liquid. If you are using fresh morels, pour the stock in a bowl and set aside.

Take the venison out of the fridge and salt it liberally. Let it rest at room temperature for 20 to 30 minutes.

If you are using fresh morels, heat a skillet over high heat for 2 minutes. Turn the heat down to medium-high and place the morels in the pan to heat. They will release their water quickly. Let this boil until the water is almost all gone, then add 3 table-spoons of the butter and the shallot. Cook for 3 to 4 minutes, stirring often. Remove and set aside. If you are using dried morels, you do not need to dry-cook them first. Cook them with the shallot in the butter.

Heat a clean pan over high heat for a minute or two and add the grapeseed oil. Heat this for 1 minute. Pat the venison dry with a paper towel and place it in the pan. Sear it for 3 to 4 minutes on one side, then flip. Let it cook through to your taste on the other side without flipping again, another 1 to 3 minutes. Remove from the pan and set aside under foil to rest.

Add the remaining 1 tablespoon butter to the pan and let it melt over medium heat. Add the flour and stir to combine to make a roux. Cook, stirring constantly, for 2 minutes. Add the wine and stir to combine. It will thicken immediately, and if it turns to a paste, add the reserved stock. If it does not turn to a paste, let the port boil a minute, then add the stock. Add the morels.

Once the morels are heated through, lay down a pool of the sauce on 4 plates, then top with venison. Arrange the morels around the meat. Grind black pepper over all and serve at once.

CORNED ANTELOPE

This began as one of those "why not?" experiments that turned out far better than I had expected. So good that every deer hunter really ought to learn this technique. You will get far more enjoyment out of the leg roasts from your deer. I used prong-horn antelope in this recipe, but any red meat will work.

The technique is simple: Brine your meat, then simmer it into tenderness. It takes several days to brine, but it isn't labor intensive at all. Once cooked, the meat will last a couple weeks in the fridge, if you can hold off eating it that long.

About those nitrites. I use them for color, for flavor, and for safety. Can you do this without pink salt? Yes, but your meat will be gray, you will lose some flavor, and there is an ever-so-slight chance you might pick up botulism—not a large chance, but as botulism is one of the most toxic substances known to man, I'd say use the nitrite. You can buy it online at Butcher and Packer and at good butcher shops.

Serves 8–12

½ gallon water

1 cup kosher salt

⅓ cup sugar

½ ounce Insta Cure No. 1 (sodium nitrite)

1 tablespoon cracked black pepper

1 tablespoon toasted coriander seeds

12 bay leaves, crushed

1 tablespoon red-pepper flakes

1 tablespoon dried thyme

1 teaspoon caraway seeds

1 cinnamon stick

6 cloves

5–6 cloves garlic, chopped

3–5 pounds venison roast

Add everything but the venison to a large pot and bring it to a boil. Turn off the heat, cover, and let it cool to room temperature. This will take a few hours.

Meanwhile, trim any silverskin you find off the roast. Leave the fat.

Once the brine is cool, find a container just large enough to hold the roast, place it inside, and cover with the brine. You might have extra, which you can discard.

Make sure the roast is completely submerged in the brine. I use a clean stone to weigh down the meat. Cover and put in the fridge for 5 to 7 days, depending on the roast's size. A 2-pound roast might only need 3 days. The longer it soaks, the saltier it will get, but you want the salt and nitrite to work its way to the center of the roast, and that takes time. Err on the side of soaking it extra days, not fewer.

After the week has passed, you have corned venison. To cook and eat, rinse off the meat, then put the roast in a pot just large enough to hold it and cover with fresh water. You don't want too large a pot or the freshwater will leach out too much flavor from the salty meat; it's an osmosis thing. Cover and simmer—don't boil—the meat for 3 to 5 hours.

Eat hot or cold. It is absolutely fantastic with good mustard and some sauerkraut on a sandwich, and it makes an immaculate hash.

A LITTLE TONGUE

This is a nice little salad that uses offal seamlessly. Unless told, your guests will probably not recognize it as tongue. The end result is a lot like carnitas, although the tongue should be sliced thin in sheets, not shredded.

Serves 4

> 2 quarts lamb, venison, or beef broth
>
> 4 bay leaves
>
> 2 sprigs fresh oregano
>
> 2 deer or lamb tongues (antelope or other smallish cervid will work, too)
>
> 2 large cloves garlic
>
> Pinch of salt
>
> 2 teaspoons mustard (something nice like Dijon)
>
> 2 tablespoons white wine vinegar
>
> ¼ cup olive oil (use the good stuff)
>
> 4 cups salad greens (use exciting greens like arugula, chicories, miner's
>   lettuce, fresh herbs, watercress, dandelion leaves, and the like)
>
> Freshly ground black pepper

In a large pot over medium-high heat, bring the broth, bay leaves, and oregano to a boil. Lower the heat to medium-low, drop in the tongues, and simmer for at least 2 hours, possibly 3. The tongue should give willingly to the point of a sharp knife. If the tongue floats, flip it periodically. Remove from the heat.

While the tongues are still warm, transfer to a cutting surface and peel off the skin with a paring knife. The skin is really the only icky thing about tongue. Underneath, it is pure meat. Slice the peeled tongue quite thinly and return it to the broth to rest.

Place the garlic, salt, and mustard in a mortar and pound it into a paste. Add the vinegar and mix well. Add the oil in little batches, stirring and mixing all the while. Make sure each drip of oil is incorporated before you add more. Continue until it looks like dressing, not like a paste.

In a large bowl, mix the greens with three-quarters of the dressing. Divide the greens evenly on 4 plates.

Remove the tongue slices from the broth and toss with the remaining dressing. Arrange a few slices atop the greens on each plate, grind pepper over all, and serve.

17

WILD BOAR AND WILD CHARCUTERIE

I'll admit it, I was nervous.

Holly and I were bouncing along a ranch road in my pickup, looking for wild pigs. We were members of a club that pooled its money to buy hunting leases on ranch land all over California, and this piece of property was known to have hogs living on it. I sorely hoped we'd find one, but I was anxious about the whole matter nonetheless.

It was my first big game hunt without an experienced guide to keep me from getting into trouble. I'd only shot one pig before in my life, and that was from 50 yards away, with a guide standing next to me. Now I was the guide. Holly was along as an observer. She'd not yet become a licensed hunter, and this was to be her "test hunt," to see if she really wanted to start this pursuit. I felt pressure to perform, to use what I'd learned in the previous hunt to bring down an animal all by myself.

We arrived in late afternoon, and began tooling up and down the ranch's hills looking for likely spots. We did not expect to see any pigs. It was over 90°F, and the pigs would be resting under the shade of the junipers until just before sundown. I knew enough to look for water holes and funnels—places where animals would move through to get to water or food. It was the food that was the issue: The ranch was a barley farm, but the barley had been cut already. Not a great sign.

Finally, we found a canyon with a streambed that wasn't totally desiccated. At the bottom, we found tracks. Lots of tracks. But I was not entirely sure whether the tracks were from deer or pigs; they're very similar. So we set up in a hidden spot on the hillside above and waited. Every few minutes, I'd hear a snap or a crackle that sounded deafening to me, but was only a bird alighting on a dead branch or a ground squirrel scampering around. The sun fell, and we headed out, back to our little motel nearby.

The next morning, we woke before dawn and drove to a different area of the ranch. We rumbled along barley stubble and up and down some precarious dirt tracks. My Toyota Tacoma is reportedly a billy goat when it comes to driving steep dirt roads, but I wasn't keen on testing that reputation. We inched down a steep hill, and about halfway to the bottom, Holly and I both spotted deer on the opposite hillside, which was blanketed in a suede coating of dried native grasses.

"Deer!" We watched, looking for bucks. It wasn't deer season, but if we saw any, we could come back in the fall and try to find them again. No bucks. But just as we finished scanning for antlers, Holly noticed something else on the hillside: little black spots, moving. I noticed them, too. "Pigs!" we both said at the same time.

Problem was, we were in a white truck out in the open, in full view of the deer and hogs. How far were they? Could I make a shot from here? I did not own a rangefinder, and I was too new then to gauge distances well. I felt a stab of nerves. What do I do now? Set up for a shot? What if it's actually 500 yards away, too far to shoot? It didn't look like 500 yards, but . . . oh hell, I just don't know!

But I grabbed my rifle and slipped out of the door. The pigs were on my side of the truck, so I ducked down and crept behind the truck. I'd take a shot off the front of the pickup, using the hood to steady my aim. My heart was beating like a rock concert, and the teeny pig in my crosshairs bounced and weaved. This was not good. I took a deep breath and tried to calm myself. I'd shot long distances before, I thought to myself, trying to forget the part about having never shot from a long distance at anything alive. I somehow steadied myself long enough to squeeze the trigger.

BOOM! In the little valley, the shot sounded like a cannon. The deer ran in all directions. The pigs merely looked up. Including the one I'd shot at. Missed. So I shot again, aiming a little over the hog's back. This time I saw the dust cloud at his feet. I simultaneously thought, "This must be a really, really long shot" and "Holy crap! They're running away!" The pigs took off at a trot over a gentle ridge. Out of sight.

I motioned for Holly to get out of the truck, and we followed the pigs as I reloaded. We walked as quietly as we could to the spot where I'd shot, and it was indeed a long distance, maybe 400 yards or so. A potentially doable shot for a veteran, but not for me. All the way I was thinking to myself, "Shit, shit, shit. This was my one chance to prove I could shoot an animal by myself and I botched it. God, I hope these pigs are still there. . . . "

Rifle ready, we got closer and closer to the ridgeline, where, if the hogs were still there, we'd be able to see them. At first, nothing. Then I saw it: a thin strip of black moving slowly from left to right through a patch of taller grass, heading right for a clearing. I raised my rifle and planted the crosshairs on the pig. I don't fully remember what happened next, but I have an image in my head of the pig coming out of the grass, looking up, and me shooting all at the same time. It fell like a stone and did not move.

I chambered another round as I walked up to the pig. I knew that hogs are hard to kill and was waiting for it to jump up again. But no, the little pig—we noticed it could not have weighed more than 90 pounds—was as dead as Julius Caesar. I learned later that I'd shot it right behind the ear, destroying its skull. It died instantly, for which I am thankful. I laughed with relief. I'd done it! I had successfully killed a big game animal. Without an expert guiding me. And we'd have wild boar to eat! Driving home, pig in the cooler, Holly noticed that we'd been hunting near where actor James Dean had died in a car crash. The connection to Jimmy Dean sausages was too close to miss. Our pig had a name, and forevermore we've referred to this, my first solo big game animal, as Jimmy Dean. I've shot other hogs since then, but none I was more proud of.

SEASONS

Wild hogs are considered an invasive species all over the United States, and there are no bag limits or closed seasons on them, although in most states you do need a hunting license and, in many cases, a special tag for every wild boar you kill.

The traditional homes of wild pig hunting have always been Texas, California, and the Deep South. But hogs are prolific and resourceful animals, and they have spread to much of the rest of the country. Wild hogs have even been spotted in northern states such as Indiana and West Virginia.

While you can hunt wild boar at any time in many states, certain seasons are better than others. Pigs, more than most other animals, taste like what they eat. So tie your hunt in with what they are eating.

Late spring in California, when the landscape is beginning to dry out, is an ideal time. The pigs have been hanging around eating greens and young grains (wild oats and barley are a particular favorite in California), and are just starting to need to move around more to find food. This means they are fat but mobile. If you try to hunt them in early spring, the hogs will still taste good, but they move around less and are tougher to find.

Late fall is another prime time, after the acorns have dropped. Watch the oak trees where you live, and schedule your hunt when they start to fall. Late September to early November is great. Any earlier and the pigs may be lean and strong-tasting because they have resorted to spicier forage in the summer, such as juniper and sages.

Winter hunting is another good option because the pigs are typically well fed, but this is the rainy season in Texas and California, so the dirt tracks into good pig country are often lost in a sea of mud.

HUNTING TIPS

I have hunted hogs for a few years, but my friend Phillip Loughlin, who is a hunting guide, is the real expert. He was kind enough to offer me some of his tips on how to successfully hunt wild pigs.

Hogs can and will cover miles of ground between bed and food. If you can't catch them on the food at daylight, backtrack closer to their beds and wait. Hogs prefer to bed close to their water source. Remember that because pigs can't sweat, they need to be near water to cool off. Even a wet spot from an underground spring will attract them, especially if it's close to their beds. This is a great spot for a midday ambush.

Cereal grains and grasses tend to generate a lot of heat during the digestive process. Hogs that have been eating these things will almost always go straight to water and mud after eating.

Avoid entering bedding areas or creating a lot of disturbance. Hogs consider the beds to be a safety zone, and if they don't feel safe, they will abandon the area. Even the slightest incursion can blow them out. It may be days or even weeks before they come back. This is not a hard-and-fast rule, however. Sometimes they act like deer and come right back when they think the threat is gone.

Hogs almost never stop moving when they're on their feet. It's not entirely futile to try to track a hog if you've got really fresh sign (and if the hogs aren't alarmed), but it can be an exercise in frustration to try to catch up. If the hogs are frightened, you can almost forget catching up to them. It's best to try to get above them and flank them. Or just go find another one.

🐗 Even if a hog is moving fairly quickly or even trotting, don't assume it's frightened. They move fast if they're not eating, especially if they are heading for bed, water, or a food source. Keep an eye on the animal if you can, and see if you can figure out where it's headed.

🐗 On open ground, spooked hogs will only bolt a relatively short distance before they slow down. If you hold your fire until they slow, you have a much better chance at a clean shot.

EQUIPMENT

Pig hunting requires precious little specialized equipment. It is often spot-and-stalk, meaning you find your way to a high point and scan the countryside with good binoculars until you spot hogs, which are often black and appear as moving black specks on faraway hillsides. So that means you need good optics. Definitely the best binoculars you can afford and possibly even a spotting scope. It also means you need sturdy, comfortable boots you can walk miles in. Brush pants are worth buying because the tough canvas or nylon front on these pants will protect you from the various prickly plants you may need to walk or crawl through to stalk or recover your pig.

Camouflage is not strictly necessary, as pigs have poor eyesight. Movement and scent are far more likely to scare them off than the sight of you wearing a pair of jeans. I typically wear brush pants or jeans; strong boots; good, breathable wool socks; and a tan or olive T-shirt. But I've successfully hunted pigs in sneakers, jeans, and a plaid shirt. A hat is a good idea to keep the sun off your head.

You will need a good rifle and scope in the West, although you might want to stick to regular iron sights in the South, where you often see wild hogs up close and personal in the dense undergrowth. It is easier to take aim at short distances with iron sights than with a scope. I shoot a .270, which in my opinion is the best all-around cartridge for big game hunting in America. This caliber will kill anything from a jackrabbit to an elk; the only animals that need a tougher round are grizzly bears and moose. Do not hunt pigs with any rifle smaller than this, because really large hogs will have a thick shoulder blade you might need to break through. Can you hunt hogs with shotguns or a bow? You bet, but you'll need to get within 50 yards. Use slugs or buckshot for shotguns, and your nastiest broadhead point for hogs. They are tough, hard-to-kill animals, and you will want to bring them down as fast as you can.

For hog hunting, keep two sharp knives handy. A hog skin will dull the best blade. Extend the life of the blade's edge by always cutting from the inside out—and never cut across the hair. Have a sharpening steel ready to touch up the blades as you work.

You'll also need several lengths of rope to help you drag the pig. Wild pigs have a very bad habit of falling into the deepest available ravine after you've shot them. And believe me, dragging a dead pig up a steep, dusty ravine in 100°F weather is not fun.

Here's how I use the rope. I cut two lengths each about 3 feet long. I use my knife to cut a slit in between the bone of the pig's hind legs and the Achilles tendon. You can feel it easily. Slip the ropes through these slits and tie them off firmly. To drag, wrap the other end of the ropes around one or both of your forearms, which gives you a lot more leverage to drag than if you just grab the beast and pull. You will also want a longer length of rope in your car or truck to hoist the pig up into the air over a tree limb. It's way easier to skin and gut a pig in the air than on the ground, although in many cases I gut the hog where it fell and then skin later.

A really big cooler is also a must. I have a 100-quart marine cooler that will fit a whole hog up to about 120 pounds. You can also skin and quarter your pig before putting it in the cooler. But because a lot of pig hunting is done in hot weather, ice and a cooler are extremely important. Hog meat can withstand some abuse in terms of temperature, but you really, really want to get that meat as cool as you can as fast as you can. Skinning and gutting promptly go a long way toward doing this.

A muslin game bag is also a good idea. If you are hanging your pig for a while—even a few hours—put it in the game bag, which is usually made large enough for a deer. This creates a barrier between the meat and flies that might contaminate it. I usually gut the pig; save the liver, heart, and kidneys in a bag; skin the animal; and put it in a game bag to hang for an hour or so in the shade. The offal goes on ice immediately. Prop open the body cavity with a stick to let it cool even faster. Then either it goes into the cooler whole, or you can cut off the legs and head before putting everything into the cooler.

WILD GAME CHARCUTERIE

I put the section on sausage making and meat curing in this chapter specifically because the wild boar lends itself so well to the caresses of salt and time. Fresh wild boar meat is nice, but cured is far better. Most of the recipes in this chapter are for cured meat, and many of them are applicable to other animals, such as deer, rabbits, or game birds.

I do a lot of wild game charcuterie, and most good charcuterie highlights the flavor of the meat. The French, for example, often flavor their cured pork with little more than salt and pepper. You can only do this with top-quality pork or with wild boar. Because its diet will be varied and unusual, the flavor of wild boar can run from the sour to the sublime. To gauge that flavor, first smell the meat: If it is a smell you like, start thinking about some of the simpler preparations so you can highlight it. If it's not, start heading toward heavier spiced things like chorizo or spicy coppa.

Most wild pigs are lean, often too lean to make salami and sausages with them solo. If this is the case, you will need to buy domestic pork fat. Try to get pork fat from a serious hog producer, because a great deal of the flavor in your charcuterie will come from the fat. Adulterating a fine flavored wild boar with factory farmed pork fat is a sin. Many farmers' markets have vendors who sell pork. Ask them for some back fat, and they'll be happy to sell or even give it away to you.

Everything that follows here will work with any wild game animal. I've made sausages and cured everything from ducks and geese to pheasants, deer, antelope, and hares. Just remember that you always want to maintain a fat-to-meat ratio of at least 1:4 and no more than 2:3. My sausage recipes are typically 4 pounds meat to 1 pound pork fat, but I've gone with as fatty as 2 pounds fat to 3 pounds meat.

SPECIAL EQUIPMENT NEEDED

- Meat grinder; I use the KitchenAid grinder attachment.
- Hog or beef casings, available at butcher shops or online.
- Sausage stuffer—I don't recommend the KitchenAid attachment; buy a real stuffer.
- Wooden rack to hang sausages to dry.
- And, most important, a cool, humid place to dry-cure meats.

If you are going to make sausages, you will need special equipment. There's no getting around it. You can grind meat in a food processor and stuff by hand with a funnel, but it results in an inferior sausage and is far more work.

To stuff sausages, I use a dedicated stuffer that can handle 5 pounds of sausage at a time. I bought mine from a restaurant supply store, but they are also available online. It cost me more than $100 but makes a huge difference. I don't recommend using a stand mixer's sausage stuffer attachment because when you push the meat through the auger a second time, it damages the meat's structure and can overheat it. Not ready to drop that much money on a dedicated stuffer? Make patties. Other options include wrapping the sausage in blanched cabbage or chard leaves, rolling them in bulgur and making Lebanese kibbeh, wrapping them in caul fat (available from good butchers, although you might need to order ahead), or stuffing grape leaves with the sausage.

BEFORE YOU START

Temperature is vital. Your equipment, meat and fat, and all your liquids need to be cold—almost freezing—before you begin. Once you begin, you need to keep putting things in your fridge and freezer to keep them cold, so make room ahead of time.

Start by putting all your grinding equipment and bowls in the freezer for an hour or so. If you are using pork fat, you can cut it into chunks while frozen. Lamb and beef fat are harder, so you cannot do this as easily.

Why all this emphasis on temperature? Sanitation and chemistry. Colder meat and fat are less likely to spoil. Chemistry comes in when you grind and mix the meat and fat. If they are too warm, the fat can smear over the meat, coating it. This destroys the structure of the sausage by limiting the meat's ability to bind to itself in the mixing stage—when you mix the ground sausage, it creates a bind much like gluten when you knead bread. If your meat is too warm, you'll make spicy cat food, crumbly and nasty. You want your meat and fat close to, but not actually, freezing.

You also need to be prepared to spend a couple of hours on this project. I can make a 5-pound batch in less than an hour, but when I first started, it took me several hours. Don't have anything pressing planned.

If you do plan on stuffing your sausages, hog casings are the easiest to buy. Nearly every good butcher has them, and they are inexpensive. Most come heavily salted in plastic tubs and must be soaked in warm water for a half hour or more to reconstitute them. You also can use narrow sheep casings or very wide beef casings, but you may need to special order them from your butcher, or buy them online from a dealer such as Butcher and Packer or The Sausage Maker. You can buy artificial casings made from edible collagen, but I hate them: They feel like eating cellophane to me.

Finally, you'll need a rack of some sort to hang your links. Sausages need to drip-dry for an hour or more before they go into the fridge. It's also easier to find air bubbles when they are hanging. Any wooden clothes rack or even a large pasta drying rack will work.

MAKING THE SAUSAGE

1. Get all your ingredients ready. Put dry spices and herbs in one bowl, liquids in the fridge.

2. Chop the meat into chunks between 1 and 2 inches across. Cut the fat a little smaller than the meat. To keep your ingredients cold, put your cut meat and fat into a bowl set in a larger bowl filled with ice.

3. When the meat and fat are cut, add the salt and most of your spices. If you want, you can leave out some of the spices or herbs and add them in the final steps, to make them more noticeable in the final sausage. Mix quickly. Cover the bowl with plastic wrap and put the mixture in the freezer for 30 minutes.

4. If you're stuffing your sausages, take out some of the casings. You need 15 to 18 feet for a 5-pound batch of links, which is three or four lengths. When in doubt, use more; casings are cheap. Soak the casings in warm water.

5. Take your grinding equipment out of the freezer and put in the coarse die. Most of the sausages I like to eat are rustic links, not finely ground "city sausages." For a fine sausage, you will want to grind everything first through the coarse die anyway. Push the sausage mixture through the grinder, working quickly. If you use the KitchenAid attachment, use it on level 4, about medium-fast. Make sure the ground meat falls into a cold bowl. When all the meat is ground, put it in the fridge and

clean up the grinder and work area. Repeat with the fine die if you want a less rustic sausage.

6. Add any remaining spices and the liquids to the ground meat. Using the paddle attachment to a stand mixer—or a wooden spoon, or your clean hands—mix the sausage well for 1 to 2 minutes. This is where cold meat matters: You can get a better bind by mixing longer, but the longer you mix, the warmer the sausage gets. It's a balancing act. You want it to look sticky and begin to bind to itself.

MAKING LINKS

If you are making links, put the mixture back in the fridge and clean up again. I cannot stress enough how important it is to work clean. Hot, soapy water is your friend.

Run warm water through your sausage casings, which flushes them and also reveals any leaks. If you get leaks, cut that part of the casing out. If you are using chard, grape, or other leaves, blanch them now. Caul fat needs to be soaked a bit in warm water, too.

Slip a casing onto your sausage stuffer's tube, and leave an end of casing that is at least 6 inches trailing off the end of the tube. You need this to tie off later. Pack the sausage into the stuffer and start cranking it down slowly. You want to push out air from the stuffer first. This is why you don't tie off the trailing end immediately.

When the meat starts to come out, use one hand to regulate how fast the casing slips off the tube. You want it to be slow and regular. Coil the link as you go, and don't be tempted to make links just yet. Remember to leave at least 6 inches of trailing end at the other end of the casing, too. When the sausage is all in casings, tie off one end in a double knot. You could also use household twine.

Now, with two hands, start at the tied-off end of the coil and pinch off what will become two links. I like my links about 6 inches long, but you could go longer or shorter. Gently pinch down and wriggle the sausage back and forth until you can feel your fingers touch. Then with a flip, roll the link you just made forward three to five times. Move down the coil and do the same thing, only this time you must flip the link backward; it's a little harder. This alternating twist will help keep your links from unraveling easily. If all this twisting is too much for you, tie the links off with butcher's twine.

Hang your sausages on the rack so they don't touch each other and find yourself a needle. Sterilize it by putting it into a flame until it glows, then look for air bubbles in the links. Prick them with the needle, and in most cases the casing will flatten itself against the link. Dry your sausages for an hour or two, then put them in a large container in the fridge overnight, with paper towels between each layer. If you are making sausages in cold weather, it's even better to let them hang overnight, but the temperature needs to be no warmer than about 42°F and no colder than about 32°F. You want the sausages to neither freeze nor develop bacteria.

Package the sausages, or eat them the next day. They will keep for a week, but freeze those that will not be used by then.

ADVANCED SAUSAGE-MAKING TIPS

Over the years, I've learned that there is an enormous amount of information vital to mastering any skill that, for whatever reason, never shows up in print. Here are a few tips I can pass along that will help you make even better sausages:

When making fresh sausages, use fresh ingredients. This should be a "duh!" thing to say, but it bears repeating. I've used fresh green garlic in many of my sausages, freshly grated lemon peel, and fresh herbs, and I noticed the difference. Dried ingredients are okay, but fresh is better.

🐇 When you do use dried spices (seeds like black pepper, fennel, coriander, etc.), toast them in a dry pan first. It makes them taste stronger, even weeks later. Don't toast dried leaves like oregano or thyme; they'll burn.

🐇 Buy the best casings you can afford. I had a near-murderous moment once when the "premium" casings I had bought broke again and again. That meant I needed to restuff the sausages—at the risk of them warming up too much, which would ruin the texture. I'm glad no one was around when that happened; I had sharp knives handy. Also, stuff your sausage rather loosely when making the initial coil. This gives you more wiggle room to make links. If your initial coil is too taut, you will not be able to twist it enough to keep the whole coil from unraveling.

🐇 Leave some spices out for the final mix. When you do this, you get some whole pieces, such as caraway or fennel seed, or larger chunks like cracked black pepper or crushed juniper berry. They make the texture of the link a lot more interesting.

🐇 Vary the length of your sausage links depending on how rich they are. This is of course a matter of opinion, but I think leaner links ought to be long and skinny, and fatty ones shorter and plumper.

🐇 Spend the time to trim silverskin, the whitish membrane that encases many individual muscles. It is a huge pain in the ass, but you need to get your knife sharp and trim away gristle and the silverskin membranes on the meat—especially if you are making sausage from the trim of a whole animal and especially if it's a game animal like a boar or deer. If you don't, the silverskin and gristle will gunk up your grinder.

🐇 The poorer the meat quality, the finer the grind. If I am dealing with hopelessly gristly or chewy meat, or meat from an old animal, I will grind it a second time through a fine die. The second grind will greatly improve your sausage.

🐇 Choose your fat wisely. Use pork back fat if possible, although there is plenty of suitable fat in the shoulder. Avoid using fatty bits that are stringy; they usually live between muscles. Also avoid the rock-hard tallow that runs along the back of a deer, antelope, or domestic lamb or goat. It is so hard it will ruin your grinder. If you do want to use the tallow, which is flavorful, finely chop it by hand first.

🐇 If you're cooking slow and low, such as smoking or slow barbecuing, add a bit of nitrite. This last tip is a bit controversial, as many people want to limit their nitrite consumption and fresh sausages typically don't need any added nitrites. But if you plan on slow-cooking your links below 200°F, I'd advise 3 to 5 grams of sodium nitrite (Insta Cure No. 1) for protection against food poisoning. It will also give you a beautiful rosy color within the meat. Add this with your other spices and salt.

The liquid you use to moisten your links matters a lot. The exact same sausage recipe made with red wine will taste different with white wine. Vinegar will change it again, as will water or fruit juice or liqueur; I've added ouzo in a few of my recipes. Put some thought into not only what kind of liquid you want to use, but also the quality of it. If you won't drink it, don't use it.

The most important thing to learn is balance. Make enough sausages, and after a while you will develop an eye for how many spices or herbs would overpower the meat, how long to make links, etc. A good sausage has all flavor elements in harmony. Savory is easy, so is salty. Sour can come from vinegar or a slow-fermented salami, sweet from any number of sources. Herbs need to play well with one another, as do spices. To garlic up a link or not? Will there be a star player, other than the meat? Not every batch I do meets these goals, and a sausage can still be good without doing so. But when you nail it, it is something special.

Which leads to my final bit of advice: Write everything down. If you don't keep accurate notes, you will never be able to tinker with your recipes, and, most importantly, you will never be able to recapture those moments of perfection.

RECIPES

HERBED WILD BOAR SAUSAGES

This is a coarse, country-style wild boar sausage recipe that stresses the flavor of the boar. I use only a few herbs for flavoring, which allows the taste of the meat to come through. Don't make this with a stanky old boar; use only younger animals or those with clean-tasting fat. And yes, you can substitute domestic pork, duck, goose, or venison in this recipe just fine.

Remember to cook the sausages slowly. Good sausages hate high heat. Indirect heat on a wood-fire grill is perfect, but my indoor alternative is to put a spot of oil in an ovenproof pan, brown one side over medium-low heat, flip the links, then put them in a 300°F oven for 20 to 30 minutes. They come out perfectly.

Makes about 20 sausages

4 pounds wild boar meat

1 pound pork shoulder (make sure it's fatty)

Hog casings

25 grams sugar (about 2 tablespoons)

35 grams kosher salt (about 2 tablespoons + 1 teaspoon)

1 teaspoon garlic powder

1 teaspoon dried thyme

1 tablespoon finely chopped fresh rosemary

1 tablespoon finely chopped fresh sage

¼ cup ice water

½ cup white wine

Put the meat in the freezer for an hour or so, or until it is almost frozen.

Take out some hog casings and set in a bowl of very warm water.

Chop the meat and fat into 1-inch chunks. Combine the sugar, salt, garlic, thyme, rosemary, and sage with the meat. Mix well with your hands and let it rest in the fridge for 1 hour.

Grind the mixture through your meat grinder using the coarse die (you can use a food processor in a pinch, but you will not get a fine texture). If your room is warm, set the bowl with the ground meat into another bowl with ice to keep it cold.

Add the water and wine. Mix thoroughly using either a stand mixer with a paddle attachment set on low for 60 to 90 seconds or your (very clean) hands. This is important to get the sausage to bind properly. Once it is mixed well, put it back in the fridge for 10 to 20 minutes.

Stuff the sausage into the casings all at once. Twist off links by pinching the sausage down and twisting it, first in one direction, and then with the next link, the other direction. Or you could tie them off with butcher's string.

Hang the sausages in a cool place. The colder it is, the longer you can hang them. If it is warmer than 70°F out, hang for 1 hour; if it's in the 40s or even high 30s, you can hang the links overnight. Once they have dried a bit—the color of the links will darken—put them in the fridge until needed. Refrigerated, the sausages will keep for at least a week. If you are freezing the sausages, wait a day before doing so. This will tighten up the sausages and help them keep their shape in the deep freeze.

MAZZAFEGATI

This is what to do when life gives you livers. *Mazzafegati* are an unusual fresh sausage from Umbria, in central Italy, and they are delicious roasted over an open fire, especially a wood fire. You can use domestic pork and pork liver for this, but wild boar gives the sausages an extra punch. You can also substitute venison and deer liver, or the meat and liver from ducks or geese. But you'll still need pork fat.

Make sure everything is very cold when you make these sausages. Liver is very moist and will bleed when ground. I chop the liver into chunks when it is still mostly frozen, to limit the amount it bleeds.

Makes 22–24 links

> 1 pound wild boar, deer, duck, or pork liver
>
> 1½ pounds pork fat
>
> 3 pounds wild boar, venison, duck, or goose meat, or pork shoulder
>
> Hog casings
>
> 1 heaping teaspoon coriander seed
>
> 1 tablespoon whole black peppercorns
>
> 3–5 tablespoons pine nuts
>
> 50 grams kosher salt (about 3 tablespoons)
>
> 2 tablespoons sugar
>
> 4 cloves garlic, minced
>
> Peel from 3 Minneola tangerines or oranges
>
> ⅔ cup sweet white wine, such as muscat

Put the liver, fat, and meat in the freezer for 1 hour, or until almost frozen.

Take out some hog casings and set in a bowl of warm water. You will need 3 to 5 lengths, or a total of about 15 feet, to make these sausages. It will be a little longer than you need, but better to have a little extra.

Chop the liver, fat, and meat into 1-inch chunks, then put back in the freezer.

Toast the coriander and black pepper in a dry pan set over medium heat until they become aromatic. Shake the pan often. If the coriander starts popping, turn off the heat and set the pan aside. Put them into a spice grinder or mortar and pestle. Grind as fine or as coarse as you'd like.

Put the pine nuts in the same dry pan you used for the spices. Toast them over medium heat, tossing and stirring often, until they brown. Pay attention, as pine nuts can go from lovely brown to bitter and burnt in seconds. Chop the pine nuts roughly.

Reserve half of the coriander–black pepper mixture. Combine the other half with the salt, sugar, garlic, half the pine nuts, half the orange peel, and the meat. Mix well with your hands and let it rest in the fridge for 1 hour.

Grind the mixture through your meat grinder twice, first using the coarse die, then the fine one (you can use a food processor in a pinch, but you will not get a fine texture). If your room is warm, set the bowl with the ground meat in another bowl of ice to keep it cold.

Add the wine, the reserved coriander–black pepper mixture, and the remaining pine nuts and orange peel. Mix thoroughly using either a stand mixer on low for 60 to 90 seconds or your (very clean) hands. Mixing is important to get the sausage to bind properly. Once it is mixed well, put it back in the freezer.

Stuff the sausage into the casings all at once. Twist off links by pinching the sausage down and twisting it, first in one direction, and then with the next link, the other direction. Or you could tie them off with butcher's string.

Hang the sausages in a cool place for up to overnight (the colder it is, the longer you can hang them). If it is warm out—warmer than 70°F—hang for just 1 hour. Once they have dried a bit, put in the fridge until needed. They will keep for at least a week in the fridge. Put paper towels under the sausages to soak up any moisture. If you are freezing the sausages, wait a day before doing so. This will tighten up the sausages and help them keep their shape in the deep freeze.

LONZINO

Does anyone not like cured meats? Didn't think so. And *lonzino*, a Spanish air-cured pork loin, happens to be a preparation perfect for wild boar. Lonzino ages into a lovely pink, slices well, and tastes not unlike a good cured ham. Is it as good as prosciutto? Nope. But given how easy it is to make, I haven't a clue why more home cooks aren't doing it. You also need good pork or wild boar. Lonzino highlights the innate qualities in the meat, so if you use a smelly old boar or a piece of factory-farmed pork, you will very definitely notice—especially if it is put up next to quality pork.

The only special equipment you need are a gram measure—precision is important in all charcuterie, but especially in this recipe—curing salt, and a cool place to hang your loins. You can get curing salt online, and your hanging place can be anywhere that isn't bone-dry (70 to 80 percent humidity is good) with a temperature ranging from 40° to 60°F.

Lonzino can hang for ages under the proper temperature and humidity settings, but I typically hang it for 3 to 5 weeks. At this stage, it will be dry at the edges, but still fairly moist in the center. The flavor is mild, like a young air-cured ham. Lonzino is silky, only a little salty, and you get a hint of the spices that help cure the meat with every bite. This is a subtle meat.

Makes 1 lonzino

40–45 grams kosher salt (depending on the weight of the loin)

15 grams sugar

5 grams Insta Cure No. 2 (also known as Prague Powder No. 2)

10 grams freshly ground black pepper

5 grams garlic powder

5 grams ground cloves

10 grams onion powder

8 grams dried thyme

2–3 pounds pork or boar loin

Mix all the dry ingredients. Rub them well into the loin, then put the meat in a plastic bag with the air pushed out, or wrap with plastic wrap. If you have a vacuum sealer, you can seal it in a bag. This keeps the meat from drying out.

Keep the meat refrigerated for 12 days. On the 12th day, remove the meat from the wrap, rinse it off, and let it dry on a rack for 2 to 3 hours. I use a portable fan set on low to get a breeze going over the meat.

Truss the meat with kitchen twine (the white stuff) as you would a roast. Leave a long loop at one end so you can hang the loin.

Hang the meat in a cool, humid place to dry. How long? At least another 12 days. The meat should feel firm throughout and be a pleasing red. You can hang it for 6 months or more, but it will become harder and drier the longer it hangs. If you want to hang this for a long time, you will need a humidifier to gently ratchet down the humidity, starting at 80 percent over a month as you cure the lonzino, then down another 10 percent each month, until you settle at 60 percent.

To store: Wrap tightly in butcher paper or, better yet, vacuum-seal pieces of it—I cut the loin into three chunks—and freeze. Unfrozen, it will last indefinitely in the fridge, but it will continue to dry out.

Note: Mold is a matter of course with cured meat. But there are molds and there are molds. Fine white mold is your friend; it is most likely penicillin. Fuzzy white mold is no big deal. Green mold is no fun, and black mold is dangerous. At the first sight of green or black mold, wipe down the meat with a cloth wetted with vinegar. If black mold persists, throw out the meat.

18

UPLAND GAME BIRDS: PHEASANT, GROUSE, QUAIL

Grouse inhabit my dreams now. I hear the thrum of their wings as they flush from dark spaces in dense alder or hazel thickets. I see their mottled shapes zip away through a picket of trees thin and thick. Sometimes I manage to kill one, threading a shotgun pellet through the maze and dropping the bird in the wet duff. Mostly, though, I swing, pull the trigger, and watch the grouse fly into another stretch of the Minnesota Northwoods.

My first grouse hunt had such a dreamlike quality. For 3 days, we walked miles in freezing rain that became snow, through a fairy-tale landscape of damp young forest dotted with odd mushrooms and lit by the scarlet fruit of the highbush cranberry.

With me was my old friend Chris Niskanen. Chris was the guy who convinced me to start hunting; he took me on my first hunt, to chase pheasants in South Dakota. I couldn't hit anything on that trip. The last time I'd seen Chris and his wife, Diana, had been 5 years previous. It felt like an eon. So much had happened in the interim I'd forgotten more news than I could recount to them. But all those years I'd held one wish: to redeem myself in front of Chris. I wanted to show him that after 5 years of practice, I could finally shoot. In some weird way, I felt like a son seeking approval from a father, even though Chris is only a few years older than I.

As soon as I stepped out of the airport and loaded my gear into Chris's truck, the years evaporated. It was like we'd seen each other last month. Good friends are like that. A few hours later, we were outside Grand Rapids, tooling down a dirt road looking for a sign that said "Thunder Hollow." It was raining steadily, the temperatures hovering around 40 degrees. Not ideal.

Chris explained grouse hunting to me as we drove. It's like pheasant hunting in that you walk a lot and do much better with a dog to point at or flush out the birds. Finn, Chris's black Lab, is a flushing dog excellent at retrieving downed birds. The difference between pheasant and grouse is that you get precious little time to react when a ruffed grouse flushes—and when you do see the fleeing bird, which is only about half the time, you must shoot it through a haze of dense undergrowth. Then you need to find the grouse on the forest floor. And, of course, grouse are the color of the forest floor. Thus the dog.

He said good hunting is not measured in dead birds, but in flushes per hour. This recognizes how hard it is to successfully kill a grouse. He said he'd been getting three or four flushes per hour so far this year, and that eight flushes per hour was nirvana. A good strategy is to hunt dusk and dawn, because that's when grouse will wander onto footpaths to eat green things like clover or strawberry leaves.

We had not walked a mile before I realized this kind of hunting stirred me in a special way. The terrain was not overly hilly, the world was still pretty green (although most of the leaves were off the trees), and the forest was dense. It felt like home. I grew up in New Jersey, and spent much of my time exploring the old forests of Watchung and Kittatinny, looking for interesting things. I might have come across a grouse there; I don't remember. But never before in my hunting life had I felt like I was in that environment again. It was a warming feeling—which was good, because the rain was turning to sleet.

"That's a grouse!" Chris stopped in the path. Sure enough, a few grouse were meandering along the path about 40 yards ahead of us, just inside shotgun range. When they saw us, they flushed and Chris let fly with a side-by-side shotgun he'd been shooting since high school. Down the bird went. "You got him!" I shouted. Chris was unsure, but I wasn't. Nor was Finn, who found the bird under a log.

We didn't find any more grouse that evening, and the rain increased as the sun went down. Early next morning, we drove even farther north, to the Beltrami Island State Forest. We turned onto some forest roads and soon found walking trails. Shortly after we started, Finn got excited. "There's a grouse!" Chris pointed to a silhouette of a bird standing on a log not too far into the forest. He gave me the shot because he'd shot the last bird. My goal on this trip was to ultimately eat lots of grouse, so I shot the standing bird. Not exactly the shotgunning prowess I'd wanted to show Chris, but I shut up and enjoyed my first-ever ruffed grouse. It would have been a pretty bird had it not been pouring rain. In the weather, the poor thing looked like a bedraggled lump of feathers.

As we walked on, Chris showed me highbush cranberries, and I began picking some with the idea that a highbush cranberry sauce would go well with my grouse. We walked farther into the thickets and bogs, and came to what must have been a homestead a century ago. Asparagus still sprouted from a patch in a corner of what was now a meadow. Chris was poking around at the edge when a grouse flushed. He shot and missed, but I could still see the bird, so I lifted on it and felled the grouse in one shot from 40 yards. *This* was what I wanted Chris to see! "Nice shot!" Chris said. Suddenly the weather seemed warmer.

Chris shot a few more grouse that day, and I repeated my performance when we tracked another bird that had walked off the path into the brush. Chris and Finn went into the brush to head it off while I crept up the path. The grouse flushed right over Chris's head. He tried a pirouette shot but only caught feathers, while I again had a clear shot and dropped the bird. It felt good.

At the end of the day, we had six grouse in the bag and had eight flushes per hour—all in the driving sleet and a snowstorm that was rapidly becoming a blizzard. Chris said this was what he was talking about when he called it nirvana. Just days before, I would have said he was nuts. Now I knew what he meant.

SEASONS

Seasons for upland game birds vary, but all fall between September and January, with the exception of quail season in Arizona and Georgia, which can extend into February. Of course, there are also the options of game preserves, whose bread and butter are pen-raised pheasants and quail. These seasons start earlier and end later than those for wild birds.

I don't hunt pen-raised birds too often. They are obviously not as wild as their un-penned counterparts, and they fly slower and are far less skilled in the art of escape. The only reason I shoot them at all is because, being pen raised, they can be as fat as a chicken sometimes. This has its advantages at the table. But it still feels like glorified grocery shopping to me, only with a freaked-out live bird, so I visit these places sparingly.

In many states, dove season opens the traditional hunting season each year, as it begins on Labor Day in most places. The season is short, sometimes only a week. I highly advise you to try it. Doves are hard to hit, plentiful, easy to pluck, and absolutely delicious.

Plan on doing most of your upland hunting from September through Thanksgiving, because the later you wait once a season opens, the smarter the birds will be. Hunting pheasant around Christmastime in South Dakota is both a chilly and chancy affair. The roosters have been chased before and will often flush too far for a clean shot.

TYPES OF UPLAND GAME BIRDS
PHEASANTS

The most common upland bird shot in North America, the pheasant is actually a Chinese immigrant, brought here in the 1800s for sport. Apparently they liked the place so much they went wild, and now pheasants can be found in most states. They don't do well in the Far North, however, where the winters can kill thousands, or in the desert, where there is not enough forage for them to eat.

With the exception of the wild turkey and the sage grouse, the pheasant is the largest of the upland game birds, weighing up to 4 pounds if it's a rooster. Most states forbid the shooting of hen pheasants, for conservation reasons. Pheasants like to be near people, especially grain farmers, as seeds are their preferred food. Find lots of seeds—wheat, corn, milo, sorghum, etc.—and chances are you will find pheasants.

When hunting pheasants, you can easily tell the rooster because it is flashy and showy, with iridescent feathers and a bright white ring around its neck. Roosters also sport extremely long tails—the best way to spot a rooster in a hurry—and they also cackle when they flush, making an "urck urck urck!" sound as they fly off.

If you want to hunt wild pheasants, get thee to the Midwest. The Dakotas, Kansas, Nebraska, and Iowa all have excellent populations.

QUAIL

There are lots of different native quail in the United States, especially around Arizona and New Mexico, which have three species in abundance. The quail that probably comes to mind to anyone familiar with the bird is either the bobwhite of the South or the California quail, also known as the Valley quail—it's the one with the funny "hat."

Quail are small (less than a pound), mottled birds with black-and-white eye patches, and, in the case of the western quail species, tufts of feathers on the top of their heads. Quail travel in large groups called coveys. You almost never flush just one quail. Like pheasants, they are seed eaters and have white meat and a mild flavor. Unlike pheasants, quail don't need farm fields to thrive. They love the open woods, and in California can often be found in blackberry bushes or in a manzanita forest.

Both sexes of quail are legal game, and the trick to shooting quail is to conquer your nerves when several dozen burst out of a thicket 5 feet from your face. What's more, California quail will flush in waves, so just when you think they're gone, several more will flush out of the bush. Finding a downed quail is also difficult, as they blend in perfectly with the ground cover. Dogs are vital help in recovering them.

The best states for quail are Texas, California, Oregon, Arizona, Oklahoma, and in the Deep South.

HUNS AND OTHER PARTRIDGES

Fortunately for residents of the northern tier of states, what they lack in quail they make up for in partridges. Imported partridges—essentially, small pheasants, from an eating standpoint—such as the Hungarian ("Huns") and chukar are all over the country. Huns are also known as gray partridges, and chukars are also called red-legged partridges, although they are a different species from the real red-legged partridge, which lives in Spain. Unlike pheasants, you can legally hunt both males and females of these species.

Chukars are birds of arid regions and rocky hillsides. Hunting wild ones requires stamina and the willingness to walk up and down steep hillsides. Like quail, they also travel in extended family groups, so you will rarely find just one.

Huns prefer the high plains of the Dakotas, Montana, and southern Canada, although they can also be found as far west as Idaho and in parts of upstate New York. They are extremely fast fliers and, once flushed, will keep flying until they're in the next county. Don't bother chasing them.

THE GROUSE FAMILY

Our largest upland game bird other than the wild turkey is the sage grouse of the western plains. Its numbers are so limited that the government is considering a ban on hunting them. But the sage grouse is just the largest in a large family of native game birds in North America that includes the blue grouse, spruce grouse, sharp-tailed grouse, ptarmigan, and the incomparable ruffed grouse, my favorite bird to eat. There's a grouse for pretty much every habitat in the northern part of North America.

Ruffed grouse are mottled, mostly brown birds with an angular "hat" that gives them a slightly hawkish look, and weigh just under 2 pounds. They live in forests and old pastures from the far northwestern corner of California to eastern Oregon and Washington and to the Rocky Mountain states; they skip the Great Plains and return in force in northern Minnesota. You can find them all through the Appalachian states up to Maine, which has arguably the best ruffed grouse hunting in America. Canada has even better grouse hunting, however, as the birds are present through most of that country.

Sharptails are similar to ruffed grouse but are grayer and more spotted, and run a little more than 2 pounds. This is the grouse of the northern Great Plains, while its cousin the prairie chicken inhabits the really open plains farther south. Prairie chickens are in steep decline, too, so your hunting opportunities for these birds are limited. Sharptail meat is darker than other grouse and can be strong-tasting. I find this an asset, especially if you pair it with the mild meat of a pheasant or partridge.

Blue and spruce grouse, which can top 3 pounds, live in the pine forests of the western states as well as the far north of Minnesota and Wisconsin and all of Maine. They are, as their name suggests, "sprucy" in flavor and are not everyone's cup of tea.

DOVES AND PIGEONS

Two of my favorite birds to hunt. Most of the doves we hunt are either the common mourning dove or the white-winged dove, both of which run less than a quarter pound. You'll need at least two per person for a meal, and four is better. Good thing they are among the most numerous birds in North America and the most prolific. Every state has this bird, although they flee the northern tier once the weather cools. Another popular dove for hunters is the imported Eurasian collared dove, which is nearly twice the size and is just as tasty as a mourning or white-winged dove. Eurasians look like mourning doves but have a black collar on the back of their necks.

Common pigeons can be fine table fare when hunted in rural areas; I don't eat city pigeons. Barnies, as we call country pigeons, eat grain and seeds and hang out in old barns. They often live to be 7 or 8 years old in the wild, which means they'll be tough. Fortunately, pigeon rillette and pigeon pâté are wonderful. Young pigeons, which you can tell by their clean-looking feet and blue-shafted pinfeathers, are excellent roasted whole.

There is also a band-tailed pigeon that lives along the West Coast. These are the largest species of pigeon in North America, running nearly a pound. Hunting is strictly controlled, however, so if you are lucky enough to get a few bandtails, treat them royally.

HUNTING TIPS

For most upland birds, you'll probably need to hunt with a well-trained dog; more on this in the Equipment section.

Make sure you get a proper fitting for your shotgun, especially if you are left-handed or are a woman. Most shotguns are designed to fit an average, right-handed man. Hire a professional to do this for you. The difference between consistently killing birds and flailing around is a well-fitted shotgun, and practice. The stock of the gun can be altered to fit your neck size, handedness, overall height, hand size, and arm length. Getting this fit correct is so vital to your overall success as a shotgun hunter that I cannot emphasize this enough.

Use the proper shot. Doves need only target loads, with light charges and tiny, No. 7 or No. 8 shot. Woodcock are the same. Quail are best killed with No. 7s or the larger No. 6s. Pheasants and pigeons don't die easily and require more powerful charges and shot as large as No. 4 sometimes. Grouse are in between; I use No. 5 or No. 6 shot for them.

Practice your shooting. Then practice some more. You might only get one or two opportunities to shoot on some of your upland bird hunts, so you want to make the most of those chances when they occur. Skeet, trap, and sporting clays all provide good, fun practice and will help build muscle memory when those unexpected flushes surprise you. Skeet was originally designed to mimic grouse shooting. Sporting clays can help with a wide variety of field shots. Trap is great practice for connecting with those rising, quartering-away pheasants.

Understand your game. Know the intimate details of how pheasants, grouse, quail, and other game birds live and eat. You'll kill more birds if you know what they eat and where they live. Spend some time on the Web sites of Pheasants Forever, Quail Forever, and the Ruffed Grouse Society, which have extensive information on the habits of game birds.

Hunt until the end of shoot time, which is often a half hour past sundown. Upland game birds, like most wildlife, are particularly active in the mornings and the evenings. You want to hunt toward the end of legal shooting time, when your chances of encountering birds are high. Many other hunters will have cleared out of the fields and forests by then, so there's the added benefit of less competition.

Learn to walk without looking at your feet. It sounds crazy, but it's true. Try walking through thick brush without looking at your feet and you'll see. It's a learned skill. Birds flush into the air without warning, and you need every millisecond you can get to see them, get your shotgun up, track the bird, and pull the trigger. Rarely do you get more than a few seconds before the bird is out of range.

When a bird falls, mark that spot. Always. Before the high five. Walk directly to that spot, and do not take your eyes off it for anything. Upland game birds are all extremely well camouflaged and can disappear in the duff if you are not focused. And no one wants to kill a bird and fail to recover it.

Be safe. Wear plenty of blaze orange afield to let others know your whereabouts. I always wear a blaze orange vest and often a hat, too. People get shot in upland bird hunting when shooters are careless, letting the excitement of tracking a bird cloud their judgment. Don't shoot at low-flying birds that could endanger a hunting dog or another hunter. A good rule of thumb is to wait until the bird you are tracking is framed by blue sky.

EQUIPMENT

This is a short list. You need a shotgun, a hunting vest, brush pants or chaps, a good pair of walking boots . . . and a dog. While it is true you can hunt upland game birds without a dog, your chances of success in actually finding and, more importantly, retrieving shot birds go up exponentially with a good gun dog.

And gun dogs aren't cheap. Yes, you can pick up a Lab or a Brittany puppy from a pound, but you have no idea what its genetics are, and even then you must spend a lot of time training your animal to be a good gun dog. Or you need to spend money to have someone else do it, and we're talking several thousand dollars.

Some people like flushing-retrieving dogs such as Labs, but most upland hunters prefer pointing dogs, which seek out game birds and freeze when they find them, allowing you to walk to where the dog is pointing before the birds fly away. It is an exhilarating thing to hunt with a pointer, and it's why many upland bird hunters seek no other game. Working with your dog can quickly become an obsession.

My advice for beginners would be to hunt with outfitters who can provide dogs, or better yet with friends who already have hunting dogs, to see if the upland bug bites you. If it does, get that dog. It'll be worth it.

Full disclosure: I don't have a dog. I don't hunt quail—California's most abundant upland bird—very often because of this, as quail are especially tough to find once downed. Pheasants are huntable without a dog, however. You need to move slowly along the edges of fencerows or farm fields, or patches of high brush. It's better to hunt in pairs, so one person drives the pheasants ahead of him (a pheasant will always prefer to run away rather than fly) while the other waits ahead in ambush. It doesn't always work.

AGING GAME BIRDS

I used to recoil at the idea of hanging shot pheasants or partridges ungutted and in their feathers for days. It did not seem terribly hygienic or sane to me. Old texts wax rhapsodic about the sublime flavor of "high" game, which usually means pheasants that have hung for more than a week. This, I'd decided, was madness. I was wrong.

Nearly everyone would probably agree with me that dry-aged beef is the finest expression of that meat. It is concentrated, savory, and tender—and very expensive because dry-aging reduces the water content of the meat, and it also results in a layer of crusty, slightly moldy ick on its outer edges that must be removed before selling or serving.

Hanging beef—and venison—is important in part because cattle tend to be dispatched at about 18 months to 2 years of age, old enough to get a tad tough on the teeth. A white-tailed buck sporting trophy antlers is likely to be 3 to 6 years old. Pork and domestic chickens are slaughtered young, and young animals are already tender.

Enter the pheasant. A pheasant is a close cousin of the domestic chicken and when eaten fresh has, as Jean Anthelme Brillat-Savarin puts it in his *The Physiology of Taste,* "nothing distinguishing about it. It is neither as delicate as a pullet, nor as savorous as a quail." Those who have eaten fresh pheasant—and by fresh I mean unhung—can't help but think, "So what? This just seems like a slightly tough and slightly gamy chicken." They are correct, especially with pen-raised birds or those shot at a game preserve.

One day, after my girlfriend Holly and I managed to put four birds in the bag after some 6 miles of tramping around, I finally decided to hang some in my salami fridge, which

is set at 55°F. (Yes, I have a salami fridge. Is that weird?) But I did not know how long to hang them. Brillat-Savarin doesn't give a timetable, but says that "the peak is reached when the pheasant begins to decompose; its aroma develops, and mixes with an oil which in order to form must undergo a certain amount of fermentation, just as the oil in coffee can only be drawn out by roasting it." Sounded pretty hard core. More recently, Clarissa Dickson Wright—one of the former Two Fat Ladies, my favorite TV food personalities—says of pheasant: "Hang it you must, even if for only three days, for all meat must be allowed to rest and mature." Clarissa's preference is a week to 10 days.

Fortunately, science exists on the topic of hanging game birds. My best source is an Australian government publication that did some rigorous experiments. Pheasants hung for 9 days at 50°F have been found by taste panels to be more acceptable than those hung for 4 days at 59°F or for 18 days at 41°F. The taste panels thought that the birds stored at 59°F were tougher than those held for longer periods at lower temperatures. Pheasants hung at 50°F became more gamy in flavor and more tender with length of hanging.

One issue solved. Food writers rarely talk about temperature of hanging because most of them think about hanging pheasants outside, which is fine if you don't live in California; even in November, it is typically too warm to properly hang game. It seems 50°F is ideal, and 55°F is acceptable. I aged my birds at 50° to 55°F for 3 days.

Furthermore, an English study from 1973 found that *Clostridia* and *E. coli* bacteria form very rapidly once you get to about 60°F, but very slowly—and not at all in the case of *Clostridia*—at 50°F.

That same study found that field care of the birds is vital. Under no circumstances should you allow pheasants to pile up in warm conditions because doing so will slow cooling so much that the dead birds will develop bacteria in their innards. This is no bueno.

Left undiscussed by the food writers is the importance of feathers and innards to the hanging process. Here's my take: The feathers provide protection for the skin against drying out during aging. Pluck the feathers right away and you can still age the bird, but the skin will be unacceptably dry. I hung our birds in the feathers.

As for the guts, I am on the fence about whether to remove them. I think they do add flavor, although at 50° to 55°F this is going to take some time to develop. For what it's worth, a pheasant's body temperature runs about 105°F. I kept the innards in our pheasants.

After they were aged 3 days, I noticed two things when I plucked and gutted our pheasants: One, they were pretty dry inside; and two, the innards in three of the four birds looked fine and wholesome, not ratty and stinky. Maybe the *je ne sais quoi* that Brillat-Savarin discusses does not appear until later.

A few things you should know. First, aging works with any game bird. The general rule is the larger the bird, the longer you can hang it. Doves and quail need just a day or so, while grouse, partridges, woodcock, and pigeons can go as long as 5 days.

Don't try to wet-pluck an aged game bird. You must dry-pluck these birds because the skin gets looser, and scalding (more on this ahead) does not seem to help with the feathers. It was a major bummer to scald one bird and rip some of the skin. Dry-plucking, you should be warned, takes forever, but the results are worth it. I'll go into more detail about plucking in a moment.

To eat the giblets or not? I'd say go for it for birds aged up to 3 days, if they have not been shot up. Any sign of ickiness in the innards and you should toss them.

So, to wrap up, here's what I found.

🐾 Keep your birds as cool and as separate as possible in the field. Use a game strap, not the game bag in your vest. Separate your birds in the car or put them in a cooler, and do not get them wet!

🐾 You can hang your birds by the neck or feet with the same results, as several studies have shown.

🐾 Hang the birds between 50° and 55°F for at least 3 days, and up to a week with an old rooster. Old roosters will have horny beaks, long, blunt spurs, and feet that look like they have been walked on for quite some time. They will also have a stiff, heavy keelbone. Hen pheasants, usually shot at preserves, only need 3 days.

🐾 Do not hang any game birds that have been gut-shot or are generally torn up. Feel around the body of the bird for shot holes, and pay special attention to the tail area. You don't want too much damage there, which can be a sign of a gut-shot bird. Butcher damaged birds immediately and use them for a pot pie or something else.

🐾 Dry-pluck any bird that has hung for 3 days or more.

🐾 Wash and dry your birds after you pluck and draw them. Only then should you freeze them.

HOW TO PLUCK A PHEASANT, QUAIL, OR GROUSE

Plucking a game bird is not hard, but it requires patience. Unlike ducks or geese, upland game birds have relatively thin and loose skin—skin that will tear very easily if you try to rush the job.

There are two methods: wet plucking and dry plucking. Dry plucking is exactly what it sounds like: You just start plucking feathers off the bird. Although many people swear by it, I never do this with fresh pheasants because the wet-plucking method works so well. I will only dry-pluck pheasants that have hung for a few days. Pigeons and doves are very easy to pluck, so I dry-pluck all I shoot.

WET PLUCKING

Quail, partridges, or any birds that have been shot up get wet-plucked. Wet plucking means scalding the bird before plucking. To do this, you need a large pot of water at scalding temperature. What is scalding temperature? Steaming, but not boiling—not even simmering. If you have a thermometer, shoot for 170°F.

Once you have the water hot enough, pluck the bird's tail feathers out, one by one. Then grab the pheasant by the head or feet and plunge it into the water. Hold it under for 30 seconds. Lift it out and drain until the water stops coming off in a stream. Repeat this three times. This means you have dunked the bird for a total of 90 seconds.

Pluck the bird while it is still warm, so only scald one bird at a time. Start with the wings, back, and neck, then move to the breast and legs. It is very important to take your time. Go feather by feather if need be, especially around the breast. You want it to look pretty and not torn.

The feathers on the wings of upland birds come off easily. But the breast, and anywhere around a shot hole, is by far the hardest part, to my mind. When you have shot holes, anchor the skin down with the fingers of one hand and pluck one feather at a time with the other. It's the only way to get them off without tearing the skin.

When you are finished, gut the pheasant (save the liver, heart, and gizzard, if you wish) and wash it well. Dry the bird with a paper towel thoroughly, then set it on another paper towel in a lidded container in the fridge for 2 to 7 days. Pheasants age well this way, although this is not the same thing as hanging your birds.

DRY PLUCKING

Start on the back and the wings as you would with a scalded pheasant. Remember to PLUCK, not pull. Use a quick snap of the wrist to yank a feather out very quickly, while anchoring the skin down with several fingers of your other hand. Under no circumstances should you try to grab more than a couple feathers at a time, or you will rip the skin.

The legs pluck the easiest. The neck has a few areas that pluck easily, but the loose or limp areas are a devil. Expect to get a few tears.

There are two kinds of feathers on an upland game bird: quill-type feathers with a stiff core, and wispy underfeathers. The underfeathers pluck very easily, while the quill feathers are guaranteed to rip the skin if you pluck them incorrectly.

To pluck quill feathers correctly, anchor the skin down and in one motion, yank each feather out first the way it is attached, then the opposite way in a kind of arc. It is *very* important to do only one or two feathers at a time when you get to these feathers, which are on the neck, along each side of the breast, and on the flanks of the bird.

The wings are pretty easy, but watch out for where the wings meet the body. This area tears easily.

Save the breast for last. It can be persnickety, but it is the showpiece of a whole plucked bird, so you don't want to mess it up.

RECIPES

Glazed Roast Pheasant, Grouse, or Partridge

There's something lovely about a well-roasted, sweet-and-savory glazed bird. Chickens are the norm, but there is no reason not to do it with pheasants. After all, they are basically ditch chickens. Any other upland game bird will work, too.

Truly wild game birds are very lean and benefit from brining for 6 to 8 hours before cooking. Many hunters shoot pheasants and partridges at hunting preserves, however, and while not exactly the most challenging to "hunt," pen-raised birds do have the advantage of being fat. And tender. This recipe is ideal with this sort of ditch chicken.

Be sure to brine the bird if it is wild, and start the cooking breast side down. Whatever fat the bird has will drip down onto the breast and help keep it moist. Also, watch your glaze once it's on. You can go from caramelized loveliness to burnt crap in about 2 minutes.

Oh, and as for the prickly pear syrup? If you don't have prickly pears, don't worry.

Use any fruit syrup, or pomegranate molasses, honey, or maple syrup. All are good, just different.

Serves 2 hearty eaters

¼ cup kosher salt

4 cups water

1 pheasant, 2 grouse or partridges, or 4–6 quail, plucked, with skin on

1 teaspoon ground red pepper

¼ cup **Prickly Pear Syrup** (see page 28), or any other syrup

Freshly ground black pepper

Mix the salt and water together and whisk to dissolve the salt. When it is dissolved, pour it over the pheasant in a plastic, glass, or ceramic container. Cover and leave in the fridge for at least 4 hours and up to 10 hours; 6 hours is ideal.

Remove the bird from the brine and pat dry. Ideally, you would leave it sitting in the fridge, breast side up and uncovered, for a day. This will help you get a crispy skin. You don't have to do this, but it will make for a better bird.

When you are ready to cook the bird, remove it from the fridge. Let it rest on a cutting board for 20 to 30 minutes while you preheat the oven to 450°F.

Dust the pheasant with ground red pepper. Place it breast side down on a rack in a roasting pan. If you don't have a proper rack, rig up something with halved onions, carrots, or the like and place the pheasant on top. I arrange potatoes around the bird, which serve as a good side dish.

Roast the pheasant for 18 minutes, then lower the heat to 375°F and roast for another 20 minutes. For

partridges or grouse, roast 12 minutes at the higher heat, then 10 minutes at the lower heat. For quail, it's 10 minutes on the high heat and 5 minutes on the lower heat.

Turn the bird breast side up and baste with the syrup. Roast for another 20 to 30 minutes, basting twice in the first 20 minutes. Keep watching the glaze, and remove the bird immediately if it burns too much. Expect some burning at the edges of the legs and wings. Roast partridges or grouse for 10 to 20 minutes, and quail 10 to 15 minutes.

When the bird is done (the thigh should be 160°F when poked with a thermometer), remove to a cutting board and tent loosely with foil. Leave the bird undisturbed for 10 to 15 minutes.

Grind some black pepper over the bird right before you serve it.

FRENCH PHEASANT, HUNTER'S-STYLE

I developed this dish from a recipe I found in Roy Andries de Groot's *The Auberge of the Flowering Hearth*. De Groot's recipe is for an old stewing hen or young rooster, but I find pheasants work just as well. And there is no reason not to use grouse, partridges, or even quail. If you decide on chicken, find a stewing hen if you can.

De Groot's recipe is French, from Chartreuse, in the alpine regions. Yet it is, at its heart, a version of the familiar chicken cacciatore. The French version is, as you might guess, a bit more refined. It has tomatoes, yes, but also a little heavy cream. The French style also has Armagnac, a kind of brandy, and vermouth, as well as shallots. Cacciatore requires mushrooms, and here I use fresh chanterelle mushrooms, which are available at some farmers' markets, but also online.

Another thing that makes the French version distinct is how you brown the chicken or pheasant. The name *rousille* comes from the local dialect in Chartreuse; it means "slightly burnt." And yes, you brown the hell out of the meat before simmering it in tomatoes and brandy.

I use only legs, wings, and thighs here. Save the breasts for another dish.

Serves 4–6 (can be doubled)

Salt

Legs, wings, and thighs of 2 pheasants or chickens

4 tablespoons olive oil

½ cup Armagnac or other brandy

1–2 cups crushed tomatoes

½ pound chanterelle or other fresh mushrooms, roughly chopped

4 tablespoons butter

10–12 small whole boiling onions or shallots, peeled

½ pound smoky bacon, cut into batons or ½-inch pieces

½ cup vermouth

2–3 tablespoons heavy cream

2 tablespoons cornstarch or arrowroot

Chervil or parsley

Salt the pheasant or chicken pieces well and let them come to room temperature for 20 to 30 minutes.

In a large, heavy skillet, get the oil hot over medium-high heat. Pat the pheasant pieces dry and brown them well. Do not crowd the pan, and adjust the heat as needed so you get a good sear without scorching. It could take 15 to 20 minutes to get all the pieces nicely browned.

Put the browned pieces into a pot or Dutch oven with a lid. When all the pieces are browned, put the Dutch oven over medium-high heat, pour in the Armagnac, and bring to a boil. Add the tomatoes, turn the heat down to a bare simmer, and cover.

Wipe the skillet out well. Bring it to high heat and add the mushrooms. Shake the pan constantly until the mushrooms begin to lose their water. They should squeak in the pan until then. Dislodge any that get stuck on the pan with a wooden spoon. Once the mushrooms have lost most of their water, add the butter and cook, stirring frequently, until they begin to brown. Sprinkle them with salt. Once they look lovely, add them to the pheasant.

Add the onions to the skillet, adding more butter if needed. Brown them well and then add them to the pot with the pheasant.

Add the bacon to the skillet; turn the heat down to medium. Fry until crispy, then add to the pheasant.

Pour the vermouth into the pot, bring it to a strong simmer, then drop the heat to low, cover, and cook for at least 1 hour. An old pheasant or rooster will take longer. Check every half hour. You want the meat to almost fall off the bone. Taste the sauce for salt, and add if needed.

When the meat is ready, turn off the heat and ladle the juices into a saucepan. Pour the heavy cream and cornstarch into a small bowl and mix well, then whisk into the juices over medium-low heat. Bring it all to a simmer and let it reduce until the sauce coats the back of a spoon.

Pour the sauce back into the pot with the meat. Toss in lots of chopped chervil or parsley. Serve with mashed potatoes, polenta, or crusty bread, and a light red, such as a Beaujolais or Grenache, or a dry rosé or big white, such as a Viognier.

GAME BIRD SALAD WITH FENNEL

Cooling salads are the way to go in summer, especially here in Northern California, where 100°F is pretty normal. Fennel has the same cooling properties as cucumbers, so I decided to base an upland game bird salad on it, adding some fennel pollen and some fresh green fennel seeds, too.

You can buy fennel pollen online, but the green seeds are not sold, to the best of my knowledge. I grow fennel, so I get them naturally. If you live in the West, where wild fennel is common, you can forage for green fennel seeds in July and August. No worries if you can't find the seeds, though, as the salad will be fine without them.

The method for cooking the bird—you can use pheasant, chicken, partridges, turkey, or grouse—is special and results in very tender meat. You poach the skinless breasts in broth very, very gently. It is foolproof. And you don't use the skin here, either. If you have the skin on your bird breasts, fry it up and eat it as a treat.

Let this salad marinate for at least an hour or two before you serve it, so the flavors will meld. It's good made the day before, too. I like to eat it with a crisp white wine and some crusty bread as a light summer supper.

Serves 2 (can be doubled)

1 quart pheasant, turkey, or chicken broth

1 whole pheasant, grouse, or chicken breast, or half a turkey breast

1 medium fennel bulb, chopped

2 teaspoons fennel pollen

1–2 tablespoons green fennel seeds (optional)

1 tablespoon mint leaves, chopped

1 small red chile pepper, finely chopped (wear plastic gloves when handling)

Peel and juice of 1 lemon

¼ cup olive oil (use the good stuff)

Salt and freshly ground black pepper to taste

Bring the broth to a simmer in a large lidded pot. Turn off the heat and add the pheasant breasts. Make sure they are submerged. Cover the pot.

Meanwhile, chop the fennel bulb into pieces the size you'd want to eat. I like them about the size of my thumbnail. Put the fennel in a large bowl, add all the remaining ingredients, and set aside.

Pheasant and grouse breasts should be fully cooked in 20 minutes. Turkey and chicken breasts are larger and will take longer. A turkey breast might require 45 minutes in the warm broth, and you might need to turn the heat to its lowest setting to keep it warm. Remove the meat and set on a cutting board. Save the broth for soup or something else. It will keep in the fridge a week or so.

When the pheasant is cool enough to handle, shred it into pieces. I like the texture and appearance of shredded meat, but if this skeeves you out, I suppose you can chop it. Add it to the fennel mixture and let this sit, covered, at room temperature for an hour or so before eating. You can also store it overnight in the fridge.

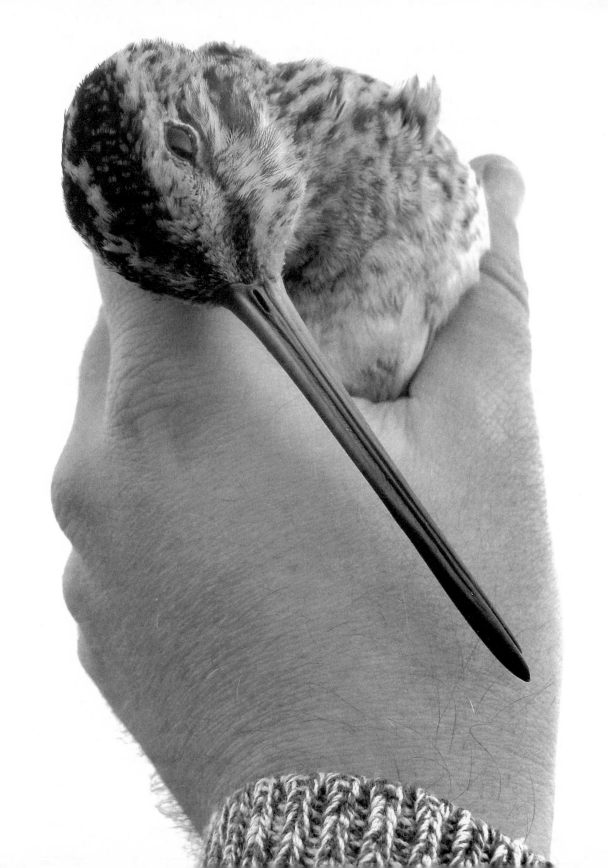

19

WATERFOWL: DUCKS, GEESE, AND THE MYSTICAL SNIPE

Nobody told me it was going to be like this.

I was standing in a swamp, staring at two ducks that had exploded off the water and were zooming away at what seemed like something close to the speed of sound. I sighed. It had happened again.

I taught myself how to hunt ducks and geese. I had no mentor, and for a long while I did not know any other duck hunters. So I read books on duck hunting (useful but abstract), watched hunting television shows (mostly useless), watched what other people did (felt like watching a foreign movie with no subtitles), and, most of all, sloshed around in the marsh by myself.

The mistakes I made could fill a book. I got too close to some hunters' decoys and was yelled at. I arrived at the marsh precisely at shooting time, the absolute worst time to be moving around. I had no idea which bird was which. I couldn't shoot my shotgun worth a damn. I had the wrong waders, the wrong boots, the wrong gun, the wrong ammo, the wrong duck call. I was a disaster.

But I learned. I began my duck-hunting life as a "jumpshooter," a person who walks around hoping to scare ducks into the air and then shoots them. It is a very effective style of hunting—so long as you have the marsh to yourself, something that rarely happens where I live.

The first waterfowl I ever shot was a moorhen, a quiet relative of the common coot that lurks in still water and eats water plants and various bugs. I was ecstatic. I'd finally, after several boxes of ammo (each holding 25 shells), brought down a bird. I skinned it right there in the parking lot of the swamp, something I later learned was a no-no.

I then became a coot killer. Coots are more closely related to pheasants than ducks, have dark burgundy meat, fishy-tasting fat and skin, and have the singular advantage of requiring a long time to get into the air when jumped, unlike actual ducks, which can be airborne instantly. I got good at hunting coots, but I soon grew tired of eating them, although once skinned, their breast meat is as savory as any duck's.

So I plunked down several hundred dollars and hunted with guides. This was a new style of hunting, in fancy duck blinds with lots of decoys all around. And the guides could call! I'd not even mastered the simple teal whistle, so I'd been largely silent on my marsh excursions. I stood rapt the first time I saw a guide call in a mallard from a clear blue sky. I missed it, of course, but it was still wonderful to watch.

Still, I learned a lot from those guides. I learned about the correct equipment, how and when to call, where decoys ought to go, what the good duck hunting days are (north wind and a bit stormy are best in California), which ducks were the best table fare (pintails and teal), and why geese are so hard to hunt. It's because there is often a very old goose somewhere in the V who has seen hunters for many seasons and no longer fools so easily. That goose, more often than not, prevents his or her friends from coming too close.

Yet even after a dozen guided trips, I was still just a newbie. That was eight seasons ago, and only recently have I felt like a solid waterfowl hunter. This is a pursuit with a long learning curve; my friend Charlie has been hunting for 50 years and says he still sees new things every time he hunts. So why bother with ducks and geese? Bite into a perfectly roasted duck, with salty-crispy skin, a layer of sweet fat underneath, all covering beautiful pink breast meat, and you will understand. There is nothing I eat that touches me in a more primal way than simply roasted duck. I put up with ungodly early mornings, frozen fingers, leaky waders, an aching neck, and the sticker shock of shooting high-end shotgun shells all to see the sun rise over a marsh covered in waterfowl. And in the back of my mind, there is always the taste of that perfect roasted duck.

SEASONS

Duck and goose seasons vary, depending on the state. You will need to check your state's fish and game department first. In general, however, many southern states have a season just for teal, a small but tasty duck, which begins in September. A few northern states have begun early seasons on resident Canada geese, too. Many northern states begin their main duck seasons in September as well, because the birds migrate through those states en route to the South and California.

Duck hunting is typically in full swing by October and November, petering off in the far north in early January, when the hunting gets really hot in California and the South. It's mostly over by the end of January, except for a few states that have special hunts for geese in spring. Many geese, snow geese in particular, have become so numerous they are destroying their nesting grounds in the Arctic and farmers' crops in the United States. Both the Midwest and Pacific regions have these spring goose hunts, which are typically in March and April.

TYPES OF WATERFOWL

There are scores of different kinds of waterfowl that are legal game in North America, everything from the tiny snipe, which looks like a stubby sandpiper, to giant swans and sandhill cranes. Knowing your birds is vital to being not just a good hunter, but a law-abiding one. Many birds that are illegal to hunt look a lot like their legal cousins, and many more have restricted bag limits. While the daily limit in California has in recent years been seven birds, if you get caught with seven canvasback ducks, your wallet will suffer and you could have your license revoked. Buy a bird identification book! Remember, it is better to pass up a shot on an unidentified bird than it is to risk running, ahem, afowl of the law.

SNIPE

I reckon I'll start small. Yes, snipe are real. They look like a short-legged sandpiper with a very long, pointy beak. They are tasty, too. But snipe are not easy to hunt, and they closely resemble a dowitcher, which is illegal to hunt. You will need to pay careful attention before shooting. A few tips: Snipe tend to be solitary or in small groups. Dowitchers tend to travel in flocks. Dowitchers have a white patch on their tail, which snipe lack. Snipe make a telltale, raspy "graaack!" when they flush; if you don't hear that, don't shoot. Final tip: If you don't have a dog that retrieves snipe—and many won't—never, ever shoot more than one at time! Snipe look *exactly* like the vegetation of the marsh, and you will lose one or both of your birds if you get greedy. Mark the spot and go straight to it. All snipe should be roasted simply.

COOTS AND MOORHENS

Coots and moorhens are two unloved waterbirds that are legal game in most states. Migratory coots and their sedentary brethren the moorhen are more closely related to pheasants than ducks, making the Cajun term for them—*poulet d'eau*, or water chicken—basically accurate. Coots, which are jet-black with an ivory bill and red eyes, tend to raft up in great numbers out in the open, making it tough to get close enough for a shot. Moorhens, which are charcoal gray with a white patch on their tail, are solitary and like out-of-the-way areas. Both are perfectly good eating, if you skin them. The fat and skin are extremely fishy tasting. Watch out for the legs, too: Because coots and moorhens are wading birds, they develop a lot of sinew in their legs. The best use for their legs is to braise them a long time and pull the meat away from the sinew.

LITTLE DUCKS

Teal, buffleheads, and ruddy ducks fall into this category. Teal are the best eating and come in three varieties: green-winged, blue-winged, and cinnamon. Buffleheads are often fishy tasting, and ruddy ducks are strong flavored but not generally fishy. The green-winged teal is one of the best-eating ducks in North America. It mostly eats seeds, and it will never be fishy. Be aware that buffleheads and ruddy ducks are diving ducks, so if you shoot one, make sure it's dead. A wounded diver duck will dive and hide from you and your dog, making it nearly impossible to find. Better to shoot at it twice than lose the bird. At the table, these ducks tend to be single-serving birds: One whole teal, ruddy, or bufflehead per person is a good meal.

MEDIUM DUCKS

This includes most of the duck species in North America: wigeon, wood ducks, northern shovelers, scaup, ring-necked ducks, gadwall, goldeneyes, old-squaw, scoters, harlequin, and whistling ducks. These birds are big enough to feed one hearty eater, but not quite large enough to satisfy two normal appetites.

Which species are tastiest depends on what they are eating. All of these ducks can be rank-tasting in a poor environment, but when eating prime forage—acorns for wood ducks, grain for most others—they can be excellent eating. The best duck I've ever eaten was a morbidly obese gadwall that had been gorging on rice. With rare exceptions, sea ducks, such as old-squaw and scoters, are fishy and need to be skinned. Northern shovelers, also known as spoonies, and scaup, also known as bluebills, can be iffy, too.

BIG DUCKS

With one exception, these are the primo ducks for the table: mallards, black ducks, canvasbacks, redheads, pintail, and eiders. Only the sea-dwelling eider is poor table fare, unless skinned and de-fatted. Pintail ducks are the most consistently delicious duck in North America; like teal, they are primarily seed eaters. Mallards are, for the most part, good eating, but since they are opportunists, they can occasionally be sketchy. Canvasbacks were once the king of ducks, but with the decimation of the wild celery they once fed on, these handsome diver ducks will now eat a variety of forage, including clams. Same goes for the redhead.

SMALL GEESE

A subset of geese that are about the size of the big ducks: Ross' goose, and the various small Canada geese, like cacklers, lessers, and Aleutians. Ross' geese look like baby snow geese, and they taste like snow geese, too. They're okay but have a bluish skin and are often very lean. Ross' geese are best skinned. The same holds true for the little Canada geese, but for a different reason. The underfeathers of cacklers and Aleutians are black and are difficult to pluck fully. This makes the semiplucked bird look like a white guy's legs in winter. Ew. Still, if you can cleanly pluck a small Canada goose, it's worth it, because the fat on those I've eaten has been tasty.

REGULAR GEESE

Canada geese are everyone's image when they think "wild goose." There are lots of different subspecies of Canada geese, ranging from the little ones like cacklers and Aleutians, to "normal" size Canadas weighing 8 to 12 pounds, to the giant, which can top out at

16 pounds. Canada geese are like mallards: opportunistic. They can be delicious, or they can be foul smelling and fit only for sausage.

Another common goose is the snow goose, which runs about 7 pounds and is white with black wingtips. (Don't mistake incoming seagulls for snow geese, because they're not legal to shoot and the taste is, well . . . you've seen them at the dump, right?) There is also a color variant of the snow geese in which the feathers are bluish; these are called blue geese, but they're really just snows. Snows are best skinned for the same reason their little cousins the Ross' geese are: weird, blue-gray skin, not much fat, and very tough to pluck. They tend to have spectacularly large gizzards that will give you a lot of meat eaten as is or ground into sausage.

The king of geese, known as the "ribeye in the sky," is the specklebelly or white-fronted goose. This goose is rare in the East but common in the West. It looks a little like the greylag goose, which is a European domesticated goose with gray-and-black spots. White-fronted geese are excellent eating, weigh between 6 and 8 pounds, and love nothing more than to eat leftover rice in Northern California fields. If you can find a spot to hunt specks, don't pass it up. These are my favorite waterfowl to eat.

HUNTING TIPS

Whole books are written about this subject, and setting down just a few tips and tricks to act as a primer is daunting. But here are some tips you will need when starting out.

The number-one thing newbies need to know when they are out in the marsh is that ducks and geese see color and see movement. When ducks are flying close and looking like they might come within shooting range, you don't have to be totally camouflaged, but you cannot get away with movement. The whole act of duck hunting is to convince wary, wild birds to drop their guard and fly close enough to your decoys for you to get a clean shot at them. Ducks and geese can live a long time in the wild. Every year, hunters recover banded birds that are older than 20 years. Imagine those ducks: They've been hunted for two decades and are almost impossible to trick.

When ducks are approaching your spread, don't move. Watch them with your eyes only. You should be able to see if they are looking your way. Assume that if they are flying toward you, they are looking at you. If they bank left or right, you can adjust your position a bit. Always watch the birds from just under the bill of your cap: This keeps your head down.

Along these lines, unless you are already a good duck hunter, don't use your duck calls when the birds are flying right at you. The saying is "butts and wingtips," meaning you use your call when the birds' rear ends or wingtips are closest to you. Call less than you think you need to unless you really know what you are doing. There are a few more duck-calling tips in the Equipment section.

Take the shot. Make sure the bird is in range, but you have to pull the trigger to kill ducks. Many new hunters overthink their shooting. In most cases, you will only get a few seconds to shoot when the bird is within 20 yards—ideal range for a shot—and trying to tag a fleeing duck at 45 yards is a lot harder. One way to gauge distance is to put some decoys out 40 paces from where you are hunting. Any bird within this radius is close enough to shoot.

Be mindful of where you are shooting a bird. I will not take shots when I know the duck will land in thick reeds or in very deep water. I don't hunt with a dog, and I know my chances of recovering a bird in deep water or in reeds—especially if it is only wounded—are minimal. Better to wait for another bird to fly by than to waste its life with a poorly thought-out shot. While you are waiting for ducks, visualize your shooting lanes so you know where you can make a shot cleanly.

Be where the birds want to be. Pay attention in the marsh. It is easy to get ducks and geese to land in a place they want to be, and very hard to get them to come to another place. I've seen hunters with no cover slam the birds when they are sitting exactly where every bird in a square-mile radius wants to land (for reasons known only to the ducks themselves). This means move around if you can.

You don't need a lot of fancy decoys, but a few will give you an advantage. Buy a dozen top-quality decoys and have them closest to you. This is especially important for geese. Why? When you call waterfowl, they will look in the direction of the call and see these decoys. They need to be convincing. As for the rest of your decoy spread, you can go cheaper. When hunting snow geese, even sheets of white paper secured in the mud will work 50 yards out from where you are sitting. Go to parks and other places where lots of ducks hang out, and remember how they look on the water: Arrange your decoys like that. Have at least a few decoys of the same species you have flying around.

Ducks and geese land into the wind, so have the wind at your back. This is the saving grace of bad-weather duck hunting, because you want the wind in your face in most other forms of hunting. Also set your decoys with lots of gaps so live birds can land into the wind, close to you, and safely. What does "safely" mean? Most ducks and geese will not fly over birds on the water when they're landing. They are afraid the sitting ducks will suddenly lift into the air without warning, knocking into them and possibly injuring the landing bird. That's why you leave large holes and Vs in your decoy pattern.

If you can, shoot the drakes. The drakes are the males and will be the brightly colored birds; the green-headed mallard in your mind's eye is a drake. Why shoot the males? That leaves more females to lay eggs next year. It is a simple conservation move. I don't get broken up over shooting hens, but I do my best to aim for the drake.

If you down a bird that is still alive, wait until everyone else in your group has stopped shooting, then chase it as fast as you can. Ducks and geese will do everything they can to escape you. Diver ducks like canvasbacks and bluebills will actually dive to their deaths, swimming down and grabbing an underwater reed to escape you, even if they drown in the process. Shoot them on the water to prevent them from getting away, but make sure no other hunters are in the line of your shot!

When you catch a wounded bird, kill it quickly and humanely. This is the hardest part of duck hunting, at least emotionally. I will "helicopter" a small bird by the head three or four times so its neck breaks, which works fast, most of the time. You can also cut its throat or otherwise break its neck. Again, this is a sad moment, as it should be. But it will help you remember to eat as much of the duck as you can, so the duck did not die for nothing.

EQUIPMENT

Waterfowl hunting is a gear-intensive activity. So much so that I would strongly advise you to first find people who hunt already and ask to join them on a hunt, or to schedule a hunt with an outfitter. I hunted low-tech for a while, with very limited results. Now I have tons of decoys, several duck calls, a spare pair of waders, a spare jacket, many hats, etc.

At the minimum, you need a shotgun, non-lead ammunition (lead ammo has been illegal for waterfowl hunting for more than 25 years), high waterproof boots, and warm clothing that will blend into your environment.

Most duck hunters use a 12-gauge shotgun, typically either a pump action or a semiautomatic. I use a smaller 20-gauge, double-barreled shotgun with a walnut stock. Why? It's what I first bought, and like any good Scotsman, I am cautious with money. I see no need to have more than one shotgun, and if you take care of your gun after you come in from the wind and rain, it will last as long as one with a synthetic stock. Whether you want the standard 12-gauge gun or the smaller 20- (or even a 16- or 28-gauge gun) is a matter of personal choice.

As for ammunition, I am a big fan of Kent Fasteel, which is very fast-moving steel ammo that won't break the bank. Buy it in No. 2 shot or larger for geese, No. 3 for ducks. The smaller the shot number, the larger the pellet. Other steel ammo is fine, but it doesn't travel as fast as the Kent. If you can afford it, however, you can go with the specialty non-lead ammo like Hevi-Shot or Kent's Tungsten Matrix or Bismuth. These are made from pellets heavier than lead, often tungsten or bismuth or other exotic metals. They hit hard and kill ducks. But they are also expensive, upward of $2.50 per shot. I use No. 6 shot for ducks and No. 4 for geese. It's lethal, but—at least on most days—I am a good shot, so I don't burn through enormous amounts of the stuff. My advice is to stick to steel until you are consistently killing birds. It's a lot easier on the wallet.

As for boots, what I really mean are waders. You can get away with a pair of good Wellies, but what happens if the duck falls into water higher than your boot top? You're out of luck. Put simply, if you want to hunt ducks seriously, buy chest waders. Do they need to be camouflaged? It helps but is not vital, so long as they're a color you'd find in a marsh.

It is far more important that your outer jacket be camouflaged, because this is most visible to the birds. A good duck jacket needs to have an inner liner you can remove on warmer days, be water resistant, have lots of pockets for stuff (food, ammo, game strap, cell phone, etc.), have a hood for the rain, and have a good camo pattern that fits where you hunt. Ask the sporting goods dealer you buy from or other local hunters. If you can get a hat to match the camo pattern on the jacket, even better. But I often wear an olive drab or green baseball cap, and it works fine. You can even use a ghillie suit the way military snipers do; these are the jackets with lots of strips of cloth hanging off them, which breaks up your outline in the marsh. I wear one on bright, sunny days. Whatever you do, remember: No bright colors, because waterfowl have excellent eyesight and can see color.

Other good items to have:

▰ Gloves, preferably waterproof and warm. It gets cold out there!

▰ A face mask or camo face paint, especially if you are white. People with black and brown skin blend in better when they are looking skyward, but a white face is a warning beacon to waterfowl. This is why many serious duck hunters grow big beards in the season. Obviously not an option for women.

▰ Thermal underwear and high wool socks (for obvious reasons).

▰ A change of clothes in your car. You get pretty sweaty wandering around in the marsh, and if you've fallen in the marsh, allowing water into your waders, you'll be grateful for the change.

DECOYS. You will want some. A half dozen is the minimum, although in some circumstances you can hunt with just a couple. I have scores of them, because I sometimes hunt in big, open water, and you need lots of decoys to attract birds. Always begin with mallards, then find out which are the most common birds where you hunt. For us in California, it's wigeon, pintail, spoonies, green-winged teal, mallards, and gadwall. You might also want to use coot decoys, which tell the ducks that no people are around. Coots are wary birds and will not swim near hidden hunters, so their presence in your decoy spread can attract ducks looking for a safe place to land.

A word on duck calls. You will not be a good duck hunter in the long term if you cannot call in ducks. In fact, calling is half the fun. I will never forget the first time I called in a drake mallard out of a calm, cloudless sky all the way into my decoys. It was exhilarating, because had I called poorly, that mallard would have passed me by. Start with a whistle, which lets you mimic teal, pintail, and wigeon. You can buy an all-in-one call that is very easy to learn, and this is the first duck call you should buy. Listen to what the ducks sound like, and listen to recordings of them online. (Ducks Unlimited, www.ducks.org, has an excellent audio library.) Practice, practice, practice. Nine times out of 10, all you need to call in ducks is that whistle, and in late season, after the birds have heard people quack at them all winter, only the whistle will still work.

So why bother with a mallard call, which is what you think of when you think "duck call"? Because it's louder, more persuasive, and can bring birds out of a clear blue sky the way a whistle cannot. And most hens of all species of duck quack (no male ducks quack, by the way), making a hen mallard call versatile. I strongly advise starting with an inexpensive call that comes with an instructional CD. Practice it like a musical instrument, which is what it is. And practice outside of the hunt. There is nothing that makes experienced hunters want to strangle someone more than an inexperienced hunter bleating away on a duck call 150 yards away. Less is more, until you know what you are doing. Learn from others and, again, practice! Calling is an art.

HOW TO PLUCK A DUCK OR GOOSE

Ducks and geese require their own techniques for plucking. On the plus side, their skin is pretty tough, so you are less likely to tear it, compared with plucking a pheasant or quail. The downside is, well, the down. Waterfowl have a layer of gossamer down under their regular feathers that keeps them warm and waterproof. It is not easy to remove by hand.

You can dry-pluck any waterfowl, but it will take longer than it would for a comparably sized upland bird, and you must deal with the fact that the wing feathers are extremely difficult to pull out. Think about it: Ducks fly thousands of miles in their migrations, while pheasants rarely fly at all, and when they do, they fly only short distances.

Wet-plucking is the way to go, only with a twist. Holly and I pluck all our ducks with the aid of canning wax, or paraffin. You should be able to find it in the canning section of your supermarket. We go through many blocks of it each year, so stock up. The trick is to get a giant pot of water steaming—not boiling—melt wax in it, and dunk your birds. Toss the waxed birds in another basin of ice cold water to set the wax, let them cool a bit, and pluck away. The wax grabs the down and upper feathers, leaving you with a nice, clean plucked duck.

Start with a large pot, like a canning pot or, if you live around Mexican communities, a big tamale pot. Let your tap water get as hot as it will go, then fill the pot two-thirds of the way up with water. Put this on a powerful burner; we use a portable burner we set up in the garage. Get it steaming, about 170°F.

Examine your ducks and geese. Chop off badly damaged legs or wings. Now rough-pluck your birds. Pull out the tail feathers, the big wing feathers (you might need to go one by one with geese), and some of the regular feathers on the body of the bird. Be careful when you do this, and anchor the skin of the duck with one hand while you pluck with the other. Do not remove the down at this stage.

Put the wax in the water. How much? Our paraffin comes four blocks to a box, and we find that a goose needs a full block. Big ducks need half, and on smaller ducks you can get away with two to three per block.

Once the birds are rough-plucked and the wax is melted, grab a bird by its head and feet, and dunk it up to its neck in the water. Swirl it around a bit on the surface, too, and make sure you get the bird well coated. Let it drip a little over the pot, then put the waxed duck into a basin of cold water; we use our slop sink in the garage. Let the bird chill for a few minutes to set the wax, then put it somewhere to drain.

Wear an apron when plucking, because it is a messy, wet business. Start with the wings, as they are the hardest part. You might need to break the wax seal on parts of the bird to peel off the wax. Again, anchor the skin with one hand while you peel with the other. Many times you are actually keeping the wax on one place while gently peeling the skin away from it. This is especially important when working around shotgun pellet holes.

After I pluck the wings, I go to the tail, then the back, then the legs. Finally, I do the neck and breast. The neck skin is loose, and this is the most likely place for a tear. The breast is the most prized part of the bird, so you will want your full attention here. It's like opening a present: The breast gives you the best look at whether you have a fat bird or a skinny one.

Only after the ducks are plucked do I gut. I do this by feeling for the hard round gizzard under the skin, then taking a cleaver or kitchen shears and cutting the tail off between the gizzard and the pelvis. Watch out for the legs, as they tend to want to get in the way. Do this near a sink with cold running water. Immediately rinse the pope's nose (the tail) and pull out any intestines or fecal matter. Don't worry, so long as you are fast and thorough, everything will be fine.

Now reach in and grab everything you can find. Pull it out. Separate the gizzard (you might need to cut the intestines with a knife), the heart, and the liver. Be careful with the liver, as you do not want to pierce the little green gallbladder, which looks like a pine nut or a NyQuil gel cap. It is super bitter and will wreck the liver. Cut out the gallbladder with a knife. If you do break it, wash the liver under cold water immediately. Wash the giblets you want to keep, discard the intestines, and wash the interior of the duck.

Use a knife or kitchen shears to remove the feet—which help make a great duck stock (the collagen adds body to the broth)—as well as the neck and head. Save the neck for stock and discard the head. You are now ready to break the bird down if you don't want to roast it whole.

HOW TO BREAK DOWN A GAME BIRD

Not every bird is worthy of a full-on roast. To me, such a bird needs to be fat, young, and not terribly shot-up. For birds with broken legs, shot-up breasts, or that are skinny or very old, I break them down into parts for separate cooking. Breasts get seared, while legs and wings go into braises. The carcasses all go into stocks and broths. I waste very little. Here's how I turn a whole duck into parts.

STEP 1: Have a sharp boning or paring knife. Can you use a chef's knife? Yes, but in my mind it is too wide to do a lot of the fine work needed for cutting up a duck or pheasant. A good alternative to a boning knife is a fillet knife for fish. It may be a little thin, but it's better than a big wide chef's knife. And make sure your knife is sharp! A dull knife is a lazy servant.

STEP 2: Start with the legs. I press on the gap between leg and breast to push as much skin toward the breast as I can: That skin helps keep the breasts juicy and tender when you cook them. Slice down in the gap and you will notice you just sliced skin, not muscle. That's the key. Gently cut downward until you reach the ball-and-socket joint where the leg is attached.

As you slice down, arc the knife under the back of the bird to get all the meat off the thigh. Snap the leg down to pop open the ball-and-socket joint, which frees the leg/thigh. Tuck the knife behind the ball and cut the leg free. As you cut past the socket joint, don't forget to arc the knife around the little pocket of meat nestled in the back of the bird known as the oyster, as this is the best part. The oyster is small in wild ducks, but is substantial in turkeys, geese, and pheasants.

STEP 3: Move to the wings. If your bird still has wings (you often lose one when wing shooting), look for the dark line where the fatty breast ends and the side of the bird begins: You make a cut parallel to that line all the way to the wing joint. If you cut in the right spot, you will go right through the soft cartilage and will free the wing from the body. Don't worry if you mess it up a few times. It takes practice to know exactly where that spot is.

Now slide the knife along the saber bone, which is a long, curved bone along the bird's back that looks like a sword. It's roughly equivalent to the bird's shoulder blade. Slide the knife along that bone until you get to the joint, which will now be totally free from the body. Finish removing the wing by cutting a little extra skin from the neck area.

STEP 4: Finish with the breasts. I like to take the breasts off in one piece. This lets me stuff them if I want, and it wastes less skin. Remember, skin equals protection for breast meat, which is prone to drying out. I begin by making a cut along a fat pad on the flank of the bird near the end of the ribs. I then gently start sliding the knife along the rib bones toward the bird's tail end. Ducks and geese have broad plates under their breasts, so you run the knife flat along this plate until you hit the keel bone.

When you get the breast freed from the ribs and breast bone, run the knife forward, along the stout bone at the neck end of the bird, then along the wishbone up toward the keel bone, which separates the two halves of the breast. Some cooks remove the wishbone before breaking down a bird, but I generally don't. Free the meat from one side of the keel bone with gentle, short strokes of the knife—incidentally, freeing the meat is how you should think about this process, rather than "slicing" or "cutting"—then free the meat from the wishbone on the neck end.

Once you have done this on both sides, gently cut the attachments along the top of the keel bone to free the whole breast from the body. I do this by letting the mostly freed breast sides hang down. To finish, remove the tenders on the inside of the breast, as they are only lightly attached to the rest of the breast and need to be taken off if you plan to sear the breast solo. If you don't, the tenders will come free while cooking and mess up your searing. Cook these tenders separately; they're great batter-fried.

MY ADVICE: Take your time. Every bird will be easier than the last one you did, and this technique for cutting up a carcass works with any bird—ducks, geese, pheasants, pigeons, turkeys, even domestic chickens. Once you get the hang of it, it only takes a few minutes to break down a bird.

RENDERING YOUR OWN WILD DUCK OR GOOSE FAT

Domestic ducks and geese are the pigs of the air. When well-fed, they lay on thick layers of clean-tasting, delicious fat that is less saturated than lard—and remember that fresh-

rendered lard is even less saturated than
butter. Other than fish fat, waterfowl fat is
arguably the animal fat that is best for you.
It is so low in saturated fat that it's actually
liquid at a warm room temperature.

I cook with it all year long. I am
blessed with ducks and geese that winter
in Northern California among the rice
fields. It is not uncommon to see pintails
or mallards with such a thick layer of
white, rice-built fat that they look like little
domestic ducks. In my experience, only
wigeon and snow geese tend to be lean. These need extra fat when cooking. Where do you
get it? By rendering the fat from your pudgy ducks.

First, pluck your birds. Once plucked, the fat is mostly in the body cavity, around the
gizzard and in the pope's nose, or tail end. There is also good fat to be had in the neck skin.
Chop the neck skin, pull out the body cavity fat and the fat around the gizzard, and hack
the pope's nose into at least two pieces; as this part contains the poop chute, you will most
definitely want to wash it thoroughly!

Wash it all in cold water and put it in a small frying pan over medium-low heat with
just enough water to cover the bottom of the pan. The fat will begin to render into the water,
which will soon evaporate, but not before rendering enough fat to allow the rest to continue
rendering slowly without scorching.

Take your time, and turn the pieces periodically until they are crispy and brown. Can
you eat them? Sure, but the skin gets pretty tough in this preparation. Take the bits out,
skim any impurities, and let the fat cool slightly. I typically pour everything through a
paper towel into a container, cover it, and keep it in the fridge. It will last a year.

EATING EVERYTHING BUT THE QUACK

Over the years, I have learned to eat pretty much everything but the quack on a duck or a
goose. I can't help it. I shot these ducks. They're dead because of me. The least I can do is

not waste them. Holly and I start this process by plucking most every bird we kill. The skin is a crucial part of the enjoyment of ducks; a skinned duck breast might as well be any red meat. I only skin fishy-smelling ducks and snow geese, which have weird blue skin that creeps me out and are not worth the effort of plucking.

I then cut off the feet. Adding the (cleaned!) feet to a duck stock is a great way to add more collagen, which adds body and heft to the broth. The key to releasing the collagen on any bird feet is to hack at them with a cleaver or heavy chef's knife. This opens the skin and allows the collagen from the cartilage to leak out when you make the stock.

I also use most of the innards. Hearts can be eaten in several ways, from stir-fries to braises or even chopped raw in tartare. If you are squeamish, use the hearts in your broth making. Gizzards are destined for the stockpot if they are small, such as those from teal or wigeon. If they are large—goose gizzards, especially—I clean them, trim them, and make them into confit. You can also grind the gizzards and use them in a Louisiana dirty rice recipe.

I don't like the texture of liver, although I like the flavor. So I grind the livers and make

them into ravioli, or chop them into dirty rice, or even make them into a fancy liver crème caramel.

Occasionally, you will find a liver that is light beige. This is, essentially, wild foie gras. Waterfowl naturally store fat in their livers, and this beige color means the bird has a fatty liver. This is a special, wonderful treat. Sear the liver quickly in some duck fat to brown it, then drizzle a little high-quality balsamic vinegar over it, and top with a fancy salt like *fleur de sel*. This is one of the great bites in the wild game world.

I even use the duck necks. Push out the bones and meat (they go into the stockpot), then clean the inside of the skin, pull out the windpipe, and voila! You have a great sausage casing. I thought I had come up with this idea all by myself and was so proud of it—until I later read that the French have been doing it with geese for centuries. Generally, I only use the necks from geese and larger ducks such as pintail and mallards.

Before they go into the freezer, consider jointing your ducks. Duck breasts are best served rare-to-medium. Duck legs and wings are best braised for a long time over low heat. If you remove the legs and wings from your big ducks, you can easily collect enough to make something lovely, like a *salmis* of duck.

Teal and ruddy ducks should always be left whole. And you will also want to leave especially fat, especially pretty ducks—pintails often fit this bill, as do big drake mallards— whole to roast.

RECIPES

PERFECT SEARED DUCK OR GOOSE BREAST

This is a basic skill you will want to master if you are going to hunt ducks. Properly searing a duck breast, wild or domestic, means crispy skin, rendered fat, and meat that is medium-rare. My method is idiosyncratic, but it works. Be sure to start with breasts that have the skin and fat on them. Skinless breasts are not good candidates for searing, as they are boring. Use them for something else.

STEP 1: Take the meat from the fridge and let it come toward room temperature. If your duck breast is very fat (all domestics fall into this category), score the skin in a crosshatch pattern, making the crosshatches about 1 inch across. This helps the fat render and will give you a crispier skin. Salt it well on both sides, then let the breasts stand on a cutting board or some such for 15 to 30 minutes.

STEP 2: Heat a large pan (not nonstick!) over high heat for 1 to 2 minutes. Add 1 tablespoon of duck fat or some other oil. Let this get hot for another minute. Do not let it smoke.

STEP 3: With the back of a chef's knife (or other knife), scrape the skin side of the duck, then pat it dry. This gives you a nice, flat, dry surface to sear on.

STEP 4: Lay your breasts down on the hot oil, skin side down. Turn the heat down to medium. You will notice the "tails" of skin and fat from the head and the tail side of the fillet contract immediately. What? You cut off those parts? Shame. Don't do it again!

STEP 5: Let the pan do its job. Cook at a jocular sizzle—not an inferno, not a gurgle—for . . . it depends. I like my duck medium to medium-rare. To do this with teal or ruddy duck will require only about 3 minutes on the skin side, and you might want to keep the heat higher. Wigeon, gadwall, or other medium ducks need 3 to 5 minutes; mallards, pintails, and domestic ducks 4 to 6 minutes; and geese definitely need to be on medium (even medium-low) for a good 8 to 10 minutes. The key is to let the breast do most of its cooking on this side. It's the flattest, and will give you that fabulously crispy skin we all know and love.

STEP 6: Turn the breasts over. When? Follow the guidelines above, but also use your ears: You will hear the sizzle change. It will die down just a bit. That's when you turn. Now—this is important—lightly salt the now-exposed skin immediately. Doing this seems to absorb any extra oil and definitely gives you a yummier, crispier skin. Let the ducks cook on the meat side for:

- 1 to 2 minutes for teal, ruddy ducks, or bufflehead.
- 2 to 3 minutes for other ducks.
- 4 to 6 minutes for geese.

STEP 7: "Kiss" the thick side of the fillet. You will notice that duck and goose breasts plump up and contract as they cook. One side of the fillet will be wider than the other, and this side will need some heat. Tip the breasts on their sides and cook for 30 seconds to 1 minute, to get some good color.

STEP 8: Take the duck off the heat and let it rest, skin side up, on a cutting board. Teal only need a minute or two, while big Canada geese might need 10 minutes. You need to do this or the juices will run all over your cutting board and not down your chin, where they should be.

You can slice from either end, either side up. You can get thinner slices by starting at the meat end, but you lose a little of the crispiness of the skin. If you are serving a whole breast, always serve it skin side up, with its sauce underneath.

SUGO D'ANATRA, WILD DUCK RAGU

This is a classic *sugo*, or ragu, made from wild ducks or geese. Basically, it is a long-simmered pasta sauce that is so intensely flavorful a little dab will do ya. The ideal accompaniment to this sauce is long pasta, such as tagliatelle, pappardelle, or spaghetti, with a little grated pecorino or Parmesan. Top it with a fried sage leaf and you're getting fancy.

There are several important keys to the success of this recipe. First, you need a good sear on the meat. Take your time, and get your duck or goose bits good and browned—if you develop a thick layer of crusty stuff on the bottom of the pan, even better. Second, you need as many ducky elements in this recipe as you can muster. I use duck fat and duck broth to go with the duck meat.

Another thing: This is an absolutely perfect use for gizzards. Gizzards are, after all, just meat. They are what a duck uses to grind the seeds it eats into digestible bits. Cleaned, gizzards are deeply ducky and satisfyingly meaty. Besides, they get ground up at the end so no one will know!

This sugo is best the day after it's made, will keep in the fridge a week or so, and freezes well for a few months.

Serves 8–12

3 tablespoons duck fat, butter, or olive oil

3 pounds duck or goose parts: gizzards, legs, thighs, wings, hearts, necks, livers

Salt

2 medium yellow onions, chopped

2 celery sticks, chopped

2 large carrots, chopped

1 bottle red wine (medium-bodied, such as Pinot Noir)

3 tablespoons tomato paste

1 quart duck broth (you can use beef)

4 bay leaves

½ teaspoon ground nutmeg

½ teaspoon ground cloves

1 tablespoon dried oregano

1 package dried porcini mushrooms (about a handful)

4 tablespoons finely chopped parsley

Grated pecorino or Parmesan cheese

Heat a large Dutch oven over medium-high heat and add the duck fat. When it melts, add the duck or goose parts and brown them well. Salt the meat lightly as it cooks. Do not crowd the pot, and take your time. Do it in batches if you need to. This process should take between 15 and 30 minutes.

When the meat is browned, remove it from the pot and add the onions, celery, and carrots. Brown them well, stirring occasionally. If you need to, add a little more duck fat. Sprinkle the veggies with salt.

When the veggies are browned, remove them and add 1 cup of the wine to the pot. Turn the heat up to high and scrape the bottom of the pot with a wooden spoon until it is clean of debris. Let the wine reduce by half.

Meanwhile, mix together the tomato paste and the rest of the wine. When the first cup of wine has boiled down, add the wine–tomato paste mixture. Bring this to a rolling boil and let it reduce by half.

Add the broth and bring it all to a boil. Taste for seasoning and add salt if needed. Add the bay leaves, nutmeg, cloves, oregano, and mushrooms, then turn the heat down to medium. Stir well and return the veggies and meat to the pot. Mix well. Cover and simmer gently for at least 3 hours, more if you are using Canada geese or very old ducks.

When the meat is about to fall off the bone, remove the pot from the heat. Take the meat out, and pull the meat off the bones. Put about one-third of it back into the pot.

Push everything in the pot through a food mill with a coarse grate attached. If you do not have a food mill, an immersion blender would work, as would a China cap and even a metal colander. As a last resort, you could buzz the solids in a food processor and return them to the pot. My advice: Buy a food mill. You want a coarse paste.

Add the remaining meat to the sauce, and thin with a little water if necessary.

To serve, boil some pasta. When it's done, mix some sauce with the pasta, then dish onto plates. Top with some more sauce, then the parsley and grated cheese.

How to Make Confit of Duck, Goose, Rabbit, or Pheasant

This is perhaps the best way to preserve and eat the legs of wild ducks and geese, which can be tough. It also works very well with rabbit and pheasant legs. The meat is tender, and the skin can be crisped up in a pan right before you serve. The effect is a little like Mexican *carnitas*, with its combination of crispy and tender.

Confit is a French method of slightly curing meat, then poaching it gently in fat until it is meltingly tender. I use a modified *sous vide* method for this, as it uses less fat than submerging the goose in 4 to 5 cups of fat.

You will need a vacuum sealer for this recipe. If you don't have one, you should— they're indispensable, especially if you hunt or fish a lot. But I will give you alternative directions at the end.

This method works every time. The only variable is how long you poach the meat. Once made, this confit will last, sealed in its bag, for a month in the fridge. It can also be frozen.

Serves 4–6

1 cup salt

1 cup sugar

2 tablespoons dried thyme

2 tablespoons freshly ground black pepper

About ½ of a freshly grated nutmeg, or ½ teaspoon dried

Peel of 1 large orange

1 teaspoon pink salt, such as Insta Cure No. 1 (optional)

6 legs or wings of geese, pheasants, or rabbits, or 12–15 legs of wild ducks

1 cup goose, duck, or pork fat, or olive oil

3–6 bay leaves

Mix the salt, sugar, thyme, pepper, and nutmeg together. Now mix in the peel, which, as it is moist, will form clumps. Keep mixing until it is well incorporated.

A word on the pink salt. This is for color and preservation. It also is an extra dose of prevention during cooking, as you will be poaching the meat in 160° to 180°F water. I use it, but if you have a morbid fear of nitrates, skip it. If using, mix it into the cure mixture.

Pack the legs with the cure mixture. Press it into the skin and exposed meat, and make sure every part has some on it. Refrigerate for 6 to 24 hours. The longer you go, the saltier it will get and the longer it will preserve.

When you're done curing the duck, rinse everything off, then dry well. Put on a rack to dry further while you make the vac bags.

Make 3 vacuum bags, each large enough to hold 2 legs or wings. Put a little of the fat into the bottom of each bag. Divide the bay leaves among the bags.

Add the meat, then divvy up the remaining fat among the bags. Smear it all over the meat and in between the pieces. Use more fat if need be. Definitely err on the side of using more if you are making this with rabbit or pheasant legs, as they tend to be very lean. I mostly use goose fat or wild duck fat. You can buy duck or goose fat, render your own, use fresh lard, or even use olive oil.

Seal the bags and place in a large pot (the largest you have) two-thirds filled with water that is somewhere around 160° to 180°F, which is below a simmer. Poach the legs for 4 to 12 hours, flipping every half hour or so if they float, which they probably will. Young, tender birds need only 4 hours. Old pheasants, hares, and ancient geese will need 8 hours or more. If you happen to have a sous vide machine, cook at 180°F for 6 to 12 hours.

Remove the bags from the water and plunge into an ice water bath to cool. Remove them to a rack to dry, and when they're dry on the outside, store in the fridge.

IF YOU DON'T HAVE A VACUUM SEALER: Rinse the cure off as above, then pat dry very, very well. Totally submerge the meat in 5 to 6 cups of fat in a Dutch oven and put, uncovered, in an oven set on Warm or not hotter than 200°F. Alternatively, you can do this on a stovetop with a weak burner set on low, or with a flame tamer. Watch that the oil never sizzles. Cooking time will be about the same.

EPILOGUE

PUTTING IT ALL TOGETHER

Many of the pursuits detailed in this book are time-consuming and can seem daunting to busy people. Believe me, I know. Until very recently, I held a day job—one where the 40-hour workweek was fictional—all while trying to juggle homeownership, a relationship, and a social life, as well as my outdoor and cooking pursuits. I've only been a full-time hunter, angler, forager, and cook for a little more than a year. When I was a journalist, the outdoors and cooking became my refuge from the rough-and-tumble world of politics. Everything I write about in this book I did on weekends, vacations, and at night after work. What I mean to say is that *you can do this.*

It's easier than you might think. Start with some aspect of wild food that inspires you and focus on that. Don't try to do it all, especially at first. You will only find frustration that way. I did not do everything at once. I still don't, even without a day job. Choose some pursuit, whether it's duck hunting or berry picking or a commitment to learning the nuances of your nearby reservoir, and work at it until the season is over or you master it to your own satisfaction. Then turn your focus to something else. This does not mean you cannot expose yourself to other pursuits along the way. Spend a day fishing while you are in serious berry-picking mode, or practice your shotgun shooting on a day you're not clamming or catching fish.

I was a competitive distance runner for many years, and I found that the only way to keep myself focused was to have goals, the most important of which was the conference championship race. Taking that metaphor into wild food, an excellent way to organize all the things you want to do is to center them on a meal. Maybe a celebratory barbecue or a birthday meal—even Christmas or Thanksgiving. My colleague Steven Rinella did this famously in his book *The Scavenger's Guide to Haute Cuisine*, in which he hunted, fished, and foraged for an epic Thanksgiving feast based on the recipes in Auguste Escoffier's *Le Guide Culinaire.*

Nothing sharpens the mind like a deadline, so set a date several months in advance. Write down what you hope to serve and set about obtaining the ingredients for that meal.

Maybe you start organizing a hunt or a fishing trip for your main course. Maybe you begin walking the riverside to find nettles for the pasta. You smoke some shad or herring or whitefish when they run in the rivers and lakes, and set that, tightly sealed, in the freezer awaiting the day. The berries of summer become ice cream or syrup for spritzy drinks. The legs of a half dozen ducks simmer slowly and submit their individuality to the power of a classic Italian ragu you can store in your freezer. Slowly, it will all come together. And when the day comes, the meal will be truly yours: You will have caught, collected, and cooked at least some part of every course. I can assure you that you will remember that meal forever.

But wild food is not just for big parties, celebrations, or holidays. Wild food can find a way to fit into your everyday life. Hunt ducks? Maybe your quick Wednesday night supper isn't a store-bought piece of chicken, but is instead a mallard breast, seared perfectly. Gather greens? Skip the spinach and sauté amaranth or lamb's-quarters. It takes the same amount of time, and the plants grow all around us. Collected huckleberries this past summer? Freeze them and use them for Sunday morning pancakes. Pull a rock cod fillet out of the freezer and steam it with vegetables. Mix some home-smoked eel or herring in with mayo, celery, and mustard for a surpassing fish salad sandwich to take to work—but be warned, you'll never go back to canned tuna again after that one. The possibilities are endless.

The important part is to get out there. Everything beyond that first act is just a matter of degree. Even adding one pursuit, even something as simple as cooking the dandelions in your yard, will connect you with the real world, with where real, honest food comes from. My hope is that this book helps set you on that path or, for those already walking it, has helped to open new avenues. Good luck, and remember that the feast lives all around us. We just need to find it.

ACKNOWLEDGMENTS

Few books are written in isolation, and this sure ain't one of them. What follows in these pages may be my adventures and my experiences, but most were done in the company of friends, family, even helpful strangers. All helped this book become what it is.

I owe the most thanks to my family: Mom and Dad, my sisters and brothers. They set me on the path as a forager and an angler, and, thanks to some lucky genetics, armed me with a restless mind and more curiosity than a litter of cats.

An almost equal debt of gratitude goes to my girl, Holly, whose photos grace this book. Holly and I have been together for a decade, and her tolerance of my many odd projects— "So. You're curing meat in the living room again, huh?"—has earned her a special place in Valhalla. She is my hunting partner, the love of my life, my best friend.

Thanks also to my agents, Jason Yarn and Lydia Wills, for their patience with me, and to Rodale Inc. for believing in this project. Moreover, I owe a debt of gratitude to those friends who helped me directly with this book: Elise Bauer, Langdon Cook, Rusty Dennen, Tim Huber, Phillip Loughlin, Chris Niskanen, Charlie Peebles, Mike Roth, Josh Stark, Stephanie Stiavetti, and Peter Tira.

Finally, I need to thank the woman who gave me the courage to set out on this journey. Pam Hunter convinced me that pipe dream could become reality, that hobby could become a life's work. Thank you, Pam. May you rest in peace.

Holly would like to thank her photography mentors Andrew Nixon and Robert Durell for their advice and encouragement, which was essential to her progress as a photographer.

RESOURCES

WEB SITES

There are endless Web sites with useful information out there, as well as online sellers of many of the hard-to-find ingredients you might need for some of these recipes and vendors of foraging, fishing, or hunting equipment.

Also useful are the addresses of the various state fish and game departments, which will be gateways for ethical, legal hunting, fishing, and foraging. To legally do many of the things I describe in this book, you will need a license, and in the case of hunting, it is almost universally required.

And of course there is my own Web site, **Hunter Angler Gardener Cook,** which is where you will find my continuing adventures in food, instructional guides, as well hundreds of recipes: www.honest-food.net

What follows is by no means exhaustive, just a list of the sites I find myself clicking to often.

ONLINE FORUMS

Where you can listen in to the conversations or ask questions of the aficionados of the pursuit, whether it's duck hunting, wine making, or charcuterie.

Duck Hunting Chat. Organized by state, this is where the duck hunters come to chew the duck fat. www.duckhuntingchat.com

The Fish Sniffer. Where the fish are and what they're being caught with (for West Coast, mostly California, anglers). Covers Oregon to Baja, Mexico. www.fishsniffer.com

WinePress. Everything from grape wine to fruit wine to mead making is talked about here. Very useful site. www.winepress.us

Sausagemaking Forum. All things charcuterie. www.forum.sausagemaking.org.

INSTRUCTIONAL SITES

Not blogs so much as sites with lots of knowledge.

Wedliny Domowe: The Marianski brothers' sausage-making site. These guys are serious charcuterie experts specializing in Polish and northern European cured meats. They are the authors of several excellent home sausage-making books. www.wedlinydomowe.com

California Oaks Foundation. This is where you can find pretty much everything you need to know about the Golden State's many oaks. It has a free PDF of Suellen Ocean's *Acorns and Eat 'em*, a great book on eating acorns. www.californiaoaks.org

Ducks at a Distance, by the US Fish and Wildlife Service. It's an online guide to figuring out what sort of duck you might see in the field. It's important, because there are restrictions on how many of some species you can legally shoot; for example, canvasbacks are heavily restricted. www.npwrc.usgs.gov/resource/birds/duckdist/

Food Blog Search. Simply the best search engine to see what the food blogging world is up to. You would be surprised to see how many others have experimented with the same odd ingredients you've brought home. I go here whenever I plan to cook new ingredients. It helps keep me from reinventing the wheel. www.foodblogsearch.com

ONLINE SUPPLIERS

These are the companies I work with when I am trying to get hard-to-find equipment or ingredients for cooking.

Butcher and Packer. The gold standard of American charcuterie suppliers. No one else comes close, and they have great service. www.butcher-packer.com

MoreWine! As good as Butcher and Packer is for charcuterie, MoreWine! is just as good for home wine making. I can get everything I need from them, and they ship quickly. www.morewinemaking.com

Earthy Delights. One of the best purveyors of wild and offbeat ingredients, from wild mushrooms to fennel pollen to hickory syrup. www.earthy.com

The Sausage Debauchery. The best source for Italian ingredients that are tough to get anywhere else. They also carry pasta gadgets like gnocchi boards and garganelli combs. www.sausagedebauchery.com

D'Artagnan meats. I don't shop with them because I hunt everything myself, but I know the people at D'Artagnan and have eaten their products for years in restaurants and in friends' homes. If you can't hunt it, you can find it here. www.dartagnan.com

USEFUL BLOGS

I read lots of blogs, but the following are those written by fellow travelers who fish, forage, or hunt regularly. All have excellent information on the nitty-gritty of their pursuit and are well written.

Holly Heyser's NorCal Cazadora. My girlfriend, Holly, is quite possibly a better duck hunter than I am, and her passions for both duck hunting and the larger questions of hunting ethics and philosophy go way beyond what you will find on my site, which focuses on the food. www.norcalcazadora.blogspot.com

Phillip Loughlin's Hog Blog. Phillip is a consummate pig hunter, and his site is loaded with tips and tricks to track down the wild hog. www.californiahuntingtoday.com/hogblog

Agrarianista. Fellow Northern California forager Josh Stark writes about his adventures foraging on marginal lands. www.agrarianista.blogspot.com

Fat of the Land. Forager and mushroom expert Langdon Cook is based in Washington state, but most of his foraging applies nationwide. www.fat-of-the-land.blogspot.com

Punk Domestics. A crowd-sourced Web site dedicated to DIY cooking, canning, and other cool food preservation projects. www.punkdomestics.com

SEASONS, LICENSES, RULES, AND REGS

You need to bookmark your state's department of fish and game site. Each state has a different name for this agency, but they all have them. This is where you can find out about seasons, licensing requirements, bag limits, areas to hunt or fish, etc. In many states, you can buy fishing licenses online.

US Fish & Wildlife Service: Hunting. A good place to start for an overview of the federal rules and regulations, which overlay those of the states. www.fws.gov/hunting

International Hunter Education Association. A great one-stop-shopping site for learning about the hunter education classes you'll need to take in your state. It also links to some online courses you can take to minimize the time you will need to spend at an in-person class. www.ihea.com

The National Rifle Association. This group maintains a one-stop site for state fish and game departments that I find very useful. All 50 states' departments are linked here. www.nrahq.org/hunting/statefishgame.asp

PRACTICE, PRACTICE

Nothing is more important to safe, ethical hunting than good marksmanship. To be a good shot, you need to shoot. But where?

National Shooting Sports Foundation. This group runs an excellent Web site that is a nationwide directory of gun ranges where you can hone your shooting skills. www.wheretoshoot.org

FURTHER READING

FORAGING

Cohen, Russ. *Wild Plants I Have Known . . . and Eaten*. Essex, MA: Essex County Greenbelt Assn., 2004.

Dubin, Margaret, and Sara-Larus Tolley. *Seaweed, Salmon and Manzanita Cider*. Berkeley, CA: Heyday Books, 2008.

Gibbons, Euell. *Stalking the Wild Asparagus*. New York: D. McKay Co., 1962.

Gibbons, Euell. *Stalking the Blue-Eyed Scallop*. New York: D. McKay Co., 1964.

Green, Connie, and Sarah Scott. *The Wild Table*. New York: Viking Studio, 2010.

Grieve, Guy, and Thomasina Miers. *The Wild Gourmets*. London: Bloomsbury, 2007.

Hahn, Jennifer. *Pacific Feast: A Cook's Guide to West Coast Foraging and Cuisine*. Seattle: Skipstone, 2010.

Harrington, H. D. *Edible Native Plants of the Rocky Mountains*. Albuquerque: University of New Mexico Press, 1967.

Harris, Ben Charles. *Eat the Weeds*. Barre, MA: Barre Publishing, 1968.

Medsger, Oliver Perry. *Edible Wild Plants*. New York: MacMillan, 1939.

Nabhan, Gary Paul. *Gathering the Desert*. Tucson: University of Arizona Press, 1985.

Phillips, Roger. *Wild Food*. London: MacMillan, 1983.

Saunders, Charles F. *Useful Wild Plants of the United States and Canada*. New York: R. M. McBride, 1920.

Sturtevant, Edward Lewis. *Sturtevant's Edible Plants of the World*. New York: Dover Publications, 1972.

Sweet, Muriel. *Common Edible and Useful Plants of the West*. Healdsburg, CA: Naturegraph Co., 1962.

Thayer, Samuel. *The Forager's Harvest*. Ogema, WI: Forager's Harvest Press, 2006.

Thayer, Samuel. *Nature's Garden*. Birchwood, WI: Forager's Harvest Press, 2009.

Williams, Kim. *Eating Wild Plants*. Missoula, MT: Mountain Press Publishing, 1977.

Williamson, Darcy. *The Rocky Mountain Wild Foods Cookbook*. Caldwell, ID: Caxton Printers, 1995.

FISHING

Buffler, Rob, and Tom Dickson. *Fishing for Buffalo*. Minneapolis: Culpepper Press, 1990.

Gall, Ken. *Handling Your Catch: A Guide for Saltwater Anglers*. Ithaca, NY: New York Sea Grant Extension Program, 1986.

McClane, A. J. *The Encyclopedia of Fish Cookery*. New York: Holt, Rinehart and Winston, 1977.

Wood, Ian, ed. *The Dorling Kindersley Encyclopedia of Fishing*. London: DK Books, 1994.

HUNTING

Bauer, Erwin. *The Waterfowler's Bible*. New York: Doubleday, 1989.

Dorsey, Chris. *150 Waterfowling Tips, Tactics & Tales*. Minocqua, WI: Willow Creek Press, 2002.

Fisher, Dave. *Outdoorsman's Edge Guide to Rabbit Hunting*. Bellvale, NY: Woods N'Water, 2002.

Fromm, Eric, and Al Cambronne. *Gut It, Cut It, Cook It: The Deer Hunter's Guide to Processing & Preparing Venison*. Iola, WI: Krause Publications, 2009.

Gooch, Bob. *The Ultimate Guide to Squirrel Hunting*. Guilford, CT: Lyons Press, 2004.

Johnson, M. D. *Successful Small Game Hunting*. Iola, WI: Krause Publications, 2003.

Lawrence, H. Lea. *The Ultimate Guide to Small Game and Varmint Hunting*. Guilford, CT: Lyons Press, 2002.

Mettler Jr., John J. *Basic Butchering of Livestock and Game*. Pownal, VT: Storey Publishing, 1986.

Reiger, George. *The Complete Book of North American Waterfowling*. New York: Lyons Press, 2000.

Smith, Richard P. *Hunting Rabbits and Hares*. Harrisburg, PA: Stackpole Books, 1986.

Smith, Steve. *Hunting Ducks and Geese*. Harrisburg, PA: Stackpole Books, 1984.

Tapply, H. G. *Tap's Tips: Practical Advice for All Outdoorsmen*. Guilford, CT: Lyons Press, 2004.

Tinsley, Russell, ed. *All About Small-Game Hunting in America*. New York: Winchester Press, 1976.

Triplett, Todd. *The Complete Book of Wild Boar Hunting*. Guilford, CT: Lyons Press, 2004.

OTHER USEFUL BOOKS

Alley, Lynn. *Lost Arts*. Berkeley, CA: Ten Speed Press, 1995.

Bertolli, Paul. *Cooking by Hand*. New York: Clarkson Potter, 2003.

Brillat-Savarin, Jean Anthelme. *The Physiology of Taste*. New York: Limited Editions Club, 1949.

Cameron, Angus, and Judith Jones. *The L.L. Bean Game and Fish Cookbook*. New York: Random House, 1983.

De Gouy, L. P. *The Derrydale Game Cookbook*. Lanham, MD: Derrydale Press, 2000.

De Groot, Roy Andries. *The Auberge of the Flowering Hearth*. Indianapolis: Bobbs-Merrill, 1973.

De Vita, Oretta Zanini. *Encyclopedia of Pasta*. Berkeley: University of California Press, 2009.

Dickson Wright, Clarissa, and Johnny Scott. *The Game Cookbook*. London: Kyle Cathie Ltd., 2004.

Farris, Efisio. *Sweet Myrtle and Bitter Honey*. New York: Rizzoli International Publications, 2007.

Grigson, Jane. *Charcuterie and French Pork Cookery*. London: Grub Street, 2001.

McGee, Harold. *On Food and Cooking*. New York: Scribner, 2004.

McGrail, Joie, and Bill McGrail. *The Catch and the Feast*. New York: Weybright and Talley, 1969.

Ruhlman, Michael, and Brian Polcyn. *Charcuterie*. New York: W. W. Norton, 2005.

Schwabe, Calvin. *Unmentionable Cuisine*. Charlottesville: University Press of Virginia, 1979.

Wise, Victoria. *American Charcuterie*. New York: Penguin Books, 1986.

INDEX

Boldface page references indicate illustrations. <u>Underscored</u> references indicate boxed text.